ARCHIVAL VIRTUE

Praise for *Archival Virtue*

"Drawing from the writings of philosophers, religious scholars, progressive activists, historians, poets, and archivists—to name a few—Scott Cline weaves together a compelling argument for why archivists need to deploy the multi-layered idea of virtue into their everyday work. In this way, he challenges archivists to use whatever area of archival administration in which they work to continually and conscientiously embrace a framework of faith, integrity, truth, duty, wisdom, trust, and justice . . . all for the common good."

— Louis Jones, *Wayne State University*

"Building on his *American Archivist* articles as well as extensive reading of philosophers, theologians, archivists, and other thought leaders, Scott Cline challenges his fellow archivists to be thoughtful about grounding our practice in things moral, ethical, just, and faithful. At a time when the profession is addressing issues of justice and power, *Archival Virtue* provides us with important new ways to frame our work into the future."

— Margery Sly, *Temple University Libraries*

"What do concepts of faith, radical self-understanding, intention, integrity, and covenant have to do with archives and the work that archivists do? Everything! In Scott Cline's seminal book, these concepts are not merely terms you would encounter in the study of ethics, philosophy, and theology, but are inextricably interwoven with the individuals and archivists who perform the everyday tasks and decisions that must be accomplished for the archival collections which affect those who encounter them."

— Vince Lee, *University of Houston*

"Weaving together ideas from philosophy, religion, literature, and history with personal reflection and practical experience, Scott Cline charts a brave and bold path for archivists to contemplate the deeper meanings of our work to preserve and provide access to archives—what it means to be an archivist, what our work means in the world, what it means for others. *Archival Virtue* is at once an invitation to connect with the spiritual elements of our work as archivists as well as a powerful invocation of the spirit that infuses the mind and the matter of archives, breathing life and meaning into archival work. Whether we dive deep or dip our toes into this book, the experience will offer new insights and bigger views for imagining and practicing archives with purpose in our current moment."

— Jennifer Meehan, *Penn State University Libraries*

ARCHIVAL VIRTUE

Relationship, Obligation, and the Just Archives

Scott Cline

SOCIETY OF American Archivists

Chicago

The Society of American Archivists
www.archivists.org

© 2021 by the Society of American Archivists
All rights reserved.

Library of Congress Control Number: 2021947702

Printed in the United States of America.

ISBN-978-1-945246-71-5 (paperback)
ISBN-978-1-945246-73-9 (pdf)
ISBN-978-1-945246-72-2 (ePub)

Cover design by Kiki Lechuga-Dupont.
Interior design by Sweeney Design.

Dedicated to my wife
Carolyn
and my children
Noah and Hannah

TABLE OF CONTENTS

Acknowledgments

This book and I owe much to many. The long arc of my career and my archival thinking have been inspired by eloquent voices. I am grateful for their kindness, mentorship, and friendship; and for their scholarship and their insistence that I explore my own. Many colleagues have read and critiqued my writing, discussed archival ideas with me, or displayed toward me throughout my career the central virtues of this volume. Among these wonderful influencers are Brenda Banks, Diana Banning, Brien Brothman, Robin Chandler, Daria D'Arienzo, Susan Davis, Ernie Dornfeld, Linda Edgerly, John Fleckner, John Grabowski, John Guido, Dennis Harrison, Tom Hyry, Rand Jimerson, Elisabeth Kaplan, Bill Landis, Candace Lein-Hayes, David Levy, Waverly Lowell, Donna McCrea, Jennifer Meehan, Kaye Minchew, Richard Pearce-Moses, Mary Jo Pugh, Burt Rhoads, Mike Saunders, Joan Schwartz, Margery Sly, and Tamar Zeffren, and all the others I have slighted by failing to include them in this list.

I want to offer a special thank you to Terry Cook and Mark Greene, both of whom I came to know, ever so slightly, late in our respective careers. Both were charitable in their encouragement and generous in their kindness; I believe we would have become good friends had they not died much too young.

I have worked with two editors at the Society of American Archivists to whom I am greatly indebted. Chris Prom and Stacie Williams have had their own unique impacts on this book. And while I am ultimately responsible for whatever appears in these pages, I thank Chris and Stacie for offering their encouragement, talking over ideas, suggesting edits, and guiding me through the process.

The Seattle Municipal Archives was my work home for over three decades. Its incredible staff continually challenged me to be the best I could be. Anne Frantilla, Julie Irick, Julie Kerssen, Sarah Shipley, Jeff Ware, Jennifer Winkler, Andrea Bettger, Steve Anderson, Gail Snow and a host of grant staff, volunteers, and students built a stellar program. And two of my administrators, City Clerks Judith Pippin and Monica Martinez Simmons, gave me the encouragement and the space to pursue my scholarly and professional interests.

I also thank all of my students at the University of Washington Information School who, for over twenty years, challenged me to continually look at the archival endeavor with fresh eyes. A special thank-you goes to Rand Jimerson's archives students at Western Washington University who twice asked me to speak at the Canadian-American Archives Conference where I was able to experiment with ideas, some that ultimately found their way into this work.

The Society of American Archivists (SAA) has been a gratifying professional home for me for nearly four decades. I have great admiration and respect for all of the SAA staff with whom I have worked over the years, but two long-term relationships must be singled out. Teresa Brinati has been a source of encouragement since I first met her in 1989. And Nancy Perkin Beaumont has become a close, valued friend and confidant in the nearly two decades that I have known her.

Two of the best editors I know are my children, Noah and Hannah Cohen-Cline. Their imprint on early versions of the first two chapters of this book cannot be overstated. But far more important, they have been constant sources of joy, kept me (feeling) young, and, with the aggregate of their own families and young adult communities, give me faith in our future. And finally, Carolyn Cohen, my wife and fellow traveler and best friend for nearly five decades, was the guiding influence leading me to choose my career path. She has given constant, loving encouragement in my efforts to formulate and convey my belief that archival work is a moral endeavor of relationship and obligation. I could not have completed this book without her inspiration.

Preface

Ernest Hemingway wrote about Dostoyevsky's work in *A Moveable Feast*, "There were things believable and not to be believed, but some so true they changed you as you read them."[1] Hugh Taylor's essays had this impact on me. When I revisited his writings compiled in *Imagining Archives*, they seemed so true, they changed me—at least they changed my archival perspective.[2] Here was the closest to a philosopher that the profession had produced. Taylor, an England-born Canadian archivist with deep Anglican roots, thought in broad, universal themes that placed archives in frameworks I had never considered. Especially striking was his unabashed speculation on the spiritual nature of archives.

This encounter came twenty-six years into my career. To that point—it was 2008—I had kept my head down and my sleeves rolled up, and I did what I was educated to do: practical, efficient archival work. I had read some of Taylor's essays over the years and I had heard him speak at conferences, but it wasn't until I was fifty-eight years old that I really began to understand what he was saying to me—not because I lacked the intellectual capacity earlier in my career, but more that I lacked the discipline to make time for considering archival meaning in all its complexity. I was too busy . . . I thought.

Prior to 2008, I had presented papers at professional conferences on a wide variety of topics related to archival functions, education, government records in general, and archival certification. Now my interest changed to the exploration of philosophical questions in the archives. It is my conviction that we need to be cognizant of the social and cultural impacts of decisions that archivists make, and we need to ask questions about the meaning of what we do, but perhaps even more important, the meaning of who we are. Addressing these questions is crucial both for our individual well-being and our survival as a profession.

I am awed by the creative thinking of today's archival theorists who are introducing ideas from other disciplines into an archival literature that addresses justice, ethics of care, anti-oppression work, maintenance theory, climate change, community archives, and an assortment of other topics. This book, I believe, complements those efforts by introducing and/or touching issues of archival being, relationship, spirituality, transcendence, justice, and more in attempting to initiate a philosophical consideration of archives and archivists.

My hope is that these ideas will resonate with a range of archivists from archival studies students to senior archivists, as well as information professionals beyond the archives field. We all need to find our spaces for pondering the fundamental questions of meaning, and to do it with intention. It is my contention that these questions strike at the heart of archival relevance in whatever future we face.

Scott Cline
Seattle, Washington
June 2021

66

*We know that the letters of the alphabet
are neutral and meaningless until they are
combined to make a word which itself has
no significance until it is inserted into a sentence and interpreted by those who speak it.*

— ISABEL WILKERSON

Introduction

This is a book about virtue—specifically, what I call *archival virtue*. This nascent exploration of virtue theory in the archival endeavor suggests those virtues that afford power and moral order in archivists' work. What, then, do we mean when we talk about virtue? Virtue is defined etymologically as moral excellence.[1] French materialist philosopher Andre Comte-Sponville describes virtues as forces for good; he claims that "virtue is good itself" and imbues humans with the power to act well. Indeed, virtue is what makes us human. He argues, "The virtues are our moral values, but not in any abstract sense. They are values we embody, live, and enact. . . . Good is not something to contemplate; it is something to be done."[2] Similarly, Ghanaian philosopher Kwame Gyekye notes that much of African ethics focuses on character that is acquired through moral action. When the Akan of West Africa say of an individual, *he is a person*, it means *he has a good character*. Further, "a profound appreciation of the high standards of the morality of an individual's behaviour would elicit the judgment, *he is truly a person* (oye onipa paa!)."[3] In other words, virtues are practical characteristics that

1

speak to good moral character. This book, then, explores specific archival virtues and, thus, the moral character of archivists, but only so far as those virtues are catalysts for moral action.

Virtue: Redeeming an Idea

Before engaging the discussion of virtue theory, I want to briefly dispose of two potential criticisms of a virtue approach and suggest how this book should be read. The first identifies virtues with one group's assertion of superiority over another; the second is the question of vocational awe and the powerlessness in considering virtue as its own reward.

The concept of virtue is horribly misused when one group claims it at the expense of another. Sociologist Michèle Lamont, writing about racism in America and France, argues that "racist beliefs arise from the moral frameworks that people use to evaluate one another" and that racists believe people of color "fail to meet these moral standards."[4] The groups in America that Lamont studied claim certain virtues to develop a sense of self that erects barriers against others; they formulate categories such as "people like us," a designation that cannot be breached. In this way, virtues are used to condemn others who are perceived as "falling short."[5] The *othering* manipulation of virtue insults the concepts explicated by Comte-Sponville and Gyekye. My arguments draw on the essence of their definitions as well as the observation of Kenyan-born scholar Dismas Masolo, who, writing about ethics, notes that virtues "are perhaps the most celebrated aspects of African communitarian practices and ideals."[6] In the following pages, I suggest a fusion of these ideas for archivists: virtue embraces the development of moral character by the individual in order to fulfill their obligation to community.

The second criticism, less socially destructive, but insidious for the archival professional, is the idea that virtue equates to powerlessness. In the early 1980s, marketing researchers Sidney Levy and Albert Robles issued a report for SAA that placed the archival community in a snare of "niceness" and low professional status. The report emphasized that archival work was virtuous, but that archivists suffered from the impotence of virtue and a belief that virtue was its own reward.[7] Corollary to this argument are bromides I have heard expressed by colleagues many times over the years: "archives is a higher calling" and "I can't believe I get paid for doing this work." This constitutes vocational awe, the supposition that information professionals have internalized assumptions about themselves and their work leading to claims that their professions and institutions "are inherently good and sacred, and therefore beyond critique." Fobazi Ettarh cautions (and she could be writing about archives), "when the rhetoric surrounding librarianship borders on vocational and sacred language rather than acknowledging that librarianship is a profession or a discipline, and as an institution, historically and contemporarily flawed, we do ourselves a disservice."[8]

Ettarh's argument is crucially right and crucially wrong. Yes, we must engage in serious critique of our professions, interrogate power, and confront injustice; and we need to stop thinking of our work as its own "moral compensation." However, I propose that we aggressively define and live our virtues as sources of power and as embedded moral characteristics that make us want to act justly on behalf of a better world. Do not mistake this for "virtue signaling," which is the self-important expression of one's moral correctness; rather, my claim for archival virtue is a call to moral action based on a belief that the instantiation of archival virtues is a form of radical empowerment that imbues the archivist with the desire to act for good itself.

Why Virtue

Othering and vocational awe misunderstand and misuse virtue. My hope is archivists will reclaim and rehabilitate the language of virtue, harness it to our obligation to the good, and restore it to a place of just power, empathy, and relationship. One's virtue, as moral philosopher Philippa Foot claims, may be judged by feelings, intentions, and actions.[9] Philosopher Lawrence Blum echoes Foot, noting that her formulation—virtues equal attitude plus action—is compelling, and that we must make room for rethinking virtues and even creating new ones to fit modern cultural and political landscapes. Writing specifically about racism, he posits three new virtues that philosophical literature, until now, has never encompassed. Blum's racial virtues are: (1) recognition and valuing the other as peer, (2) civic racial egalitarianism, and (3) seeing others as individuals and not solely or predominantly as members of racial groups.[10] These three virtues should be recognizable, along with others, in the discussion presented in the following chapters.

Blum writes, "The strength of a virtue account is its capacity to express the range of psychic phenomena involved in forms of goodness and badness. A racist is not someone who only has bad intentions, but someone who has had bad and inappropriate feelings as well."[11] Here, I contend that Blum is citing the redemptive power of virtue in the struggle between good and evil and the extension of human dignity. Virtues express power and utilizing power for the good is our responsibility.

This conception of virtues runs deep in various global philosophical systems. Gyekye argues that almost all African ethics is character-based, and that in many African languages the word for *character* is interchangeable with *ethics* and *morality*.[12] Excellence of character is what virtue theory describes. Further, Odumayak Okpo, writing about leadership ethics, suggests six principles (virtues) of ethical leadership: integrity, honesty, service to others, justice, courage, and respect for others, all of which appear in Western lists of virtues.[13] Virtues are embedded also in the moral philosophy of Eastern cultures and the global South. Kedar Tiwari, for example, shows that in classical Indian thought the dharmic life was characterized by a list of necessary virtues;[14] while David Wong points out that in the *Analects of Confucius*, the cardinal concept of *ren* relates to moral excellence that many translations convey as the idea of complete ethical virtue.[15]

Archival literature is full of what we do and how we do it. The questions raised in these pages touch on personal and professional virtues; they grapple with who we are, and why we have chosen what we do. This exploration of the personal virtues that archivists might bring to their work argues that those beliefs and feelings should manifest through moral action.

Philosopher Paul Woodruff explains it this way: "People who do good are aware of moral rules, but so are people who do bad. The difference is virtue. Virtue is the source of the feelings that prompt us to behave well."[16] Virtue combines emotion and action with a commitment to who we want to be. This book is an attempt to construct a lexicon of archival virtue.

Virtues, as personal qualities that compel good behavior, are concerned with the common good. We exist in overlapping communities; our strengths and moral character are conceived in this social reality. Communities, to be stable and strong, rely on the virtue of their members. Therefore, just as individuals bind together in social and cultural groupings, their virtues combined can shape morally responsible communities, including archives workers.

Why Philosophy

Philosophy is the art of conception creation. The French philosopher Luc Ferry argues that we cannot make sense of the world without philosophy; that we are all products of thoughts, actions, convictions, beauty, prejudice, enlightenment, and animus developed over millennia of intellectual history; and that philosophy helps us sort out that tangle and figure out how to live life.[17] Ferry claims that the central question of philosophy relates to human finitude, our consciousness of that finitude, and how we confront its inevitability. [18] This aspect of philosophy concerns mortality and how we overcome the associated anxiety and reality of our own ultimate fate. It is the attempt to extract meaning from our short existence on earth and to determine how we live lives that honor the past and present and are remembered into the future.

Archives, like philosophy, also concerns death—we deal with records about people, institutions, and activities that have literally and symbolically passed, or are here today, but are reckoning with their own finitude. Archives is also about revelation—in the sense of revealing to view or making known—where lives and actions otherwise hidden or silenced might be revealed through archival processes. In addressing these concerns, a philosophy of archives should illuminate theory, practice, and methodology. By this understanding, Verne Harris, Terry Cook, Brien Brothman, Eric Ketelaar, Joan Schwartz, and others joined Hugh Taylor's swim in philosophical waters. In recent years, a new cohort of authors including Michelle Caswell, Marika Cifor, Ricardo Punzalan, Jarrett Drake, and others have introduced to archival thinking a wide range of philosophical and critical scholarship encompassing feminist theory, critical race theory, decolonization studies, affect theory, new materialism, epistemology, and more. This profusion of ideas forms a continuum that is leading to new ways of thinking about archives, to serious critiques of archival practice, and to healthy analysis of the power structures in and through which we work. I believe that a virtue theory approach to the idea of *archival being* provides an added philosophical element to this growing literature.

The philosophers and theologians I cite are largely, though not exclusively, Western. Critics rightly point to the exclusion of non-Western thought from the Western philosophical canon and argue that it has buttressed white supremacy.[19] However, my assertion is that the philosophical ideas from the classical period to the present are, for the most part, not the problem; the development of an institutional structure of philosophical study that excluded the greater part of the world and constricted the discipline is at fault. As Isabel Wilkerson's quote heading this introduction suggests, it is interpretation and misuse of those ideas that are subject to criticism. As I have already argued for virtue, we need to reclaim the language and ideas of Western philosophy, read them with communitarian sensibilities through a duty-based lens, and apply them in pursuit of the moral good.

The controversial activist-turned-academic and prolific author Julius Lester is a case study in how to read philosophy. Lester was an outspoken Black Power advocate in the 1960s and 1970s.[20] He converted to Judaism in the 1980s, and for many years, he held joint appointments in Afro-American Studies and Judaic and Near Eastern Studies (JNES) at the University of Massachusetts–Amherst. His complex biography and personal identity[21] and his evolution as a scholar can help us understand a different way of looking at Western philosophy. In one of his essays, Lester wrote: "My education did not confirm me as a Black man; it confirmed me as one who had the same questions as Plato and Aristotle. And my education told me that as a Black person, it was not only right to ask those questions, it was even okay to put forward my own answers and stand them next to Plato and Aristotle."[22] Like Lester, it is important that we all engage and challenge ideas, ask our own questions, contemplate the different answers we surface, and from our own authentic perspectives, measure those questions and answers alongside the likes of Plato, Confucius, Kant, Lester, Vine Deloria, Gyekye, and Hugh Taylor.

Many of the philosophical precepts of the West are also found in the philosophical discourse of global communities. A distinctive difference is that Western philosophy has been understood to focus on the individual, especially related to individual liberty, whereas, for example, the African philosophical concern is communitarianism. The latter is expressed in the sub-Saharan *ubuntu* philosophy through the maxim "I am because we are."[23] Among the main points of this book are the ideas of human dignity, humaneness, and the inextricable connectedness that places the individual in a web of community. I adhere to the definition of ethics expressed by Ghanaian Kwasi Wiredu: "The observance of rules for the harmonious adjustment of the interest of the individual to those of others in society."[24] My hope, through virtue theory, is to read Western thinkers in a communitarian manner. With this in mind, two key definitions are necessary for concepts that flow through this book: *justice* and *the common good*.

Justice

Numerous lists of virtues have been compiled since humans began considering the meaning of life; most of these lists have in common the identification of *justice* as the virtue that stands above all others. As Comte-Sponville argues, "justice encompasses all the other virtues, even though it substitutes for none." He observes, "But who could be so complacent as to think that he knows exactly what it [justice] is or that he himself is completely just?"[25] At this point, we must ask two pertinent questions. First, is justice truly an archival concern? To daylight my personal bias, my answer is *yes*, it is a primary archival concern. Although still contested in some quarters, there is a growing consensus that justice, in its many forms, is an important principle in modern archives theory. And this leads to the second question: In the archival context, what do we mean by the term *justice*? This, by any estimation, is not a simple question.

Justice is a pivotal framework in the following pages, informing archival virtues and dispositions, and falling within the categorization of *justice as morality*. The conception of justice that most resonates with me is the seemingly simple and profoundly elegant definition from David Wallace who argues that justice is "the demand of respect for the other."[26] An expansion on this definition frames justice as the "ideal vision that every human being is of equal and incalculable value, entitled to shared standards of freedom, equality, and respect."[27]

Wallace, of course, complicates his efficient definition by noting that a theory of justice in the archives must take account of the literature external to our profession by

> embracing ambiguity over clarity; accepting that social memory is always contestable and reconfigurable; understanding that politics and political power is always present in shaping social memory; considering that archives and archival praxis always exist within contexts of power (be it political, economic, organizational, or individual); recognizing the paradox of archives and archivists as loci of both weak social power and significant social memory shaping potential; and acknowledging that social justice itself is ambiguous and contingent on dissimilar space, time, and cultural contexts.[28]

Justice, therefore, is a complex, contested term with many dimensions and manifestations—it is plural. Caswell et al. argue that any discourse on justice is "a contribution to an ongoing conversation rather than a one-size-fits-all solution."[29] As part of that conversation, I begin with the simple idea that justice honors everyone's freedom—individually and in community—and demands everyone's obligation to cherish human dignity. And sustaining human dignity is justice in practice. I agree with Punzalan and Caswell that justice in the archives is a worthy goal and that "as shapers of the historical record, archivists have a professional obligation to work toward a more equitable future."[30] To which I add Lae'l Hughes-Watkins' coda that it is not just an equitable future we strive for; we are obliged to work "also toward a moral one."[31] In its plurality, justice, as a preeminent virtue, assumes the form needed in specific situations. This moral engagement with justice points to another term that requires contextual clarification: the *common good*.

Common Good

Common good is also a contested term. It has recently been described as a passive and nonaccountable articulation of neoliberal thought that supports commodification of information and treats it as consumable and transactional. To counteract this co-optation by neoliberal discourse,[32] I suggest applying a lens of moral engagement to better understand what the common good is.

Robert Reich, writing about political-economy, argues that "the common good consists of our shared values about what we owe one another. . . . A concern for the common good . . . is a moral attitude." He further notes that the common good is "a pool of trust" formed over time, "a trust that most other people share the same basic ideals."[33] Adapting the common good to archival theory asks us to commit collectively to a vision for a just and equitable society, to embrace difference and change as norms, to construct relationships that obligate us to *the other*, to broker dialogue and civil discourse, and to make hospitality an archival value. This is but a partial list of what we owe to one another. Whether archivists and archives are willing or can commit to these essential actions is our central moral vector.

The common good should be recognized in its communitarian affect. It does not derive from the goods or the preferences solely of individuals, but is, according to Gyekye, "that which is essentially good for human beings as such. . . . For the common good embraces the goods—the basic goods—of all the members of the community. . . . The pursuit of the good of all is the goal of the communitarian society. . . . A sense of the common good—which is a core of shared values—is the underlying presupposition of African social morality."[34] And, I might add, of this book.

In critiquing the common good, Hannah Alpert-Abrams et al. suggest *collective good* as a substitution; they call it "a framework that brings together theories of common good and collective action."[35] Their preferred term has compelling appeal. Nevertheless, I believe my definition of common good is consistent with their argument. I use *common good* throughout this book, but if readers choose to read it as *collective good*, I believe we will arrive at the same destination.

Context

I am writing in a time of crisis, in America and worldwide, including the existential threat of worsening climate change, political and social upheaval, ongoing protest after the killings of George Floyd and Breonna Taylor, questioning whether we are at an inflection point in reckoning with America's legacy of slavery and racism, and a virulent global pandemic. As I am completing these words, Covid-19 has struck over 32 million and killed nearly six hundred thousand in the United States alone. The official unemployment rate during the pandemic reached as high as 14.7 percent, although the real figure was probably closer to twenty percent. No one knows for sure what any of those figures will be before the pandemic is defeated.

Nevertheless, this book was conceived with a sense of optimism, in part from witnessing the heroic response to Covid-19 by first responders; but also, in microcosm, the response within our profession. Among those deeply impacted by the pandemic are many part-time, hourly, contract, temporary, term-limited, and otherwise contingent archives workers, most of whom are young colleagues, including many who are also coping with college debt. The response to this acute economic challenge speaks to the soul of the profession and to the ideas of moral obligation expressed in this book.

In mid-March 2020, an ad hoc working group of twenty-one archivists met to determine how they might help alleviate some of the economic adversity. They conceived the Archival Workers Emergency Fund and requested support from the SAA Foundation. The Foundation board reviewed the proposal, worked with the group to finalize details, and, in short order, adopted it. The purpose of the fund was to provide financial assistance for archival workers experiencing acute, unanticipated financial hardship due to the crisis. The Foundation authorized initial seed money and began soliciting donations. The working group, in turn, initiated an aggressive fundraising campaign through its networks. At this writing, nearly $145,000 has been disbursed to 173 applicants.[36]

The archival community's response to this crisis is characterized by a sense of responsibility for one another, respect for archival labor, an ethics of care, and a compassionate justice. This outpouring of support describes an awareness of our individual and collective obligation to one another. Although this case required an inward facing response, archivists also externalize their commitments to doing the right thing through building relationships and journeying toward, advocating for, and sustaining moral order in our slice of the world. The pandemic, and its universal implications, underscores the radical uncertainty of our times. The response by the archives community, however, illustrates an abiding faith in the future.[37]

This book is about archivists, as individuals and as a community, more than it is about archives. It is also about power, but not in any conventional sense. Following the publication of Jacques Derrida's *Archive Fever*, in which he argued *the archive* is a site of cultural and political power,[38] archival literature abounded with essays illustrating the power of records to shape contradictory or competing notions of cultural mythology, promote political hegemony, bolster democracy and democratic institutions, construct social memory, and legitimize bureaucracy. This literature, primarily from the first decade of the twenty-first century, also illuminates the power of the archivist in employing the profession's core functions, especially in appraisal, selection, representation, and managing access to collections.[39] More recent studies examine additional modes of power, including the emotional power of archival materials, archives' complicity with dominant power structures, archival institutions as agents of power, archival activism, and the communal power inherent in participatory and community archives.[40]

Others have eloquently defined what archival power is and provide examples of how it manifests in the workplace. My intention is to discuss the characteristics—the virtues—required for archivists to navigate the intricate networks of power in a work world that should be, but is not always, characterized by sociality and encounter. The book, then, is also about the challenge of understanding personal contexts, a necessity if archivists are to successfully contest and employ archival power. My arguments send us into the politically and culturally charged spaces of moral commitment, truth, difference, and just behavior in the pursuit of archival ideals.

Structure of this Book

This book is divided into three sections, each with a particular focus, and comprising eight chapters.

Part one, titled *Archival Being*, is about existence; it describes the existential posture that archivists assume in the world and in the province of relationships in all their complexity. Chapter one posits the possibility of a way we are—I call this *archival being*—and teases out some of the personal virtues that help create archival being, enveloped in a notion of *archival faith*. Chapter two explores our obligation to form reciprocal and genuine relationships, to enter into *archival covenant* with those around us.

Part two, *Archival Citizenship*, deals with certain archival practicalities and how we engage with our professional world from the position of understanding and living our archival being. Chapter three looks at what archival citizenship might encompass and especially how we engage in relationships. Chapter four touches on certain archival functions through the lens of *memory as justice*. Chapter five asks us to consider the employment of practical and moral wisdom in the pursuit of an *archival validity* characterized by *truth*, *beauty*, and *justice* as archival practices. This section focuses on our understanding that life is about encounter and our recognition of sacred obligation to community that hones our work in fostering the common good.

Part three, *Archival Spirituality*, explores the intersection of archival being with our practical role in the world, applying a reflective lens of spirituality to our profession and ourselves. Chapters six and seven, respectively, open our world to an understanding of *archival transcendence* and *archival spirituality*, even in the most mundane aspects of our work, and in the corridors of institutional power. The concluding chapter suggests that the ideas expressed throughout the book are inexorably directed toward the pursuit of *moral order* in the archival world. It asks us to become comfortable with promoting discourse and action that embrace the language of justice, truth, and faith in the archives.

Underlying the arguments in the following chapters are the essential questions of what attitudes, dispositions, and characteristics archivists must exhibit in successfully embracing power and mediating the complex relationships between the record, creators, users, communities, and the archivist on the stage of our daily work. I wrap this exploration in a quilt of virtues. It is not a protective cover; it is a garment of struggle. I believe there are necessary virtues required of archivists as they navigate and negotiate power structures while concurrently building meaningful relationships that foster a sense of the common good and create a profession whose collective outlook is the vision of a moral society.

Being Part of the Conversation

The challenges presented by the global information revolution confront archivists with demands for assimilating increasingly complex technical knowledge. Archives conference presentations, literature, and workshops rightly and overwhelmingly emphasize the specialized "how-to" aspects of digital archives praxis. However, since entering the field, my fear, and that of many colleagues, has been that the necessity for keeping up (or falling less behind) with the technical requirements of the digital ecosystem would overwhelm scholarly forays into questions of meaning in our work. In stark terms, we worried that the meaning of what we do might be sacrificed on the altar of the connected world.

Today, I am encouraged by the growing number of archivists who are exploring new ways of interrogating archives, searching for meaning and value, deliberating about justice, and focusing on the human relational attributes of archival work. Over three decades ago, my first supervisor, John Grabowski, framed this as "coming home to the why of our profession from a sometimes obsessive sojourn with the how."[41] Although the *why* and the *how* are not mutually exclusive in archival thought, and should be brought into balance, I make no pretense toward that balance; the following chapters focus on meaning and relationship and are meant to be a journey home to the *why*.

Gerald Ham, former state archivist of Wisconsin, reminds us that the archivist is duty bound. Ham, like Taylor, put us on a philosophical, if not moral, path when arguing that if the archivist "is passive, uninformed, with a limited view of what constitutes the archival record, the collections that he acquires will never hold up a mirror for mankind. And if we are not holding up that mirror, if we are not helping people understand the world they live in, and if this is not what archives is all about, then I do not know what it is we are doing that is all that important."[42] He communicates concepts of duty and responsibility that must direct our work. If we share Ham's vision, then archival work demands our participation in creating a just and representative archives; the pursuit of fairness, sacred obligation, and moral order in our work and society; and engagement with meaning, relationship, and the common good as ideals in our lives, the archival endeavor, and the broader world.

The approach to meeting this challenge can be summed up in an observation by Carlo Rovelli, the Italian physicist who developed loop quantum gravity theory, an attempt to reconcile general relativity and quantum mechanics in the hope of developing a grand theory of everything.

When asked about competing theories and the possibility that his work might be wrong, he responded that being right or wrong is not the point, but rather the important thing is being part of the conversation.[43]

My question in this conversation is whether there is an archival posture, an existential exteriority, that we assume in the world. In trying to answer that question, this book presents concepts that largely have been discarded from common professional language. These are the terms of virtue and theology—morality, faith, truth, spirituality, transcendence, and many more—what one commentator calls "soul words."[44] I believe we must recapture the essence of moral energy and language.[45] The world of archival ideas is a messy place in which Terry Cook argued, "we must stop being custodians of things and start being purveyors of concepts."[46]

I am not espousing a fixed essentialism that defines archivists. However, I do believe there are essential qualities—*virtues*—common among archivists. The purpose for these philosophical musings is to spur archivists to care deeply about who they are and why they are archivists, to look beyond the temptation to see themselves as the work they do, to grapple with ideas about their place in the world and their obligations to it, and, as Julius Lester suggested, to engage in their own art of conception creation. This book asks us to engage in the difficult work of self-examination and values clarification. The questions raised by that pursuit are about meaningful lives and personal values and how those personal values intersect with core professional values. What does it mean to be an archivist? What meaning do we, as humane beings, bring to the archives? How does that affect and define our place in the world? How do our personal values influence our understanding of obligation and care? How do they guide our relational encounters?

I hope the book is read with the understanding that we are, as individuals, part of a larger organism. Our cultural, social, educational, economic, and familial experiences, and our reactions to them, forge our views and inform our choices. These play out not only in our personal lives, but also in our professional work and relationships. The virtues, attitudes, and dispositions that we live are lived in community, in archival polity, in relationship with *the other*. Thus, personal virtues become meaningless if they are not externalized and employed on behalf of a greater good. Laboring to understand the impact of our experiences and how we can use that understanding to develop a fair and caring approach to archival work that focuses us on obligation and relationship is the project before us.

PART ONE

Archival Being

Children learn more from what
you are than what you teach.
— W. E. B. Du Bois

It takes more courage to examine the
dark corners of your own soul than it
does for a soldier to fight on a battlefield.
— William Butler Yeats

We become what we behold.
— Hugh Taylor

66

We are what we imagine. Our very existence

consists in our imagination of ourselves.

— N. Scott Momaday

CHAPTER ONE

Being and Faith

What does it mean to be an archivist? This question is not meant to survey the education required to do the work of archivy, nor does it anticipate a description of those functions in which an archivist engages day-in and day-out. Rather, the query is an attempt to discern whether there are essential qualities to being an archivist and what those might be. A useful illustration for beginning this exploration is found in a story from the Chassidim, the eighteenth-century eastern European pietistic, mystical revival movement in Judaism. The tale speaks to virtues and authenticity in one's work:

> The story is told that a disciple of Shmelke of Nikolsburg asked his rebbe to teach him the mystery of serving God. The tzaddik told him to go to Rabbi Abraham Hayyim, who in those days was still an innkeeper. The student did as he was instructed and took up residence in the inn for several weeks. During all this time he failed to observe any special indication of holiness in the man. He seemed only to attend to his business.

Finally, in desperation, the disciple went up to the innkeeper and asked what he did all day.

"My most important job," said Rabbi [Hayyim], "is to make sure the dishes are cleaned properly. I do my best to make sure that no trace of food remains on the dishes. I also clean and dry the pots and pans carefully so that they do not rust."

"That's it?" asked the student incredulously.

"That's it," replied the innkeeper.

Whereupon the disciple returned home and reported what he had seen and heard to his master.

"Now you know everything you need to know," Rabbi Shmelke said.[1]

It would be naive and foolish to equate the quest for holiness with the secular and profane world. Yet, for archivists this story is more than a homily on piety; it offers a compelling model for archival behavior—that is, being profoundly present in their work and undertaking it with a sense of obligation.

Archivists are deployed to preserve the historical record, they exhibit a body of knowledge and a toolkit of skills unique to that work, and they think in ways peculiar to the field. However, archivists are more than the archival way of thinking and a skill set. What, then, does it mean to say, "I am an archivist"?

More than seven decades ago, Hilary Jenkinson wrapped the archivist in a mantle of truth. Ever the essentialist, Jenkinson mused, "Of all the persons who pay service to the cause of Truth the good Archivist is the most absolute, the most complete, the most selfless devotee. It is his duty and privilege not merely to be as truthful as he can himself, but to be the guardian for the benefit of others of countless truths of all kinds—truths of which he himself does not perceive the existence."[2] Jenkinson's positivist ideal of the archivist as the guardian of truth does not weather the scrutiny of postmodern critical analysis, but it does raise and deserves an answer to the question: Is there a way of acting and experiencing the world shared (or at least ideally shared) by all archivists?

Archival Being

The answer to that question cannot be dismissed by arguments about the archival perspective, nor the knowledge and skills that archivists must possess to preserve the historical record and support a just democratic process; nor can it be wrapped in modern management and leadership theory. Rather, I believe there are certain virtues common to all archivists (and likely, all information professionals) at the core of forming what I call *archival being*.

This conception of *being* aligns closely with the judgment of twentieth-century French philosopher Emmanuel Levinas who conceives *being* as "self with other."[3] Levinas explains: "With the appearance of the human—and this is my entire philosophy—there is something more important than my life, and that is the life of the other."[4] This selfless expression of obligation and relationship is at once an overreach in sentiment and an impossibility in practice. Nevertheless, it is the recognition that we exist in relation to others and that we bear a presumptive duty to moral engagement with *the other*. This idea of encounter and its sibling, radical empathy, are explored in greater detail elsewhere in these pages.

An extension of Levinas's argument is that the human begins in the exigent state of saintliness—not the accomplishment, but the virtue. Use of the term *saintliness* should not be disregarded as a religious relic; Kwame Gyekye might call it moral character.[5] For Levinas, saintliness is a first and undeniably necessary condition of ethical living; ethics presupposes saintliness as the ideal. One should always endeavor to act in a manner that gives ethical priority to the life of *the other*.[6]

Using this as a starting point, archival being can be characterized as the manner in which archivists are engaged in the world, both individually and collectively, as professionals and as a profession. Archival being is the idealized, fundamental, permanent reality exemplifying what archivists do as well as the attitude and commitments they embrace in shouldering archival work in its many manifestations. Archival being is characterized by authenticity—that which compels archivists to embrace being archivists as a central distinguishing element in their lives. Authenticity, in this instance, is the intersection of how we think and feel about our lives and our commitments to certain courses of action.

Existentialist Jean-Paul Sartre, a contemporary of Levinas, contends that we each choose the type of person we want to be and that this commitment is the key to unlocking an authentically meaningful existence. In this context, he asserts there is a human reality to our existence formed by a set of givens.[7] This human reality—one might say this human condition—is a work in progress. Sartre insists that I create myself constantly through my choices and my actions.[8] In our professional lives, our givenness—our human reality—is that we are archivists who, like everyone else, make decisions and take actions everyday with the goal of living and working authentically. Achieving some level of authenticity does not automatically ensure that we are good archivists, but it inevitably compels us to embrace being archivists as our unequivocal concern. An essential quality in our quest for meaning and the drive for authenticity is embracing *archival faith*.

Archival Faith

Integral to the apprehension of archival being is foremost a consciousness of archival faith. The conception of archival faith is not entirely new, but neither has it been articulated specifically as faith. The archival endeavor and the archivist's way of being are bound inextricably with creation, endurance, and death (in an archival sense), and in a perception of the record and the user that transcends daily existence. A physical and corporeal sense of history links archivists to an existential faith that, in turn, permeates the profession. Does not what we do assume a faith in our continued existence? Is not our work, itself, a profession of faith?

Human beings live by an act of existential faith which Christian theologian Schubert Ogden describes as a basic confidence or assurance that life is worth living. This basic faith, he posits, grows from our trust that existence is generally somehow justified and made meaningful through our connections in the human community. We exist as social beings in relation to those around us and "temporally in relation to ancestors and descendants."[9] Terry Baxter expresses this faith in the most optimistic language I have found in archival literature: "I'll have to confess here my unfettered optimism. I believe that our species will be here millennia from now, that we will have peace, that we will be unified in mission and purpose, and that we will have learned love and respect for all of our comrades."[10] He goes on to link his distinctive secular faith with a personal sense of meaning, seeing himself "as a single but necessary link in the human chain . . . and that I am, along with each of you, absolutely necessary for the generations to come."[11]

The archival endeavor is a faith-based profession, not in the religious sense, but rather as an organic, universal faith in the future of the species. At its deepest, most fundamental level, archives presupposes a genuine faith in humanity, a faith that there will be a future and generations to which archives will matter. If we do what we do because the records we maintain[12] are to be used and that they will matter, we affirmatively assume a future—whether a thousand days, a thousand years, a thousand centuries. It is this belief, this consuming faith, that motivates our work; it is a mindset that archivists have, whether conscious or unconscious, when engaged in their work. This archival faith is integral to our work; it is embedded in our professional being.

For those of us born in the long shadow of Hiroshima, Nagasaki, and Auschwitz; and who grew up under Sputnik skies and unfettered nuclear proliferation, any commitment to a long-term view of our existence— that is, a faith in our future—is a tenuous, if not illogical, proposition. Add to this list the existential crises of climate change and pandemic, the social epidemic of racism, and the intimate threats occasioned by student loan debt, and faith in our future could be described as folly. [13] If we choose faith, we must, at some level, suspend reason in order to believe in something higher than reason. Søren Kierkegaard, the nineteenth-century Danish philosopher, writes that we can live and survive in this world only on the strength of the *absurd*, which, he argues, man "grasps by faith." He contends, "Faith is therefore no aesthetic emotion, but something far higher . . . it is not the immediate inclination of the heart but the paradox of existence."[14] In embracing the absurd, archivists toil in the preservation of the past and present for the benefit of future generations.

As James O'Toole and Richard Cox have noted, "The wide diffusion of literacy throughout human culture has meant that an ever-widening circle of people creates records and continues into an indefinite future to make use of the information these contain."[15] This indefinite future is at the heart of geographer Kenneth Foote's discussion of collective memory. In contemplating the need to identify the location of nuclear waste sites for the life of their toxicity, he observes: "Warning future generations about the location of waste sites is a serious public policy issue and raises the possibility of archives being used to help communicate across spans of time greater than any single civilization has ever endured." Perhaps as long as ten millennia.[16] If we trust in the existence of those imminent generations, and if our goal is to preserve records into a distant and indefinite future, then throughout our work we are knowingly committing acts of archival faith.

A lived archival faith, as a process, demands that we continually affirm a human dignity that recognizes the "equal and incalculable value" of every human being.[17] It cannot be separated from our everyday actions; indeed, renewal of archival faith and affirmation of human dignity are central to the archival endeavor. We rekindle that faith, and should live it passionately, each day through the activities we employ in speaking to the future.

In order to channel archival faith profitably for the benefit of the future, we must convert beliefs into meaningful action. This entails constituting our work lives in such a way that our actions are consequential at all times. But holding this faith also means being accountable for our actions, and recognizing that sometimes we fail to be guided by archival faith and that failure can produce harm. Nevertheless, archival faith is an essential element of archival being; one does not exist separately without the other. Archival faith is ultimately a meta-virtue that informs the body of our work and lives at the heart of archival being. I believe there are three virtues central to the understanding of archival faith and archival being; they inform our essence as individual practitioners and as a profession; and they permit us to engage our work in an authentic manner. They are *radical self-understanding, intention,* and *integrity.*

Radical Self-Understanding

Radical self-understanding is a personal and collective analytical process that requires deep contemplation and self-examination practices. According to twentieth-century philosopher and theologian Abraham Joshua Heschel, there are two ways of thinking: conceptual and situational. The former entails the act of reasoning to enhance our knowledge of our role in the world; it deals in terms of principles, assumptions, and doctrines. Applying this mode of thinking in the archival setting might lead us to consider the role archives and archivists play in the broad sweep of information and knowledge maintenance, as well as the archival role in developing a historical understanding of the world. Conceptual thinking is distant; it is a universal outlook and is often characterized by detachment. Situational thinking, on the other hand, involves an inner experience and strives for understanding issues of personal existence. It is not about analyzing concepts, but rather is concerned with the personal encounter and exploration of situations and our need to understand that encounter. Situational thinking is particular, it is about what archivists encounter every day in the workplace; it is intimate. As Heschel notes, "Unless we are in love or remember vividly what happened to us when we were in love, we are ignorant of love."[18]

Both conceptual and situational thinking are necessary to wholly comprehend and appreciate the world and our place in it. By engaging in conceptual and situational thinking and applying them to our endeavors, we make the leap toward *radical self-understanding,* what also has been called the "self-cognition of the human spirit."[19] Radical self-understanding, according to Heschel, is a process, not a product; it is "thinking about thinking . . . a process of analyzing the act of thinking, as a process of introspection, of watching the intellectual self in action."[20] The term *radical* is employed in its literal meaning of "root" or relating to the origin of something. In this sense radical self-understanding results from deep reflection on the nature of one's work (and/or life) in order to obtain a critical appreciation, not only of the doing, but also of the reason for doing. "Radical self-understanding must embrace not only the fruits of thinking, namely the concepts and symbols, but also the root of thinking, the depth of insight, the moments of immediacy in the communion of the self with reality."[21]

Radical self-understanding requires the work of *self-clarification* and *self-examination*. Self-clarification is reminding ourselves "of what we stand for" and then evaluating how that affects our experiences, informs our insights, and shapes our attitudes and fundamental principles. In the archivist's circumstance, self-clarification is uncovering the meaning of our profession and its claims in society, distinguishing its inherent values, and separating principles from opinions. Self-examination is the individual "effort to scrutinize the authenticity of our position" and test the limits of our deep convictions about our values and principles.[22]

Heschel draws this philosophy of self-cognition in part from the earlier work of German philosopher Edmund Husserl, who argues that philosophers cannot possibly engage in authentic philosophical explorations unless "we reflect back, in a thorough historical and critical fashion, in order to provide, before all decisions, for a radical self-understanding."[23] He reasons that philosophers can truly comprehend their work "only through a critical understanding of the total unity of history—our history."[24] For archivists, radical self-understanding requires a genuine and deep exploration of the profession's *why* and *what* questions: why do we engage in archival work; what is its meaning; and, indeed, what does it mean to be an archivist? The archival concern then is uncovering the depth-meaning of archives and distinguishing its principles and values. Self-examination attends to the personal values held by archivists as individuals that, in turn, fundamentally influence their work. In the aggregate, these values are elemental in forming archival being or what might even be called the archival soul.

Following this argument, archivists can engage their work authentically and discern its very nature through a deep understanding of self and of the social, cultural, political, intellectual, and historical processes that shape our profession. This ongoing examination of our existence and our actions is a crucial task in the faithful pursuit of radical self-understanding. The process of striving for understanding is the basis of thinking contextually and for overcoming the prejudgments we all bring to the table.

The discussion of professional values initiated by Mark Greene in his 2008 presidential address to the Society of American Archivists was an exercise in self-clarification at the association level. Greene argues, "Values are the embodiment of what an organization stands for, and should be the basis for the behavior of its members." He suggests that in defining core values, it is necessary to identify them in relation to archival power.[25] His call for SAA to formally define the "core values" of the archival profession was answered in May 2011 when the SAA Council adopted the Core Values of Archivists.[26] Recognizing that these values are dynamic, the profession has engaged in collective radical self-understanding through ongoing evaluation of the Core Values, including a session at the 2019 annual meeting; the publication of a book of essays in which several authors provided fresh perspectives, suggested changes to the wording of specific values, and reinterpreted the meaning of the values;[27] and, ultimately, in August 2020, a revision to the 2011 statement.

Deep and critical engagement with the history and meaning of the profession, including a commitment to consuming its past and present literature, is a constitutive piece of radical self-understanding. This can be an individual—but should also be a collective—process; the recognition that communities, whether religious, social, or professional, have a collective responsibility to strive for self-cognition. In this sense, contemplation and reflection collectively and as individuals are responsibilities that all archivists have to themselves, the field, and their communities. Archivists create opportunities to achieve radical self-understanding through interactions at national and regional meetings, publications, and participation in other professional forums. We meaningfully embrace

radical self-understanding in our daily work and professional relationships when we approach it as a focused and enduring process and commit
to it with intention.

Intention

Returning to the instructive logic of the innkeeper's story earlier in this
chapter, the smallest action—reboxing an accession, tallying data from
a reference slip, for example—is often taken for granted and treated as
routine. Yet, each of these activities can be engaged as if it is the critical
point on the holistic continuum of the archival endeavor. This attention
to detail—to the seemingly mechanical aspects of our work—admittedly,
is not an easy, nor admired, task. Modern society, including our own profession, moves at such a rapid pace and consuming intensity that we have
"no time to think," and even less for deep contemplation.[28] Framing this
problem as a professional danger, Richard Cox suggests that "Archivists
and records managers often portray themselves (not necessarily on purpose) as too busy to read, to think, or to stay current with their field."[29]

Distraction and too many competing chores could have been Rabbi
Hayyim's undoing. The job of the innkeeper was intense and full; working around the clock, bombarded from all sides by multiple customer
demands, food preparation and clean up, waiting tables, cleaning rooms,
washing linens, dealing with suppliers, keeping the books—not dissimilar in breadth and complexity to the daily tasks of the archivist. Yet, we
learn from the innkeeper's example that one can maintain a clear focus
through the intention of one's thoughts directed toward one's actions.
Indeed, David Levy, an information science professor concerned with
issues of contemplative balance, argues that "to pay attention, to be more
mindful or aware, is to be more intimately connected with what is going
on within and around us." He evokes the power and possibility of self-
observation and reflection.[30] In Jewish thought, this is the concept of
kavannah.

Kavannah entails directing the mind toward doing a thing with intention, meaning, or purpose, "toward the accomplishment of a particular act, the state of being aware of what we are doing, of the task we are engaged in." But kavannah is more than merely a state of mind. An act may be performed in full participation of the mind and yet be discharged as little more than a perfunctory duty. Heschel emphasizes that to commit an act is one thing, but "to partake of its inspiration another. . . . Those who dwell exclusively on the technicalities of performance fail to be sensitive to the essence of the task."[31] The archival analog is to recognize the implication of each thing we do—no matter how insignificant or mundane or how crucial or essential it may seem—for the communities, colleagues, and institutions in our professional spheres, and to engage our work with purposeful intention.

A danger in this argument is the potential mischaracterization of intention as a form of quietism—the abandonment of the will or the passive acceptance of things as they are without questioning. Michelle Caswell suggests this danger, noting a general disrespect for archival labor, in part because archivists have constructed "their own feminized service roles as 'handmaidens to historians.'"[32] Intention, in my reading, however, is a source of archival power, benefitting our work and those with whom we engage. If intention—whether defined as kavannah or mindfulness—is identified with a retreat entirely into personal reflection and pulling out of engagement, then we lose the power of our virtues as demands on our social experience and we can fall prey to ethical anguish.[33] Reflection, meditation, and inwardness alone are not paths to the ethical; rather, they are valuable tools if they lead to better engagement. Authentic intention is not self-effacement, but rather is a powerful self-limitation to create space for *the other*. Intention reaches beyond the self and seeks to benefit others; it is outward-focused and should cultivate commitment to moral action. The innkeeper's actions, the model of intention, were certainly directed in that manner. Archivists are truly involved in the essence of their tasks when they recognize that the human-directed nature of archival work is essential to embracing the obligation of producing value in society. To produce value, we must act with value.

Integrity

Hugh Taylor, pondering the knowledge, attitudes, and skills archivists need to make their way in the rapid currents of the information age, noted that "only by exploring and extending our professional reach to the limit of our integrity, as I have tried to do, will we escape that backwater which, though apparently calm and comfortable, may also be stagnant with the signs of approaching irrelevance."[34] Taylor, whose most important work strikes me as a quest for radical self-understanding, does not define what he means by integrity; but he does formulate the critical argument that integrity is associated with relevance, both of archives and archivists.

In practical usage, as well as in philosophical thinking, integrity has different—but associated—meanings. As a virtue term, integrity relates to the quality or content of a person's character. Integrity requires that the individual stand for something, act unhypocritically and consistently based on that stance, and operate within a framework of respect for the judgment of others. In this sense, the individual deliberates within a community of people to discover what in life is worth doing.[35] Integrity requires living one's life according to one's beliefs and best judgments, including in the professional arena; it is a matter of personal character. Integrity has a dimension of morality and moral purpose that relates to the wholeness of one's character. Indeed, integrity is the pursuit of moral purpose; it reflects a person's dedication to the pursuit of a moral life including accepting the responsibility of the demands of such a life.[36] The notion of moral purpose arises throughout this book. Morality and moral philosophy are not traditional archival concepts and seldom in the past found their way into the literature. However, the increased focus on justice theory as an archival imperative, the community archives movement, and the introduction of affect theory and feminist ethics of care into archival discourse are normalizing the language of moral action.[37]

Within limits of the archivist's professional context (the social and cultural milieu in which we live and the types of institutions and power structures in which we work), it is incumbent upon us to act with integrity, convey our beliefs to our employers, and continually educate ourselves and others about the power of virtues. When we do this, we are demonstrating professional integrity. Professional integrity, then, is governed by established standards of behavior and adherence to professional principles in conjunction with the moral and ethical beliefs of the individual; in other words, professional integrity in great measure is acting with personal integrity in the work environment.

Taylor's correlation of integrity with relevance begs the question: What makes archives and archivists relevant and how do we maintain that relevance? A key factor identified by a few archival writers is trust—user communities must have trust that the records they examine can be believed and that the repository in which they are found can be trusted to care for the materials.[38] A crucial part of that trust equation is the perceived trustworthiness of the archivist. (Trust and trustworthiness are explored in more detail in chapter three).

Trust, trustworthiness, and integrity are elements of living one's life in a moral and ethical manner. If we engage our work in this way, we are ultimately compelled to ask the central question of moral philosophy posed by eighteenth-century philosopher Immanuel Kant: "What ought I to do?"[39] This is not an abstract query, nor is it simply a rhetorical question. Rather this question—"What ought I to do?"—is the most fundamental question we should ask at every turn. Rabbi Hayyim's answer was to clean the dishes so no food was present and the pots and pans did not rust. Every action requires a decision procedure, a mode of determining the correct action to take. To reach that decision, one must be engaged with everything one does and continually ask that essential question. When we do this, we operate within a moral and ethical imperative that ultimately associates archival practice with "the constant occupation of justice."[40]

Archival Commonality

The wide variety of professional environments, the power relationships in which archivists reside, and the social and cultural differences between archivists and archival institutions on the surface seem to suggest that an essential archival character is elusive, that there is no essential nature inherent among archivists. This is not unique to the archival endeavor. Authors in virtually every learned profession have written essentialism out of the theoretical equations of their disciplines: education, child development, gender studies, post-colonialist studies, philosophy, sociology, the hard sciences, etc. For example, sociologist Stephan Fuchs argues that essentialism is a binary, black or white theory: "Operationally, essentialism is the failure to allow for variation. Where nothing is allowed to vary, nothing can be explained. . . . Allowing for variation means dissolving natural kinds and their essential properties into relationships and forces."[41]

Yet these attacks are often themselves binary; they are formed by striking a singular anti-essentialist position lacking any nuanced consideration of commonality among subjects. This distinction is important if only to suggest that there is some non-rigid point between the extremes that satisfies both the pluralist drive to charter our differences and the compelling comfort of the concept of natural kind or essences. This middle ground exists in archives in the very definition of our mission and the idea of the archival perspective; it can be characterized by the theory of exemplification. A set of entities in which all members have one or more common characteristics, yet differ in other regards, meets the definition of exemplars.[42] In this respect, it is easy to argue the case that a certain commonality exists among archivists, that there are shared essential characteristics that shape archivists and inform archival work. These include, but are not limited to, our set of professional values, an archival perspective and unique way of thinking, an ethic of preservation and access, and a powerful public service orientation (whether to a broadly defined public or more narrowly within a corporate setting). These characteristics are the foundation of an archival culture that inspires our relationships and strengthens bonds of archival commonality.

Commonality, paired with difference, is a cardinal locus on the compass of archival being. One commonality among archivists is the instantiation of personal values, although those values may be pivotally different from person to person. Personal values and commitments are critical in shaping each archivist's worldview. In suggesting that we exhibit a healthy skepticism about the claims and promises of the information age, Richard Cox expressed an intensely personal statement of how he scrutinizes technology's effect on society. "For me," he writes, "it is my hope in personal redemption, which provides a foundation for evaluating how and what I do, and how and what I teach . . . it is the basis for what I choose to say, especially in the realm of ethics and morality, about how people should approach the promises of the information age."[43] His comment is an intensely clear and candid statement of a personal meta-value. It is important for archivists to understand fully what their fundamental beliefs and motivations are and how these inform their thoughts, speech, and actions.

Connectedness

Andrea Hinding, a past president of the Society of American Archivists, in her delightfully titled "Of Archivists and Other Termites," concludes that we need to see our "collective work as cultural, as one crucial part of a web of connectedness among people and across time. . . . Seeing archives as part of a larger phenomenon gives us another way to find meaning and value in our work."[44] Perhaps Hinding was presaging the community archives movement and its power to transform through ideas such as symbolic space, affect and emotion, imagination, and political activism.[45] Heschel captures the view of meaning and value expressed by Hinding with his definition of appreciation as an attitude of the whole person: "It is one's being drawn to the preciousness of an object or situation. . . . The music in a score is open only to him who has music in his soul. It is not enough to play the notes; one must be what he plays . . . one must live what he does."[46] Rabbi Hayyim did precisely this. He discovered the sacred in all of his actions, great and small, and he recognized that those actions connected with and benefitted others. This, I hope, describes how most, if not all, archivists live their lives and do their work.

O'Toole and Cox point to broad knowledge "as the foundation for the archivist's perspective." Their catalog includes knowledge of creators and the context of records creation; of the records themselves and their lifecycle; of how recorded information might be used; and of archival principles and techniques. And they add to this a powerful ethical stance in forming the archival perspective.[47] Looking beyond the archival perspective, archivists should recognize and embrace a vibrant sense of archival being built on the foundation of archival faith. Being and faith are constructed with the tools of radical self-understanding, intention, and integrity. There may very well be additional virtues that resonate with archivists as elemental to their sense of archival being. Indeed, the virtues given voice in subsequent chapters are part and parcel of archival being. The fundamental ontological attitudes of being and faith, when crafted together, form the foundation upon which the important work of relationship is fashioned.

Archivists need to reach well beyond the archival perspective for an understanding of archival being. In his 1990 SAA presidential address, John Fleckner helped move us on that trajectory. He posited a meaning of professionalism that situates archivists in a universal vision of service. He wrote, "As 'professionals' we have something to profess, something more than devotion to the latest techniques. And further, that in this act of professing we tie our own self-interest to the well-being of the larger society so that our profession is not merely that of a self-interested clique, but instead a legitimate claim on behalf of the greater public interest."[48] Putting this vision into play requires an archival self-consciousness that is turned toward *the other*—whether colleagues, users, our institutions, or broader communities.

CHAPTER TWO

Archival Covenant

The biblical Ruth is a heroine of profound emotional resilience. Recently widowed, Ruth casts her lot with her mother-in-law, Naomi, through the poetic phrases "wherever you go, I will go; wherever you lodge, I will lodge; your people shall be my people, and your God my God."[1] Her proclamation is a gesture of fidelity to a mutual cause; Ruth, publicly declaring her devotion to Naomi, enters a relationship of moral commitment. Ruth's action is a common ceremonial or ritual manifestation of covenant.[2]

The expression of covenant is as old as the human ability to form relationships. Perhaps the simplest definition of *covenant* is "a pact . . . of mutual obligation."[3] Although accurate in its way, this definition approaches neither the complexity of the concept nor the intensity of its binding nature. In many modern contexts, covenant has been likened to contract; but there is a critical difference between the two—it is the difference between a transaction and a relationship. Jonathan Sacks, former Chief Rabbi of Great Britain, makes the simple, but elegant, distinction: "A contract is about interests. A covenant is about identity. It is about you and me coming together to form an 'us.' That is why contracts benefit, but covenants transform."[4] While contracts are concrete agreements of limited duration, covenants are compacts of enduring relationships. At the interpersonal level, individuals can relate to one another in an infinite number of ways and thus have infinite aspirations for the relationship. Attendant to this reading is an understanding that covenant also manifests in infinite obligations to *the other*.[5] In Sacks' formulation, the language of covenant includes words such as dignity, integrity, trust, love, faithfulness, cooperation, morality, and a host of other emotionally powerful and affirming terms that describe a coming together of partners to share and to achieve. My conception of covenant in the archives conforms to these ideas.[6] Covenant evokes an overwhelmingly positive connotation associated with religious culture, political theory, and interpersonal relationships characterized by obligation and reciprocity.

Covenant is a foundational idea in archives, framed in personal and professional values and ideals, emanating logically (or perhaps naturally) from a developed sense of archival being that opens our minds and hearts to relationship, duty, and service to others. Archival being is an existential posture and life orientation in the work environment. Covenant, as a natural and rational extension of archival being, is an ideal affecting interpersonal and group relations that are direct products of a full understanding and assimilation of archival being.

What I call *archival covenant* informs individual and collective obligation in our work. The following section offers a more detailed definition of covenant grounded in political theory but with direct application to interpersonal and professional relationship. The primary focus of the chapter is the very personal nature of covenant in the lives and work of individual archivists and the exploration of three concepts that are central to archival covenant and implicit in the archival endeavor— *genuine encounter, sacred obligation*, and *piety of service*.

Defining Covenant

Sacks expresses a lyrical contour of covenant, but a more fully formed definition is required to shape the concept for our purposes. Since ancient times, covenants have fashioned important religious, political, and social relationships such as treaties between sovereigns and compacts between peoples and their gods. The oldest known formal covenants are the Hittite vassal treaties in which inferior rulers of independent tribes or small kingdoms pledge fealty to a superior king who in response promises to protect the vassals.[7] A prescribed public spectacle accompanied an agreement, acting as a symbolic gesture to solemnize the covenantal relationship. In ancient times this might be the sacrifice of an animal to authenticate the covenant and indicate there is no going back to pre-covenant conditions.[8] In various religious traditions, the most common definitions of covenant extend from theology and entail a people's adherence to divine law and a deity's promise of protection. Whether political, social, or theological in nature, covenant in its earliest manifestations was an agreement between unequal parties that required obligation by both partners, not simply special privilege for one party.

Covenant later came to assume (although not exclusively) an egalitarian character of compact between equal partners who forge a relationship to achieve shared goals. These might be treaties between entities of equal status or personal bonds between individuals. In all cases, a covenant defines the relationship between the parties and lends that relationship an enduring quality and sense of commitment and obligation. In the modern era, the ancient, symbolic gesture gave way to signatures on an agreement or a public declaration.

Political scientist Daniel Elazar, the most prolific contemporary exponent of covenant as political theory, argues that it is a core idea in the development of the liberal republican state. But his definition, with its emphasis on the voluntary limitations of power accepted by all partici-pants, can be read to include interpersonal relationship. He argues that covenant is

> a morally informed agreement or pact based upon voluntary
> consent, established by mutual oath or promises, involving
> or witnessed by some transcendent higher authority, between
> peoples or parties having independent status, equal in
> connection with the purposes of the pact, that provides for
> joint action or obligation to achieve defined ends (limited or
> comprehensive) under conditions of mutual respect, which
> protect the individual integrities of all the parties to it.[9]

Key in this definition is the notion that covenant is a voluntary ordering and linking of parties that preserves their respective integrity and creates individual space for the parties to remain free, yet unequivocally subject to certain obligation. Covenant binds people together in relationships that foster mutual respect and natural duty to community, polity, civil society, and self.[10] This political definition of covenant, drawn largely from a biblical context, articulates the substance of almost all forms of covenant from the Hittites to modern republican constitutionalism to the sacred bonds between close friends and lovers.[11] Elazar's definition productively aligns covenant with an archival ethos built on relationships of moral commitment and obligation.

Moral Commitment

Covenant is firmly rooted in the locus of moral philosophy and personal and professional virtues. James O'Toole, visualizing theology and faith as a theoretical basis for archives, raises a series of questions that interrogate the moral, ethical, and justice dimensions of archival work. He asks:

> If I accept the philosophical and symbolic understandings of
> faith, how am I supposed to act, particularly in those areas of
> life that are seemingly far removed from transcendent concerns
> and are rooted instead in the messy business of life? What ethical
> standards ought I apply in my personal, family, community,
> economic, and political life? Which actions are right and which
> are wrong? What is moral and ethical behaviour in archives? In
> managing archival collections, do we pursue self-interest only

or is there some larger community (public, professional, other) whose legitimate needs ought to affect our behaviour? How, for example, do we develop the moral sense of archivists?[12]

Although the purpose of O'Toole's article is to formulate a moral theology of long-term historical accountability, his questions raise significantly broader concerns. He contemplates principled personal and professional relationships and ideals of conduct in human affairs.

More recently, archival scholars have introduced work steeped in feminist theory that lends fresh perspective on ideas of moral authority. The exploration of attentiveness, care, love, empathy, emotion, and vulnerability explicitly enters the sphere of moral responsibility. Michelle Caswell and Marika Cifor make a powerful case for what I would suggest is covenantal obligation. The authors write, "An ethics of care, which we situate here under the larger tent of feminist ethics, stresses the ways people are linked to each other and larger communities through webs of responsibilities." They continue, "A feminist ethics framework posits interlacing and ongoing relationships of mutual obligation that are dependent on culture and context."[13] Thus, archivists have affective responsibility toward those with whom we develop archival relationships: creators, records subjects, users, and our larger communities. The feminist ethics of care is among the most promising additions to archival theory precisely because it incorporates morality and moral language in scholarly discourse, opens the door to emotion in archival practice, and is compatible with a philosophical turn toward archival covenant.

Genuine Encounter

Archival work is a series of direct and indirect existential encounters—with creators, donors, users, and colleagues; with the materials we maintain and the tools we use; with the policies, procedures, and standards we employ; and with the past, present, and future. At the interpersonal level, covenant arises from encounters of mutual respect, response, and reciprocity—what can be called radical engagement, but more appropriately might be termed *genuine encounter*.[14] Martin Buber, an Austrian-born twentieth-century philosopher of dialogic existentialism, taught "that no encounter with a being or a thing in the course of our life lacks a hidden significance." This includes the "people we live with or meet with, the animals that help us with our farm work, the soil we till, the materials we shape, the tools we use."[15] Thus, every encounter has a potential immanent importance that we can sanction by our ability to make it genuine.

Buber communicates a model of genuine encounter articulated in his short work, *I and Thou*. He argues that there are two approaches for connecting with the world: through experience, which he calls the I-It interaction, and through encounter, the I-You. In the former, we engage a being or thing as an object (an "It") to be used or analyzed for our own benefit—for instance, viewing a researcher only as an addition to our user statistics or a donor as a notch on our acquisition belt. In the I-It experience, we are observers, apart from the person or object, separated by concern for ourselves alone. If our donor relation work focuses only on capturing a prized collection and does not recognize the "You" inherent in the donor, then we exist solely in the realm of experience and our response diminishes the human being. In the I-You relationship, we become fully attuned and present and encounter occurs with our undivided consciousness. We encounter the entire essence of the other being (the "You") as if that being is the whole universe. Buber expresses this idea in a slightly different manner in the following passage: "When we walk our way and encounter a man who comes toward us, walking his way, we know our way only and not his; for his comes to life for us only in the encounter."[16] When genuine encounter occurs, both the "I" and the "You" are transformed by what Buber calls the "event of relation." The donor, then, is treated "as an end also and never only as a means."[17]

Nowhere in archival literature is this expressed so beautifully as in Linda Long's moving discussion of the death of her friend and donor Tee Corinne. What can only be defined as a covenant of love developed between the two; Long, curator of manuscripts at the University of Oregon, describes it as a relationship of reciprocity and trust. "In a combined professional relationship and friendship, we were able to develop trust in each other," Long recalls, and then notes, "the experience taught me that the archivist is the keeper of someone's life."[18] This is not to suggest that all donor relations should evolve to the interpersonal level that Long experienced. While friendships of lasting quality are not uncommon between archivists and donors or users, Long's experience is not the norm. Nevertheless, encountering another in an I-You relationship can lead only to mutual respect and response, which ultimately engenders trust.

In 1982, when I was a manuscripts curator at the Western Reserve Historical Society (WRHS), I suggested to Bertha Rosenthal, the widow of Rudolph Rosenthal, a prominent rabbi in Cleveland for forty-six years who had died in 1979, that his records be transferred to WRHS. Staff at the society had previously been unsuccessful in attempts to collect the papers. Upon arriving at the Rosenthal home, I discovered the reason. Bertha was still deeply mourning her husband three years after his death. She could not bring herself to go through his records and when she spoke of him, she broke into sobs. I gave her the space to cry, and when she was ready, I engaged her in conversation about her husband, his career, and their life together. This conversation elicited more tears, but it established a genuine bond between the two of us. She told me to take whatever the WRHS wanted. We stayed in touch as staff worked with the records, and as a gesture of appreciation she invited my wife and me to her family Passover Seder. Our encounter did not approach the intimate friendship of Long and Corinne, but we did build a relationship of mutual respect and trust.

Living only in the realm of experience precludes meaningful participation in the world; it entails living in a shroud of exclusive self-interest. At worst, it focuses one on the self and can lead to hyper-individualism, self-gratification, and the development of what theologian Eugene Borowitz calls "the sanctity of personal choice," which ultimately privileges "flabby ethics." It is in the construction of personal relationship, which requires positioning the self in the context of others, that we accept obligation without sacrificing selfhood and autonomy. This is the sociality of the self, the placement of the autonomous self squarely in the context of social responsibility and living in reciprocal respect.[19] The construction of covenantal meaning is where relationship can be formed by imposing the I-You modality on the intersection of post-enlightenment self-interest and postmodern social responsibility. It is in the action of stepping beyond the self to recognize the needs of *the other* where the archivist's sense of service is best recognized.

Archivists are purveyors of context; we endeavor to discern and disclose the continual making and remaking of the record. In doing so, we overlay our own biases and beliefs, which are shaped by our surroundings and experiences, by our own personal contexts. South African archivist Verne Harris maintains that the only ethical response to personal experiences and surroundings is the Derridean concept of hospitality—by which he means respecting *the other*, welcoming the stranger, and embracing what is beyond the limits of our cognitive grasp. Indeed, Harris argues, ethics is hospitality.[20] Another useful construct is found in Brien Brothman's discussion of archives as a gift. He reviews the concepts of *gift* and *giving* in social theory and then argues that archives represent a gift between generations, thus opening the potentially fertile ground of archival covenant with the dead and the as yet unborn.[21] Similarly, relating in the I-You intimacy articulates archival contextualization on an interpersonal and moral plane. Understanding your own context—engaging in the monumental effort of radical self-understanding—is developing your strong and authentic "I"; understanding the context of another is recognizing the authentic "You." Understanding and engaging both at once is *genuine encounter*.

Sacred Obligation

Two decades ago, David Gracy penned the unstartling but important observation that "use is the purpose for which archives are kept." Writing about access and use, Gracy answers the question: What is our first obligation?[22] Perhaps in contradistinction, Richard Cox and Helen Samuels have argued that appraisal is the archivist's first responsibility upon which all subsequent archival work depends.[23] There is no question that the core archival functions are of a piece; together they form a whole in which each function relates to and in some way informs the others. One should not prize a given function with an essential primacy, as they are all critical elements of the archival whole. Nevertheless, my point, credibly born of years in government service, is that access and use maintain the distinction of first among equals. The core functions of appraisal and selection, arrangement and description, and preservation are performed to meet that first obligation—providing access to records. But I suggest reframing the question as "who is our first obligation?" The context in which the question is asked—whether in the research room, a classroom, the budget office, a donor's home, at the processing table, a community space—may produce different answers (some perhaps fraught with serious professional implications); nevertheless, those answers should always evoke encounter and relationship.

Relationship is the key to authentic covenant and, ultimately, covenant is a relationship of moral responsibility. Kant calls this the categorical imperative; for archivists it might best be termed *sacred obligation*. The term *sacred* is not necessarily used in its theological or religious sense, but rather should be defined more broadly to mean devoted exclusively to a single thing; entitled to reverence and respect; highly valued and important. We can gain clarity from the language of obligation in the 1995 patient-physician covenant, which should resonate with archivists. It states:

> Medicine is, at its center, a moral enterprise grounded in a covenant of trust. This covenant obliges physicians to be competent and to use their competence in the patient's best interests. Physicians, therefore, are both intellectually and morally obliged to act as advocates for the sick wherever their welfare is threatened.[24]

The covenant, drafted in response to increasing depersonalization in medical care, argues that medical professionals constitute a moral community whose practitioners cannot meet these obligations effectively without the "virtues of humility, honesty, intellectual integrity, compassion, and effacement of excessive self-interest."[25]

Christine Cassel, a physician and one of the authors of the patient-physician covenant, asserts that there is a "sacred responsibility of physician to patient" that unambiguously obligates physicians to serve those who seek medical assistance, to sublimate self-interest before the welfare of the patient, to be accountable to the broader public, to contribute to the welfare of humankind, and to represent moral and ethical values to society. She concludes that the physician's role "can and ultimately does have spiritual dimensions."[26] One can easily imagine reading "archivist" in place of "physician" in Cassel's essay. I believe archives is a moral enterprise, that the community of archivists is implicitly shaped by a covenantal ethics that is responsive in character, that there is a spiritual element in our work, and that archival covenant incurs prerogative through the notion of sacred obligation. This assertion recognizes the common responsibilities of responsiveness and obligation shared by physicians and archivists for their respective "others." It is not meant to equate technical areas of practice between the professions. Unquestionably, the existential stakes are much higher in medical relationships.

The challenge of the patient-physician covenant is making it a reality for all patients, providing equality of treatment, an ideal we know has not been met. This is the same challenge archivists face. The idea of sacred obligation rests on the notions of trust and reciprocity of need that are integral to the idea of a responsive covenantal ethics and responsible encounter. Mary Jo Pugh, former editor of *American Archivist* and a widely read scholar on archival reference, gives play to these very ideas when discussing the human dimension of reference work and the necessity for understanding individual needs: "Sensitivity, clarity, and a genuine spirit of public service are needed to ensure successful interpersonal relationships in archival reference work."[27] Wendy Duff makes a similar point: "Putting users at ease and setting the tone help build a relationship."[28]

Pugh and Duff express sensibilities that converge at the borders of genuine encounter and sacred obligation, even if their language does not precisely cross over. Putting this to practice, Stacie Williams provides a model for what genuine encounter looks like. Williams writes of an encounter at the reference desk in which a regular patron from Eastern Europe raised many questions that on their face could be challenged as racist, or more charitably as insensitive. The researcher inquired: "Who is Oprah Winfrey? She is from humble background, yes? How did she get to be so famous and rich and not others? What kind of last name is Winfrey? She is brown like you and not darker, so she has different blood, yes?" Williams could have used her power to brush off or discount the patron's questions as offensive. Instead, she embraced the experience as an opportunity for education and connection, and framed the encounter as an example of how an archives can better serve when it has a diverse staff. As important, I believe Williams' response illustrates (whether consciously or not) a sense of sacred obligation and is an example of the I-You encounter.[29]

A significant characteristic of the patient-physician covenant is the recognition that the relationship generally is between parties of unequal power. The patient seeking care is confronted by the power of a physician with expert knowledge and skill. The patient must trust that that power will be used for his or her benefit. William F. May, a medical ethicist, argues that both parties, despite their inherently unequal power positions, need the covenantal relationship. He writes, "A covenantal ethics helps acknowledge this full context of need and indebtedness in which professional duties are undertaken and discharged. It also relieves the professional of the temptation and pressure to pretend that he is a demigod exempt from human exigency."[30] Archivists, too, exert power and must take ethical care when we conduct appraisals, describe records, and provide access—we are controlling available evidence and information, and, to a certain extent, what knowledge can be created.[31] Thus, building trust erected on a foundation of the archivist's trustworthiness is a vital archival function.

Covenant relationships ideally would exist in all relevant spaces of archival life. Just as there are inherently unequal relationships between physicians and patients, archivists also find themselves on the lower rung of the power equation in relation to employers, employing institutions, and, in certain circumstances, donors. Institutions and bureaucracies are not always democratic—and especially not loving—communities. There is little equality in the employer-employee relationship, but that does not exempt one from the hard work of trying to forge appropriate levels of trust that will support covenantal relations; this should be a particular concern for those who hold power over others within archival institutions. Painful personnel and budgetary decisions are a fact of life in the workplace, but I would hope that the compelling virtues of all parties involved would ensure that those decisions are made within a framework of care and respect. Interpersonal covenant based in reciprocity of need and responsiveness requires cognizance of the inherent dangers in unequal power. Mitigating this danger is possible by maintaining an unyielding and unrelenting awareness of sacred obligation in all of our relationships. This is an essential element for inspiring trust.

Piety of Service

The construction of interpersonal archival meaning is accomplished through recognition of *the other* in a genuine relationship, placing one's self within the context of responsible sociality, and recognizing our moral obligations as individuals and professionals. Integrating these interhuman and cognitive lessons and stepping beyond the self to appreciate the needs of *the other*, we actively display fidelity to natural duty and responsibility. The authors of the patient-physician covenant adjure that sacred obligation articulates ethical duty. Similarly, for Buber the responsibility to engage others in relationship—in genuine encounter—is the paradigm of duty. If archivists integrate these notions of genuine encounter and sacred obligation and infuse them in our professional activities, then we cast archival duty as commitment to *piety of service.*

Let's, briefly, unpack this term. *Service* is defined in a broad sense to encompass all the acts of serving that form the archival field and its functions. It includes the concept of contributing to the welfare of others as well as the many acts of serving the past, present, and future, and the records and materials in our care. This creates a logical association with and assumption of duty and obligation.

Piety, as applied here, is derived from interpretations by seventeenth-century philosophers Baruch Spinoza and Gottfried Leibniz. Spinoza associates piety with love and knowledge, arguing that it motivates one to perform acts of justice; Leibniz contends that piety is the highest grade of justice and that being pious means living one's life honorably. To be sure, Leibniz was a devout Christian who argued that piety and justice depended on two conditions: (1) that the soul is immortal and (2) that God is the ruler of the universe. My use of the term is not in its religious sense. Equating piety and justice takes some interpretive license as neither Spinoza nor Leibniz conceived of justice in precisely the manner found in contemporary archival authors, nor, for that matter, in the general outlines I offer throughout this work. Nevertheless, both Spinoza and Leibniz attach special warrant to the virtue of justice.[32] Justice, in this reading, forms a critical expression in the vocabulary of covenant; as it relates to archival piety of service, it communicates moral duty. French philosopher Andre Comte-Sponville maintains, "We must do our duty . . . but never at the expense of justice or in opposition to it. . . . In fact, how could we ever simultaneously be dutiful and unjust, since duty presupposes justice—indeed duty is justice itself, in the form of requirement and obligation."[33] Archival duty, then, assumes that justice in its many forms is a workplace concern. I recognize that for many of us this may require reimagining justice in the archives.

Archival discourse on justice is wide-ranging, covering traditional concerns such as accountability, governmental transparency, and protecting individual and group rights; broader exploration of human rights and reconciliation; locally oriented focus on nontraditional community archives; and anti-oppression work. Not surprisingly, some authors locate justice squarely in a political-archival nexus.[34] For the argument at hand, I think of justice, also, as extending archival covenant to those who may never step into our research rooms or even know what archives are, but nevertheless are affected by the record; and to those seeking what Aristotle called the good life, the life one would like to live consonant with conscientious sociality and in full possession of political rights and obligations. Political philosopher Michael Sandel makes the case that justice is about determining what constitutes the common good and is served when citizens are given what they need to live the good life.[35] Kwame Gyekye makes a similar case for the African conception of the common good which he argues embraces "the needs that are basic to the enjoyment and fulfillment of the life of each individual." Further, it is "an essential feature of the ethics espoused by the communitarian African society."[36]

Archival appraisal and description and ultimately access can be processes for giving people—as individuals and in the aggregate—the tools they need to reason about the common good and to cultivate civic virtue. Whereas David Gracy is correct that use is the reason to keep archives; I further believe promoting the common good is the reason for use. Or, argued another way, the common good is the archives' *raison d'etre*.

When we perform our archival duty and commit to piety of service, we engage in acts of justice all the time. Providing our best service, being cognizant of our obligation to equity and fairness, understanding our own biases and limitations, and being transparent in our actions are all part of acting justly and thus extending justice. This in no way diminishes concepts of universal justice; rather it is recognizing Buber's assertion that no encounter is without its significance. We do not always know what value particular records or information might have to a researcher; whether they might be significant in building a case for righting a wrong, giving voice to those who have been silenced, providing a lesson in civic responsibility, helping construct personal and familial history, or simply giving pleasure. As philosopher Susan Neiman observes, "You needn't think that knowledge of the truth can right all wrongs in order to think it can right some. . . . Simple information is never enough to change the world, but it's always the first place to start."[37]

Covenant and Meaning

The intent of this chapter is the exploration of meaning in our individual lives and how we transmit personal values to our archival work and create value through our actions and relationships. Historian Gordon Wood argues in the introduction to *The Idea of America*, "the meanings that we give to our actions form the structure of our social world. Ideas or meanings make social behaviors not just comprehensible but possible. We really cannot act unless we make our actions meaningful."[38] Covenant, by its nature, conveys meaning. We construct covenantal meaning in the archives through genuine encounter, sacred obligation, and piety of service in a common mission on behalf of the public good. We embrace it, in Buber's words, "for the sake of the work which [we are] destined to perform upon the world."[39]

What is the nature of the work to which Buber refers? Both Jewish and Christian texts variously demand that we love both the stranger and our neighbor. Historically, love has not been a subject discussed in graduate archival seminars (although this could be changing with scholarly explorations of affect theory, radical empathy, and emotional justice). Love is covenantal, as Linda Long's friendship with Tee Corinne illustrates. Archivists Colleen McFarland Rademaker and David McCartney provide additional guidance for living our archival lives in covenant and love. Interpreting the ideas of author C. S. Lewis, Rademaker describes four types of love—romantic, affection, friendship, and charitable—and how they helped her "better understand the longings of my own heart amidst the voices of those representing themselves or merely represented in archival collections."[40] McCartney emotionally recounts a growing and maturing relationship with the deceased activist Steve Smith, a man he never met. Through historical research about Smith and interviews with Smith's family and friends, McCartney developed a close, personal bond with Smith. After meeting and interviewing Smith's wife, McCartney writes unselfconsciously, "I walked out to my car and wrote down everything I could remember, filling two pages of a legal pad. And then I sobbed, uncontrollably, for a few minutes."[41] The point of these two stories is summed up by Rademaker who suggests that attention to love and friendship as archival values would help archivists "more fully realize the humanity of those represented in the historical record." In addition, it might position archivists to assist others in recognizing or experiencing "love within the historical record."[42]

The archival profession does not have a written covenant. Nevertheless, one is implied in the substance of our work. Like the patient-physician covenant, it is a covenant of trust; but it also is more. Let me conclude by returning to the reflections of Rabbi Sacks. Addressing a convocation of Anglican bishops, he distinguished between a covenant of fate and a covenant of faith. The former is created in the face of suffering, a common enemy, or shared fears. A covenant of faith is made by "people who share dreams, aspirations, ideals. They don't need a common enemy, because they have a common hope. They come together to create something new. They are defined not by what happens to them but by what they commit themselves to do."[43] We are a profession defined by a vision of archival covenant and archival faith—Sacks' covenant of faith—and by our commitment to a broad societal good and the welfare of humankind.

Exhibiting the virtues that inform archival covenant—genuine encounter, sacred obligation, and piety of service—should result in archivists being compassionate, empathetic, and kind. Archival covenant, like archival being and archival faith, is an animating ideal, a defining characteristic of our profession with the power to transform our workplaces and relationships. More importantly, developing and nurturing covenantal relationships is a central ethical challenge of the archival endeavor. Archival covenant can illuminate and inspire our professional engagement and serve as a moral compass as we strive to benefit society. The covenant ideal is fertile ground for enriching our personal and professional lives. It is a means for attaining what sociologist Emile Durkheim calls "the life of a moral community."[44]

PART TWO

Archival Citizenship

❝

There is a source of power in each of us that
we don't realize until we take responsibility.
— Diane Nash

It is one thing to be for a cause
and another thing to be in a cause.
— Abraham Joshua Heschel

Sometimes you are erased before you are
given the choice of stating who you are.
— Ocean Vuong

66

We need, in every community,
a group of angelic troublemakers.

— BAYARD RUSTIN

CHAPTER THREE

The Archival Citizen

Bob Moses, a young field representative for the Student Nonviolent Coordinating Committee (SNCC), embedded himself in rural Mississippi in 1961 to direct a voter registration effort among African Americans. On August 29, 1961, while accompanying two men to the Amite County Courthouse in the town of Liberty, Moses was severely beaten by the cousin of the local sheriff. Bloody and dazed, he managed to lead the men to the courthouse, only to have the registrar close the office early. At great personal risk over the course of the next four years, Moses worked in the most hostile counties of the state attempting to register African American voters. He suffered threats, beatings, and jailing, and still remained committed to the work of voter registration. Through the quiet force of his personality and a powerful sense of justice, he kept local and SNCC volunteers focused on their work despite extreme danger. In 1964, leading up to the presidential election, Moses helped organize the Mississippi Freedom Democratic Party which sent an integrated slate of delegates to the Democratic National Convention to challenge the legitimacy of the all-white official state delegation.

A decade later, Moses matriculated at Harvard University, studying the philosophy of mathematics. In 1982, with proceeds from a MacArthur Fellowship, he established the Algebra Project, a foundation dedicated to improving math education for students of color. Moses returned to Mississippi to teach math at a high school that served as a laboratory for his ideas regarding math instruction. The success rates in statewide math exams increased 50 percent in schools where the method was implemented. By 2006 the Project curriculum was offered in over two hundred schools to more than forty thousand minority students, and was an incubator for creation of the Southern Initiative Algebra Project and the Young People's Project. Today, the Algebra Project is a leader and partner among many regional and statewide math literacy programs that formed the national alliance, We the People—Math Literacy for All.[1]

Moses's biography illustrates the best of the responsibility inherent in moral citizenship. The project of human dignity and the extension of basic civil and human rights should be the inheritance for all individuals and groups who are a party to the American experiment. Moses advocated fulfillment of these rights-based promises; but, of equal importance, he recognized and accepted his responsibility to act on behalf of the common good. Indeed, the actions of his life are constructed on a bedrock of responsibility and service. This chapter broadens the idea of sacred obligation (the sublimation of self-interest in service to *the other* and a commitment to the welfare of humankind) that was introduced in chapter two; it is from that perspective I will develop the concept of *archival citizenship* and being a good archival citizen.

American political culture is engulfed in protest and uprising stemming from America's failure to reckon with systemic racism. Among the needed societal changes America must grapple with is development of a truly inclusive public philosophy that can overcome destructive national myths and build a culture of equity, opportunity, and community. Political philosopher Michael Sandel defines public philosophy as "the political theory implicit in our practice, the assumptions about citizenship and freedom that inform our public life." He goes on to note that "The inability of contemporary American politics to speak convincingly about self-government and community has something to do with the public philosophy by which we live."[2] To overcome this shortcoming requires careful deliberation and healthy discourse among citizens about the nature of the common good, how to attain it, and how to fashion an inclusive political community.[3] It is not my intention to posit a public philosophy of archives, but I offer some assumptions about archival citizenship, what characteristics or virtues archival citizenship might entail, and how incorporation of these ideas in our practice—and our being— can benefit the archival endeavor.

In his actions, Bob Moses exhibited the virtues of courage, fidelity, justice, compassion, good faith, and more. His life story illustrates several characteristics that can be the basis for a conception of what it means to be a good archival citizen. These include (but are not necessarily limited to) *trustworthiness, professionalism, difference,* and *care.* These virtues, if put into play by archivists as individuals and in community, can create a sense of citizenship and belonging that benefits the profession and our various stakeholders. To make this case, it is necessary to briefly define what I mean by citizenship in a larger perspective, then focus on citizenship as an element of archival being.

Citizenship

Canadian archival educator Terry Eastwood, writing on the role of archives in a democratic society, draws on and restates political theorist Robert A. Dahl's standards for democracy in a form applicable to archival work. Those central ideas are: supremacy of the people; consent of the governed; rule of law; existence of a common good or public interest; value of the individual as a moral, rational, active citizen; and equal civil rights for all citizens.[4]

Democracy, at the birth of the American republic, represented a radical "new social order with new kinds of linkages holding people together."[5] Yet, the system disenfranchised a majority of the population, it dehumanized the nonwhite residents, it established and then failed to eradicate slavery, and committed near annihilation of indigenous peoples. Applying the idealistic language that forms the central myth of this country as a standard, it is undeniable that the long, slow, and tumultuous movement toward equality and freedom for all is a work in progress that requires answering the call to justice.

In this argument, the virtue of justice is central to the democratic ideal and any meaningful conception of citizenship. Justice in archival theory and as an archival imperative has gained much currency in the past two decades, following the work of Verne Harris, Rand Jimerson, Anne Gilliland, Wendy Duff, David Wallace, Michelle Caswell, and others. These scholars have discussed at length the justice role the archives can and should play in the life of a community and the care archivists need to take in ensuring plurality in their collections, institutions, and public interactions.[6] This, in turn, requires that archivists develop a sense of archival citizenship and be good citizens.

Employing the simplest definition, a citizen "is a member of a political community who enjoys the rights and assumes the duties of membership."[7] Citizens, in this vision, embody the values of discipline, education, independence, and respect for expertise.[8] Michael Sandel casts citizenship in the light of moral philosophy, arguing, "It requires a knowledge of public affairs and also a sense of belonging, a concern for the whole, a moral bond with the community whose fate is at stake. To share in self-rule therefore requires that citizens possess, or come to acquire, certain qualities of character, or civic virtues. But this means that republican politics cannot be neutral toward the values and ends its citizens espouse."[9] These definitions assume some balance between citizen rights and citizen responsibility.

Citizenship theory in the second half of the twentieth century was driven by social movements that focused on individual and group rights in a conscious attempt to meliorate discrimination by sanctioning government authority on the one hand, and protecting citizens from government overreach on the other. Some have argued that this rights-based movement had the unintended consequence of shifting the conception of citizenship away from a balance between rights and responsibility.

The critics of rights-centered politics argue that rights-talk is anemic, shallow, and careless; legitimizes self-gratification over self-discipline; and is strident and inflexible. And most damning, it is a language that, despite its claims, is "not truly about human dignity."[10] This argument is primarily associated with conservative political thinking, but is, I believe, potentially a far more radical approach to citizenship than one might think on first blush.

Extending and defending rights are vital elements of citizenship; there is unquestionably great social value and political necessity in that. There have been long, bitter, and still ongoing struggles to secure the social, political, and economic rights that everyone should enjoy. But a rights-only definition of citizenship creates a poor model, one that alone cannot build a better society. The complete equation includes an equal dose of responsibility and a sense of duty—to one's community, to the larger and smaller polities, and to *the other*. Indeed, engaging in the struggle to secure rights is, itself, a responsibility! Robert Bellah and his coauthors, writing about citizenship, pay tribute to individual rights, but suggest they must exist within a framework of what they call the politics of community: "In the first understanding, politics is a matter of making operative the moral consensus of the community, reached through free face-to-face discussion. . . . Citizenship is virtually coextensive with 'getting involved' with one's neighbors for the good of the community."[11]

Bellah's argument regarding the good of the community may fall short of "the communitarian society," but it does have some common ground with Kwame Gyekye's observation:

> A morality of duty is one that requires each individual to demonstrate concern for the interests of others. The ethical values of compassion, solidarity, reciprocity, cooperation, interdependence, and social well-being, which are counted among the principles of the communitarian morality, primarily impose duties on the individual with respect to the community and its members.[12]

Duty and responsibility conflict with rights only when one argues that my rights are more important than yours or that it is my right to do what

I please, no matter the consequences to others. The responsibility and duty of citizenship is to help secure those rights not yet achieved and to foster and strengthen equality and freedom as a value of the common good. We need to balance rights and responsibilities and ensure the project of human dignity becomes the cornerstone for our thinking about archival citizenship.

Infinite Responsibility

A team of Malaysian researchers recently conducted a quantitative analysis of education textbooks in their country to determine what values are most cited in relation to shaping "good citizens." Among the most important values found were respect, helpfulness, and caring; but by far the dominant value was *responsibility* expressed as self-obligation, accountability, and self-discipline.[13] Political philosopher Yascha Mounk observes that we live in an age of responsibility. However, in the political sphere about which he writes, especially related to welfare reform, the idea has mostly been characterized by a punitive, blame-the-victim conception of personal responsibility. Marika Cifor and Jamie A. Lee make a similar point in their critique of neoliberalism: "The notion we are each individually responsible for all aspects of our lives, has been deployed to legitimate the decimation of social welfare provision and the privatization of many government services, producing a dramatic upward redistribution of wealth."[14]

It is important to note here that when I talk about responsibility, it is not about the conservative or neoliberal conceptions Mounk, Cifor, and Lee critique; my conception of responsibility is that of obligation to *the other*. Mounk, likewise, sets out to reclaim the language of responsibility and to make it constructive:

> Responsibility for ourselves—so central to the punitive conception of responsibility—thus remains important even to a more positive vision. But that positive vision also recognizes that an important part of responsibility is outward-looking. It therefore

> needs to give pride of place to the many ways in which citizens
> value taking on responsibility for others.

He makes the case that in the decisions and actions people take every day, they entwine existence "with the fate of things that lie beyond themselves."[15]

This idea of responsibility has an archival frame in the arguments that an archives' role is to hold governments accountable, enable citizens to know their past, protect civil and human rights, and support the public interest in myriad ways. Jimerson made that case in his 2005 SAA presidential address and further called for archivists to commit to ensuring that the records of marginalized and previously underrepresented groups are included in the archives and that archivists work to open our documentary heritage to all people. Mounk's "things that lie beyond themselves" is precisely the territory Jimerson explored when he wrote "Archives are therefore responsible to all citizens in a democratic society." He further argued that the power that archivists hold should be used not just in the public interest, but "for the good of humankind."[16]

John Fleckner also embraced the responsibility paradigm when he wrote, "What we archivists do is essential to the well-being of an enlightened and democratic society. No, not every step or each day is so vital, but the sum of all our efforts makes a critical difference. . . . The archival record—and here I mean the total of what we look after as well as the underlying principles of records keeping—is a bastion of a just society."[17] Jimerson and Fleckner cast their language in universalist expressions of justice and an archival service ethic. In what I believe is a logical progression, a new generation of archival theorists are exploring justice and obligation in particularistic ways related to community and participatory archives and anti-oppression work. In chapter two, I described the justice and service ethic as sacred obligation and piety of service; those commitments can be repurposed here as critical elements in archival citizenship.

Service, duty, and responsibility are woven into the fabric of the archival endeavor to form a tapestry of justice in the archives. Justice as a proposition in archival theory is still challenged by some who ask: Is speaking of justice akin to wrapping the archivist in the veil of activism?

The term *activist archivist* was once a pejorative, or, at least, a criticism of one's professionalism. To be an activist, one was throwing off the veil of neutrality and objectivity and stepping outside of narrow records concerns, as Archie Motley did in the early 1980s with a call for SAA to take a stand on the issue of a congressional nuclear freeze resolution. My position is that archivists are activists when they do their jobs conscientiously, with attention to justice-based discourse, with the common good in mind, and with moral purpose.[18]

What is meant by *activist archivist* in this context? It is a continuum that runs from direct action in the realm of political justice, such as being a whistleblower—as South African Verne Harris was regarding the destruction of the records related to apartheid—to Aristotelian justice found in the seemingly mundane action of supplying a third grader the required materials for her to create an exhibit, an act that gives her what she needs to live the good life, at least for a specific moment in time. Andrew Flinn and Ben Alexander note that activist approaches to the archival endeavor "embrace a view of archival practice as a form of social, cultural and political activism."[19] This undoubtedly goes too far for some archivists and certainly for some archival institutions, but a focus on archival virtue as "good itself" pushes us toward a kind of activism that, at the very least, raises questions about what supports the common good and creates a just archives. It seems axiomatic that the social good is supported when the records we maintain are inclusive, the archivists who maintain them reflect the population, and the people who use our records come from all sectors and cultural backgrounds in our communities.

It is one thing to be responsible at the societal and institutional levels, to direct archives to support the common good, to foster accountability, to promote knowledge and understanding about democratic institutions; it is quite another to bring our sense of responsibility to the face-to-face encounter. Nearly two centuries ago, Tocqueville observed that the despot "applauds as good citizens those who have no sympathy for any but themselves."[20] His observation points to another form of responsibility, one that is deeply existential and framed by Emmanuel Levinas as *infinite responsibility*. This is Levinas's first philosophy, the ethical demand that obligates us to *the other*. For Levinas, once we see the face of another person, whether we know anything about them, we are unavoidably and inescapably responsible for their needs.[21] This is an inexorable state of being rather than rational cognition; we feel the needs of the other person whose rights become our responsibility. Unlike covenant, this responsibility is not reciprocal; it is an obligation to the uniqueness of other people independent of reward or response.

Archival Citizenship

Assuming it is even possible to consider an archival life of infinite responsibility, or the notion of sacred obligation, how is this operationalized in our work? What does a commitment to archival citizenship entail? What does it mean to be an archival citizen? What are the characteristics (or virtues) that one displays when acting as an archival citizen?

At this point I want to be as clear as possible about what I mean by archival citizenship. It should not be confused with the concept of "citizen archivist," a term applied to people, generally without formal archival education, who take on communal or collective responsibility for community archives projects.[22] For my purposes, archival citizenship adheres to professional archivists and their agency in employing moral judgments and taking moral actions in their work. In addition, we should be careful in crafting definitions. When I talk about citizenship, it is not to be folded into a modern political context that situates citizen and citizenship in a nationalist, militarized, and xenophobic chauvinism. Archival citizenship in my philosophical model is the state of being driven by an inherent sense of the common good and is directed both individually and collectively by a belief in sacred obligation. Our polity is wide and deep and pulls from beyond the borders of professional archivists. Archival citizenship is broadly defined to encompass all of the approaches and avenues evident in the work of archives, whether large or small institutions, professional associations, community archives, community partnerships and alliances, ad hoc archives, postcustodial arrangements, or any other creative or nontraditional approach to archival management. In discussing archival citizenship, it might appear that I am inwardly focused on the individual archivist as citizen, but I am not speaking solely about individualism. Rather, as with the rest of this book, my argument stresses that individuals are inextricably a part of a whole, and that the virtues and responsibilities that inform citizenship adhere to the archival field as a community.

The first section of this book made a case for the virtues that are particularly important in defining a meaningful and expansive archival being: faith, radical self-understanding, intention, integrity, covenant, genuine encounter, sacred obligation, and piety of service. Personal virtues are ways of walking in the world and negotiating myriad relationships; and they are integral to our professionalism. Indeed, they are the bedrock for constructing a work-life of archival citizenship that we can fully live in archival space. Added to those just cited are the four virtues and/or actions that necessarily must be visible to our various constituencies to demonstrate archival citizenship and its attendant responsibilities: *trustworthiness, professionalism, difference,* and *care.*

Trustworthiness

Trust is fundamental to the archival endeavor. Articles abound in our literature discussing trusted archival institutions, trusted digital repositories, and trust in the archivist.[23] Canadian archival educator Heather MacNeil argues that professional identity historically sits atop the twin pillars of trusted custodians and trusted repositories. MacNeil suggests that trust, most often understood in terms of authenticity, accountability, professional competence, and belonging to a community of dependable professionals, has been sorely challenged by "new information and communications technologies and changing intellectual currents inside and outside the field of archives." This and other challenges mean archivists must be open to new narratives about the relationship between records, archivists, and trust.[24]

No matter the framing, trust ultimately resides in a complicated world of relationships. Terry Eastwood notes, "The relationship between archivists and members of society is essentially a fiduciary relationship, one held or given in trust."[25] Complicating the fiduciary or trust relationship is a general disdain that has developed in recent decades for large institutions, governments, officials, and professionals. Geoffrey Yeo observes, "Just as the days are gone when the banker's word was trusted as his bond, so also the days are gone when the word of the professional was invariably trusted as authoritative and objective."[26] However, Yeo goes on to suggest "that the professional archivist and the archival institution still have key roles to play in securing trust. Reputation is important here; [but like] other experts, archivists and recordkeepers now have to earn the trust that is reposed in them; they can no longer merely assume it."[27]

Archival codes of ethics and professionalism are often described as the foundations of trust in the archives.[28] Certainly, we must be aware of and guided by ethics codes, but more, we must at our core be moral human beings. If we desire that records be trusted objects, archivists must be trustworthy professionals. The label *trustworthy* describes something that I am, and who I am as a trustworthy human being is a process of continual renewal.

Developing trust, whether of the record, the repository, or the archivist, is ultimately a matter of establishing oneself as being trustworthy. The idea of archival faith is a useful framework because faith is essential to developing a personal value system of integrity and trust. It is necessary for archivists to have an intimate sense of archival faith if they expect that constituents will have a sense of trust in them. If we desire trust from others, we must be able to answer the following questions in the affirmative. Are you a person whose word can be trusted? Have you conducted yourself with integrity? As an archivist, have you conducted your work with integrity and honesty? Do you feel responsible to *the other* in the same way you imagine *the other* is responsible to you? Do others think of you as worthy of their trust? Can you be trusted to do what you say you will do? Do your constituencies have faith that your actions are in their interests?[29] Trustworthiness will determine whether we can claim that our institutions are trusted repositories and that we ourselves are trusted professionals and trusted partners in our communities.

Professionalism

Professionalism is an idea that needs a careful accounting. Most often it is associated with competence, knowledge, education, skill, quality, and conduct. However, when viewed through a critical theory lens, professionalism exhibits a dark side. Jarrett Drake, for example, argues that "professionalism emphasizes 'the work' . . . without a meaningful critique of how 'the work' mandates a replication of patriarchy, oppression, and violence many in our world experience." Citing profession and professionalism as tools of social control, he goes on to suggest that "professionalism further asks that we remain content with the status quo, predictability, and propaganda."[30]

Like Drake, Dominique Luster acknowledges the criticism that professionalism "fails to address the negative impacts of majority culture, power dynamics, and systemic bias"[31]—a criticism not without merit. But Luster chooses to passionately fight to change this assessment of professionalism. She tightly interlaces trust and knowledge to define what constitutes professionalism: "If we truly wish to develop a sense of professionalism of service to our materials and communities, we need to be serious about gaining public trust and putting it front and center in our discourse." She contends that purpose and ethics statements should include language demonstrating commitment to the preservation and access to records of importance for all groups in society, especially marginalized communities. Luster suggests, not in so many words, that professionalism is a process: "We must continue to develop practices that contribute to the expansion of racially conscious and culturally competent archival theory, particularly around preservation of traditionally marginalized community records."[32] In other words, professionalism is an ideal toward which we must persistently strive.

I believe professionalism should be understood as an archival virtue that contains within it all the Core Values adopted by the Society of American Archivists.[33] As a virtue, professionalism concerns identity (as Luster suggests), but more importantly, it demands moral character and the exercise of moral judgment. Professionalism, in this reading, requires self-examination and institutional analysis and critique; it demands a commitment to a just archives and embracing the ever-broadening idea of what the archives is. As I have written elsewhere, "If we are to act with professionalism, we need to be cognizant of our responsibilities to society, our roles as public citizens, our sacred obligations to *the other*, and the ideal of building genuine relationships with all who cross our professional paths."[34] To be good and faithful archival citizens, we can do no other.

Difference

The reality of our world is that difference is everywhere. It is so ubiquitous that, in an ideal world, we should simply see it as the ordinariness of life. As simple as that sounds, the concept of difference is complex. Rather than recognize difference as the way of things, we hold fast our individual and collective narratives in ways that pit one narrative against another.[35] These narratives, then, can become walls that are difficult to scale. Employing the lens of race, Mellody Hobson, recently appointed Starbucks board chair, argues that honest conversation is a tool to surmount such barriers:

> I think it's time for us to be comfortable with the uncomfortable conversation about race: black, white, Asian, Hispanic, male, female, all of us, if we truly believe in equal rights and equal opportunity in America, I think we have to have real conversations about this issue. We cannot afford to be color blind. We have to be color brave. We have to be willing, as teachers and parents and entrepreneurs and scientists, we have to be willing to have proactive conversations about race with honesty and understanding and courage.[36]

This reality of difference receives considerable exploration and discussion in the archival sphere whether it is couched as diversity, inclusion, or pluralism; wrapped in critiques of colonialism, racism, and oppression; is specific to historically "othered" communities; or is a call for a just or liberatory archives. As the archival community struggles to ensure that employees, records, creators, and users reflect the broader society, and archives serve the many conceptions of justice in society, it is incumbent on archivists to do their best to obtain an understanding of what difference means.

One approach I have found personally useful is engagement with what is often called anti-oppression theory, which, in part, is the idea that individuals and groups cannot be classified into binary social identities. At the heart of this theory is the work of Kimberlé Williams Crenshaw on critical race theory and intersectionality.[37] Crenshaw introduced the term *intersectionality* in 1989 to describe (1) a person's overlapping and interlocking social identities and how one's identity arises from the component identities and (2) how institutional structures make certain identities the consequence or vehicle for vulnerability and oppression. To understand how these two notions apply to specific discrimination and/or oppression, one must study the context—what kind of discrimination is going on, what are the policies that abet discrimination, what are the institutional structures that sustain bias?[38] Crenshaw's writing focuses primarily on the intersection of race and feminism, but her thinking has application in a much broader context.

During my tenure at the Seattle Municipal Archives, I participated in the city's Race and Social Justice Initiative (RSJI) workshops whose goals were eliminating racial disparities, promoting equity, and ending institutional racism in city government.[39] Workshop leaders were brutally frank in describing the difficulty of combatting institutional racism, implicit bias, and oppression; appreciating the complexity of identity; and understanding the nature of intractable privilege. One exercise they facilitated employed the Matrix of Oppression.[40] The RSJI matrix lists identity categories, privileged groups within those categories, targeted groups, and the name of the related oppression. In one workshop, the

Matrix of Oppression

Identity categories	Privileged groups	Targeted groups	Oppression name
Race	White people	People of color	Racism
Sex	Bio men	Bio women	Sexism
Gender	Gender conforming bio men and women	Transgender, genderqueer, intersex, gender ambiguous	Transgender oppression
Sexual orientation	Heterosexual people	Non-straight, LGBTQ	Heterosexism
Class	Wealthy	Poor/working class	Classism
Ability/Disability	Able-bodied	People with disabilities	Ableism
Religion	Protestants	Non-Christian	Religious oppression
Age	Adults	Young, old	Ageism
Education	Educated (college)	Uneducated	Elitism
Citizenship	Citizen	Non-citizen	Nativism
Indigeneity	Non-Native American/Euro	Native American	Colonialism

facilitator asked everyone attending to identify which group (privileged or targeted) they belonged to in each of the identity categories. One of my colleagues found that he was privileged in five categories and targeted in six; he was confused about what to do with this ambiguous outcome. That is precisely the question.

Diversity, inclusion, and intersectionality are complex concepts; they are not easy ideas to grapple with, nor should they be. After all, each of us must connect with our authentic personal idea of self—whether race, ethnicity, gender, religious orientation—and all the other aspects of identity that influence our being. More problematic is that others, in turn, will prejudge the identity category they perceive that you belong in. As Michelle Caswell cautions, "Difference is messy; working with and through difference is even messier."[41] Our task is not to simplify; it is to recognize the difficulties inherent in defining social identities and oppression and to engage in the very hard work of understanding that difficulty while striving to effect change. For the RSJI approach, the city's Office of Civil Rights has appropriately identified the oppression of racism as the primary focus of their work.[42] If applied in the archives, RSJI could include an education component, creating a means for analyzing and monitoring all aspects of archival work that traditionally have privileged one group over another, establishing strategies for real systemic change, and engaging in honest discussions of racism and other bias.

RSJI is just one methodology in anti-oppression work and I am not suggesting that it is better or more appropriate than any other. There are many examples throughout the profession of archivists addressing both self-education and anti-oppression praxis. Just a few include the exploration of social justice curricula in the UCLA archival studies courses;[43] a social justice reading group at the University of Texas at Austin LLILAS Benson Latin American Studies and Collections;[44] the work creating a document describing information maintenance theory;[45] metadata guidelines developed by the Archives for Black Lives in Philadelphia's Anti-Racist Description Working Group;[46] the SAA Education Office developing coursework for managers focusing on diversity, equity, and inclusion competencies; and many more too numerous to recount in these pages.

There are strident voices who challenge concepts of diversity and inclusion as simply part of the problem. David James Hudson, a librarian at the University of Guelph, argues that diversity is an ill-defined concept that has limited use in anti-racist work, and that anti-racist narratives constructed around diversity are "disconnected from the complex structures of racial subordination through which our lives are regulated."[47] Likewise, Jarrett Drake makes the case that archivists need to "transition away from the language of diversity and towards the language of liberation through the concept of an archive of the oppressed."[48]

Where the debates and discourse on language, theory, and practice go is a process and the outcome is an unknown. Nevertheless, that a body of archivists is confronting race and justice issues in new and creative ways throughout the profession is a healthy sign for an active archival citizenship. Anti-oppression work with its creation of various toolkits to help us recognize and combat implicit bias, institutional racism, and the other *isms* of oppression will move us toward the profession's stated desire for inclusiveness (or liberation, if you will) in our archives, our collections, and our communities—and strengthen our ability to form broader meaningful relationships.

Care

Being trustworthy and dealing with constituents honestly and with integrity assumes a sense of obligation, but it also assumes a level of caring harmonious with a conception of covenant. Care for and/or about *the other* is consistent with responsibility and genuine encounter, and is necessary in developing a mature archival citizenship.[49] Andrea Hinding mined the work of philosopher Harry Frankfurt to suggest that caring is a crucial act of agency and self-consciousness, an indicator that the person who cares has faith in a future that matters. Caring about something conveys a sense of importance to it and forces one to act with a personal sense of integrity. Noting that archives is a memory profession, Hinding posits, "I think acts of memory are a form of caring, or perhaps a different but related act which is similar in importance to caring."[50] Hinding makes two critical points. In the archival context, when she speaks of memory as a form of caring, she takes us to the place of "caring about" others. And if one who cares assumes there will be a future, that person is expressing archival faith.

A logical extension of Hinding's caring paradigm is care ethics and empathy. Caswell and Cifor posit that in the realm of human rights and social justice, we need to adjust our thinking away from consideration of legalistic rights-based thinking and adopt an approach based on a feminist ethics of care which stresses relationship and human linkages of mutual obligation. The authors suggest that this obligation and responsibility can be met by ongoing engagement with radical empathy in our thinking and acting. They argue that "radical empathy is thus a learned process of direct and deep connection between the self and another that emphasizes human commonality through 'thinking and feeling into the minds of others."[51]

The ethics of care approach to social justice in archival practice can replace the "abstract legal and moral obligations of archivists as liberal autonomous individuals (as heretofore conceived through scholarship and professional codes of ethics) with an affective responsibility to engage in radical empathy with others, seen and unseen."[52] Much work still needs to be done to determine how feminist ethics might change archival roles and relationships. Taking a step toward that determination, Hillel Arnold notes that "care ethics values lived experience, emotion, and the body as legitimate agents of moral knowledge." Drawing on Caswell and Cifor, he creates experiential frameworks for the four primary relationships archivists enter—with creators, the subjects of records, users, and the larger community—and then ties them to Joan Tronto's four ethical elements—attentiveness, responsibility, responsiveness, and competence. In this framework, relationship becomes the central archival function; as Arnold argues, "It means thinking of archival work as care work."[53]

The feminist ethics of care is an enticing approach to our work. It is a powerful viewpoint that meshes seamlessly with the virtues-approach in this book. It argues that our work with others is not characterized by transactions and should not be commodified; rather, our work is about relationships. The theory explicitly links the bonds of relationship with an ethical orientation. This is the assumption of the reciprocal I-You encounter in archival covenant with healthy doses of Levinas's infinite responsibility. However, unlike Caswell and Cifor, I do not believe that moral obligations are abstract; rather, when one displays radical empathy, it is an integration of the concept of care with the concrete actions of sacred (moral) obligation to *the other*.

A Healthy Archival Citizenship

Good archival citizens conduct their affairs with fairness, integrity, transparency, responsiveness, and, above all, the consciousness of obligation. But, then, we must ask whether the strength of archival citizenship is measurable. My intent is not to take a deep dive into how we might measure archival citizenship, but rather to offer suggestions that archivists might consider. Sociologist Michael Schudson provides some guidance in addressing this question applied to political citizenship, suggesting seven aspects that should be measured. These include (1) voter turnout, (2) people's trust in government and social institutions, (3) the stock of social capital measured in connection to social groups, (4) quality of public discourse, (5) extent of the disparity between rich and poor, (6) capacity of the least advantaged to make their voices heard, and (7) whether guaranteed rights are increasing or decreasing.[54] If we modify these and apply them to archival citizenship, then some can be seen as internal measures related to our relationships within the archival community; and others are external measures related to how archivists are viewed by and how they support society.[55]

Applying Schudson's framework to the strength of archival citizenship, we can use the first four aspects as internal measures, as a means to evaluate our relationships within the profession. *Voting* (and the methodology for selecting candidates), as in the political arena, is a mechanism for selecting leaders of archival associations and is part and parcel of developing a vision for an inclusive profession. *Trust* and trustworthiness have been discussed at some length above. Suffice to say, if the external measures discussed below are met—or at least honestly and earnestly approached—trust in the archival endeavor and in archivists is more likely to be freely given. *Membership (social capital)* for archivists generally relates to participation in professional associations and the strength of those groups, although it can also manifest through belonging to more informal and loosely structured communities. My personal conviction is that archivists should join together in varied associations and interest groups to enrich their professional lives and practice, strengthen the profession, and build enduring relationships of mutual benefit. Finally, the *quality of public discourse* within the profession is an internal measure of our strength. Healthy dialogue and criticism are vital to building a just archives. Productive discourse flows from considered knowledge, reasoned argument, and a commitment to relationship even when we hold fast to passionate disagreement.

The remaining three measures in Schudson's framework ask whether there is a quality of care for the poor (lacking which society has failed), whether the least advantaged groups can make their voices heard, and whether the rights of the disadvantaged are increasing. We can consider these as external measures to evaluate the strength of archival citizenship in the larger world. The archival lens for these three questions is found in discussions of justice and anti-oppression work. If archives include the voices of underrepresented or previously silenced groups in their collections, if employment ranks reflect society, if archivists are committed to reaching in to communities that have traditionally not used (or have been excluded from) the archives, if we work with an immediacy of genuine encounter and care; then, perhaps, we can answer those questions affirmatively and make the claim that the archival community is improving and that we are accountable to a fundamental, moral standard in our work and our professional worldview. But, even if we are doing these things and believe we are being successful, we must ask the crucial questions, and listen to the answers, related to how this work is being perceived from outside our ranks. The consideration is not how we feel about ourselves, but how others—the historically marginalized, powerless, and silenced communities—feel about us, whether they believe there is sincere effort moving toward an archives that values and promotes justice.

Thinking Together Well

Archival citizenship is fundamentally about relationships and community, and the necessity of working together for the common good. Cognitive scientists Steven Sloman and Philip Fernbach argue that humans are not independent agents who can act rationally on their own. The authors make the persuasive case that individual thinking is a myth; instead, we think in groups. Because no one can know everything, all sectors of society depend on group knowledge. If it can be said that there is human exceptionalism, it is built on our ability to think together and to do it well.[56]

The archivist, to be a good archival citizen, must ensure that archives as institutions or other forms of community do this internal and external work well. This means archivists must accept the responsibilities of citizenship, develop a commitment to pluralism (in all its social and archival meanings), craft a conception of justice, cultivate compassion and empathy, actively identify as archival citizens, participate in the archival community, support the common good, engage in quality discourse, and exude the virtues that make us worthy of trust.

By any conceivable measure, Bob Moses exhibited the traits of good citizenship throughout his life. The account of his work, outlined at the beginning of the chapter, illustrates a commitment to changing established narratives of oppression that one group uses to dominate another. The importance of narrative is described with power by Sandel:

> Political community depends on the narratives by which people make sense of their condition and interpret the common life they share. . . . The loss of a capacity for narrative would amount to the ultimate disempowering of the human subject, for without narrative there is no continuity between present and past, and therefore no responsibility, and therefore no possibility of acting together to govern ourselves.[57]

Archivists toil in narrative. Our ability to conduct our work as conscientious archival citizens on behalf of the common good depends on constructing and evolving our own complex narratives to best understand our personal and community contexts, acknowledge our commonalities and differences, and bring those intellectual and visceral postures into our discourse, both internally to our work and externally to our relationships in the world.

I say, if this war is to be forgotten,
I ask, in the name of all things sacred,
what shall men remember?
— FREDERICK DOUGLASS

CHAPTER FOUR

Memory as Justice

In poem 21 of the cycle titled "Patriotic Songs," Israeli poet Yehuda Amichai writes:

> Jerusalem is a place where all remember
> that they have forgotten something
> but they don't remember what.[1]

In this opening stanza to a poem exploring dreams, love, and justice, the poet tenders a circular vision of memory and the intricately interwoven duality of remembering and forgetting. The poem is an assertion that there can be no remembering without forgetting, and more, that "forgetting can be a way of remembering."[2] Elsewhere in his work, Amichai writes of his friend, Dicky, who fell in war, "A hole in his belly. Everything / poured out of him." Amichai continues:

> But he has remained thus, standing
> in the landscape of my memory,
> like the water tower at Yad Mordecai.[3]

Dicky died horribly, but in Amichai's memory he remains alive, just as the destroyed water tower also remains standing. Of course, Amichai knows his friend is dead and that the water tower was demolished, but as a literary conceit, the narrator configures the "standing" memory to replace the reality. It is a momentary forgetting of facts—and remembering of hopes—that possesses the power to provoke new memory construction.

Archives and memory are not the same, but many archival scholars agree there are important connections between the two.[4] Archives and memory are both critical to creating and nurturing social and cultural identity; both are fragmentary, they present incomplete and imperfect windows to our world and can never tell the whole story; and they are fundamentally flawed as purveyors of the truth, although they can shine light on many truths. Both entail remembering and forgetting.

As others have shown regarding archives and collective memory, and Margaret Hedstrom has stated explicitly, they form "more than a metaphor, less than an analogy." Hedstrom argues, "The appropriation of memory concepts in archival science suffers from simplification and over-generalization. A common trope in archival science equates the term archives with memory in a way that is useful rhetorically but which ignores the circumstances and conditions under which archives and collective memory may intersect."[5] It is in the actions that forge memory—remembering and forgetting—that we approach the material usefulness of the metaphor. Barbara Craig suggests this when she writes: "All archives originate in the conscious act of memorializing some thing by the giving, receiving, and keeping of documentary records."[6] The acts of remembering and forgetting transport us beyond the metaphor; they are durable actions archivists perform in their daily work.

Remembering

Individual memory is the product of encoding events, facts, and experiences, both cognitively and as sensory or "felt" experience; the recall of those; and the construction and evolving reconstruction or re-experiencing of memory. Collective memory, on the other hand, grows out of shared group experiences and values, and plays a significant role in the composition of group history and cohesion, national identity, and a community's understanding of its values, norms, and traditions.[7] This chapter is not a detailed exploration of the differences and similarities between individual and collective memory, but rather it asks how the two are intricately related to the archival endeavor and archival justice.

Memory, as a product of experiences susceptible to competing claims and influences, is ambiguous, complex, and challenging to describe or define with precision. Dutch archivist Joan van Albada notes the complexity by offering seven definitions of memory:

- the mental process or faculty of representing in consciousness an act, experience, or impression, with recognition that it belongs to time past
- the experiences of the mind taken in the aggregate and considered as influencing present and future behavior
- that which is remembered, as an act, event, person, or thing
- the period of time covered by the faculty of remembrance
- the state of being remembered, posthumous reputation
- that which reminds; a memorial; a memento[8]

Eschewing academic definitions drawn from memory studies, Albada uses these dictionary definitions[9] in concert with a list of synonyms (recollection, remembrance, reminiscence, retrospect, retrospection) and antonyms (forgetfulness, oblivion, oversight, unconsciousness) to suggest the multiple meanings of memory and to connect memory to his understanding of archives as a living thing:

> Archives to me represent a kind of living organism with which one can communicate, an organism that can be belittled, burned, falsified, nurtured, exploited, used, and abused. However, this organism is not an organism in its own right; the organism reflects us—the archivist, the administrator, the records manager, the family, the politician, the owner, and the thief, the corrupted ones and those who will be corrupted.[10]

Albada's definitions are syntactically correct—that is, memory is defined as a noun and the synonyms and antonyms he cites are also nouns. However, his concern is not about nouns; his thinking about memory (and archives) turns to the related action verbs of remembering and forgetting. Archives are living artifacts of human creation and continual re-creation through the actions of archivists and users. Great care must be taken in how we relate to and maintain the living archival record, and to recognize that memory, too, is a living organism whose voice speaks in the active language of remembering and forgetting, and whose touch can reverberate through the body.

Memory, whether individual or collective, is the product of a crucial human struggle to make sense of our surroundings, our past, our hopes, our dreams, our failures, and our passions. Individual memory "is among the most fragile and capricious of our faculties."[11] Its failure can result from cognitive impairment, but can also be purposive. The same holds true for collective memory. Historian Jeffrey Burds makes this case about competing stories in relation to multiple ethnic groups' collective memories in Eastern Europe and the difficulty of understanding the region's history during and following the Second World War. In cases where inter-ethnic violence was prevalent, contested memory is a particular obstacle, not only to understanding history, but to peaceful coexistence between neighboring groups.[12] Collective memory is bound by social and cultural frameworks consciously fashioned to sift through our individual and collective experience. Memory is a repository in which our stories are appraised, selected, and arranged by what is to be remembered and what is to be forgotten. In one sense, collective memory is a codified aggregate of the individual memories of group members. And individual memory is shaped by one's participation in the larger social and cultural groups.[13] The critical questions are: Who owns the stories and narratives of memory? And what experiences and memory form essential truths? And whose truths are they?

Richard White confronts the vicissitudes of individual memory and the contestation of cultural narrative in the exploration of his mother's memories, of her stories of Ireland in the 1920s. Recounting one of his mother's defining stories, White asserts:

> Sara Walsh's earliest memories come from before she was old enough to have memories. They are in a real sense four hundred years old. They are memories of the Time of Troubles. . . . When Sara talks of the Troubles, her voice gets cold, her diction clipped. She sees the butt of a gun driving into her mother's back. She sees the IRA man, the rebel Eddie Carmody, dead at the Doctor's Cross. That she actually saw the first and not the second, does not much matter. They have fused.[14]

White presents his mother's stories as individual memory, but they are in effect the personal manifestation of collective memory. Her memories were born of the collective experiences and traumas of her family and the residents of Ballylongford over several centuries, as they confronted the social and political conflict in colonial Ireland. They are, in Albada's construction, living things that profoundly affect the mind and the body. Societies that depend on collective memory for the existence of central ethnic, cultural, even national narratives and mythology spawn members like Sara Walsh, who remember events they could not conceivably remember from first-hand experience.

Sara's memories are perhaps more physical feelings born of the inherited cultural oppression and injustice—a shared trauma—than they are individual remembrance. This felt memory, made "first hand" by a common history, conveys a power that transcends any possible cognitive encryption. Does it matter that Sara had a memory that she could not have had from first-hand experience? Is chronology important? Can collective memory be "wrong"? Are competing memories negating? (Surely the collective memory of the English Black and Tans would contradict those of the Walsh clan.) Or can competing memories be woven into inclusive meta-memories? Does the intersection of archives as persistent documentation with collective memory create an additional contestation? Ultimately, the conflict is about more than supremacy of narrative; it is about meaning and justice and who determines what those are. Although White has employed historical research to contest the accuracy of some of his mother's memory, he acknowledges and makes space for the meaning of memories that are passed from generation to generation. As White suggests regarding American memory, "Beneath these personal stories simmers an ongoing contest over what America is and means and who gets to define it."[15]

How we choose to interpret and assimilate stories—and construct memory—depends largely on our cultural, social, and political frameworks. In addition, collective memory becomes not a metaphor, but a social reality consciously molded and transmitted through the social institutions of the group.[16] As Tywanna Whorley argues, "Memory is deeply implicated in concepts of accountability. The Tuskegee Syphilis Study did not just happen to the 625 men and their families living in Macon County, Georgia. The African American community connected with the experience because of the racial identity of the victims. Their sense of a collective past is used as a means to force the U.S. government to be accountable for its actions."[17]

Forgetting

The human capacity for remembering is limited; we cannot with fidelity remember everything, nor should we want to. But we need to take care in what we choose to forget by crafting mechanisms and procedures that make forgetting useful.

The construction of collective memory requires forgetting those stories that do not sustain a group's identity. But to forget productively requires an understanding of both traditional views of forgetting and its inherent dangers. The Bible, whose influence—no matter what your belief system might be—cascades through almost all strata of Western culture, contains a literature in which remembering and forgetting, on first blush, are not viewed as complementary. The word *zakhor*, generally translated as *remember*, appears in its various grammatical forms 169 times in the *Tanakh*, the Hebrew Bible. Its ubiquity in the biblical narrative suggests that remembering is a moral and religious imperative, associated with redemption, revelation, and justice, while forgetting is generally a negative action that has no positive or essential uses.[18] Throughout its pages, the Bible identifies what is essential to remember. By inference, however, we can assume that some things are not important to remember, thus there are things that are permissible to forget.

In modern times, Nietzsche takes the latter assumption a step further:

> Life in any true sense is absolutely impossible without forgetfulness. . . . we must know the right time to forget as well as the right time to remember, and instinctively see when it is necessary to feel historically and when unhistorically. This is the point the reader is asked to consider: that the unhistorical and historical are equally necessary to the health of an individual, a community, and a system of culture.[19]

Nietzsche is arguing that forgetting is just as important as remembering in fashioning a meaningful life. Social, cultural, organizational, and even national forgetting can be sustained through two effective processes—*clearance*, the complete wiping away of a selected portion or of an entire past; and *erasure*, the constant filtering out of information deemed unnecessary or unworthy of preservation. Both forms can be both useful and dangerous.

Informatics professor Geoffrey C. Bowker, writing about the nursing profession in the context of organizational theory, illustrates that selective forgetting via *clearance* was used in elevating nursing's professional standing in the health care field. Nursing, in a sense, was an invisible profession because there was no standardized vocabulary acceptable to the dominant medical (i.e., physician) lexicon, leading to nurses' notes being stricken from medical records at the earliest possible opportunity. In creating a new classification system and developing new nursing theory, the profession wiped away—forgot, as it were—all vestiges of the old system as irrelevant to modern nursing science. The new classification system, it was argued, would provide a good ordering of organizational memory for the future.[20]

In a few select instances, forgetting through clearance is useful in the construction of cultural identity. Anthropologist Janet Carsten shows how certain Malay cultures fashion identity through the process of living together, sharing food, and engaging in a variety of relationships *in the present*. She notes that identity is not transmitted from generation to generation. In fact, "the past, or where they have come from, has no special value or authority" and "aspects of the past . . . simply have no relevance." Carsten suggests that migration patterns of the Malay make genealogical concerns irrelevant and that "forgetting is an important part of the creation of shared identity."[21] In this case, the community decides for itself what is forgotten.

One of the most comprehensive and absolute examples of clearance is evident in the Chinese dynastic practice of destroying the records of previous dynasties after completion of "veritable and approved" histories. These actions were seen as necessary and desirable in the orderly political and social transition from one dynasty to the next. The consequence, however, is that little documentary evidence exists of dynasties predating the Qing (1644–1912).[22] At the time, the destruction of records—the forgetting of evidence and information—served what was viewed as a positive function (at least, by the new dynasty), but today we view this forgetting with alarm as it restricts our understanding of China's history. More problematic, in this example, is the blatant application of power in the effacement of a contending history. The Malay and Chinese examples raise the question of who gets to choose what is remembered or forgotten. In the former, the cultural narrative and collective memory (and forgetting) is controlled by the community; in the latter case, remembering is controlled by a dominant bureaucratic and political power.

Erasure—the expunging of unworthy or unneeded information—is, in some ways, a more acceptable approach to forgetting from an archival perspective. Erasure through appraisal and selection (including decisions not to select and/or to destroy nonarchival records) can make it easier to remember by expunging that which is not worth remembering. At the institutional level, records disposition schedules are employed to aid legal forgetting. Yet, even that application is fraught. Records schedules are tools created and employed within a prevailing power structure that may inadvertently or purposely privilege one dominant memory system over another. Who decides what is unworthy of remembering?

David Wallace, citing the danger of intentional erasure, notes that "erasure, if enacted, results in two failures: the original removal of persons (and/or their stories) from existence and the removal of this removal from remembrance. A morals dimension of memory requires the recovery of the effacement of these victims—recovering them from the abyss of erasure."[23] Michelle Caswell calls this removal of people and their stories "symbolic annihilation" and asks the following questions whose answers should be self-evidently obvious: "What does it mean to be omitted from history textbooks? What are the implications of not being able to find any (or very few) traces of the past left by people who look like you, share your cultural background, or speak the same native tongue? What impact do these archival absences have on how you might understand your place in society?"[24]

Silence

Intentional erasure and cultural effacement create silences in the archives. The point here is that forgetting, when done with care and concern for *the other*, is an aid to effective remembering; when employed to dominate (whether explicitly or implicitly), it is a tool for silencing or historically disappearing *the other*. Forgetting, when self-imposed, can support a positive need to forget; but when imposed by others it is generally a devastating silence caused when voices are removed from political, cultural, and social discourse. When it creates silence, forgetting, in its constructive sense, fails.[25]

During the final decade of the apartheid government, the expatriate South African novelist J. M. Coetzee published the novella *Foe*, a stylized retelling of *Robinson Crusoe* from the perspective of a woman, Susan, who was shipwrecked on the island during Crusoe's last year of life. She subsequently is rescued and takes Crusoe's man Friday to England where she enlists the author, Foe, to write the story of Crusoe and Friday. Friday, a former slave whose tongue had been cut out, thus rendering him silent, becomes the central figure in a discourse on truth. Susan addresses Foe on the subject of Friday's silence:

> Friday has no command of words and therefore no defence against being re-shaped day by day in conformity with the desires of others. I say he is a cannibal and he becomes a cannibal; I say he is a laundryman and he becomes a laundryman. What is the truth of Friday? You will respond: he is neither cannibal nor laundryman . . . he is himself, Friday is Friday. But that is not so. No matter what he is to himself . . . what he is to the world is what I make of him. Therefore the silence of Friday is a helpless silence.[26]

The silence imposed upon Friday by those he must serve and depend on is an injustice that forever shapes his life.

Verne Harris has ably described the use of "tools of forgetfulness" in the silencing of Black South Africa under apartheid. He enumerates state destruction of records, hidden information, and records used against citizens; and—more ominously—censorship, banning, detention, imprisonment, harassment, and assassination in the service of state-imposed amnesia. He argues that the contest for whose memory would survive or, at least, be dominant, "was a struggle of remembering against forgetting, or oppositional memory fighting a life-and-death struggle against a systematic forgetting engineered by the state." Still, Harris contributes a nuanced analysis of state manipulation, noting that remembering and forgetting are not binary opposites, that the landscape of memory is complicated, fluid, and always a site of struggle:

> The realities, of course, were a little more complex. Forgetting, for instance, was an important element in the struggles against apartheid—forgetting the half-truths, the distorted interpretations, and lies of the apartheid regime. And the notions of "oppositional memory" and "state memory" themselves are problematic. They are artificial constructs, obscuring the sometimes fierce internal contestation in both spaces. Then there is the question of memory and imagination. Memory is never a faithful reflection of process, of "reality."

It is shaped, reshaped, figured, reconfigured, by the dance of
imagination, so that beyond the dynamics of remembering and
forgetting, a more profound characterization of the struggle
in social memory is one of narrative against narrative, story
against story. [27]

Not only is the struggle over contested memory waged between competing groups and ideas, the battle over accepted narratives often plays
out within a single group in the effort to engineer its own social reality.
Jeannette Bastian has suggested that even relatively stable and accepted
collective memory is not complete without counter-memory—the struggle between two ideas for the right to be a nation's popular myth. [28] The
questions raised are what to remember, how to remember, and who gets
to choose what is remembered. Cultural historian Catherine Hall, writing about the bicentennial of the British abolition of slavery, observes
that "until this year British responses to the slave-trade and slavery might
well have been characterized as a collective forgetting." She notes that in
the British Caribbean there was great reluctance to commemorate abolition because it was "a matter of anger, shame, and humiliation. . . . Is it
the horrors of the middle passage and of the plantation and the collective
responsibility that Britons bear for this—or is it the pride in abolition?" [29]
The answer is assuredly *both;* each shapes the other in the continual
movement of becoming.

The archivist's role in the struggle over contested narrative is to act
with care, obligation, and honesty. Jessica Tai et al., likening the silences in
archives to ghosts, make the case "that archivists not only have a responsibility to help fill the silences of the institutions in which they work, but
are also personally accountable to ghosts—possessing an ethical imperative to portray the silenced in a way that not only honors them, but
acknowledges their long run of historical and cultural contributions." [30]
Yes, care must be taken to ensure that the traditionally dominant cultural, social, and political groups are not solely privileged in the terrain
of memory and history. But, just as Harris and Bastian acknowledge the
complexities of contested memory, we must acknowledge the danger of
recovering the silenced voice at the expense of silencing another. Rather,

the archives should be a cacophony of discourse, but one that seeks to create a hospitable environment that welcomes and honors contestation without domination and constraint.

Archival Remembering and Forgetting

Earlier in *Foe*, Susan implores Crusoe to speak of his years on the island, to recount his story of strength and perseverance for the benefit of humankind. She argues that he must remember and tell his story. But Crusoe responds: "Nothing is forgotten. . . . Nothing I have forgotten is worth the remembering."[31] Friday and Crusoe embody two modes of forgetting: systematic forced silence and refusal to speak. Friday is made invisible; Crusoe selects what knowledge of his life will survive. Archivists, in our day-to-day work as mediators of the record, find ourselves on a middle path—not forcing silence nor refusing to speak, but actively making choices about whose voices will be heard, about what will be remembered and what forgotten.

Appraisal is the tool archivists most commonly employ in the acts of remembering and forgetting. We describe appraisal as the professional action designed to preserve society's most important functions, processes, and events. Yet, appraisal is about choosing the appropriate things to forget as much as the important things to remember. Indeed, archivists actively forget more than we remember. Our students learn that archival selection and appraisal results in the preservation of 2–5 percent of the records universe. I suspect that none of us begin our work day consciously asserting that we are going to consign 95–98 percent of evidence, information, and thus potential knowledge to the realm of silence. Still, just as historian Yosef Hayim Yerushalmi notes that not all history is worth remembering, archivists understand that not all records are worth preserving. What we preserve—what we can reasonably preserve—represents only a miniscule measure of our documentary heritage.

Terry Cook has argued that archivists shoulder a heavy social responsibility when conducting appraisal. We exercise the power to decide "what is remembered and what is forgotten, who in society is visible and who remains invisible, who has a voice and who does not." He argues that these heady decisions are an act of creation, the creation of archives.[32] We also need to be cognizant that these decisions are acts of destruction and forgetting. Yet, rightly, in making these existential decisions, in exerting our power of remembering and forgetting, our focus should be on how we consciously are creating the archives; how we are becoming, in Verne Harris's phrase, record-makers.[33]

Current archival discourse is asking, in urgent language, questions about who is heard and seen in the archives, how archivists can address the silences that have been all too prevalent in our collections, and how they can assist communities in their own work at recovering memory and history. This is not an entirely new discussion. The development of the new social history in the 1960s and 1970s prompted archivists to begin collecting records of previously undocumented populations.[34] This refocusing of collection development policies was designed to "give voice to people who had been hidden from history."[35] Collecting policies in individual institutions were accompanied by larger theoretical and methodological discussions for how to document all of society. These included the total archives approach in Canada whose goal was to integrate public and private archives as well as disparate media with text-based collections; documentation strategy which promised a planned, systematic approach to collection development and societal documentation; a greater focus on service to underrepresented communities of common identity; and a host of new appraisal theories.[36]

As archivists became more attuned to selecting records of previously underrepresented communities, their decisions were still determining whose history would be documented and what in that history would be remembered through the written record. This process often engaged communities in informing collection development, but was still largely archival institution-centric.[37] The bottom-up collecting choices associated with the new social history, Margaret Hedstrom asserts, "challenged the role of archivists as neutral and objective custodians." Explorations of this collecting power and the attendant issues of the role of the archivist in determining what knowledge and what written histories would be possible, coupled with a growing interest in memory studies, has created an archival turn that has "helped to interject a larger social mission into archives and to align archives not only with the preservation of the past and production of history, but with the social causes of accountability, justice, identity formation, and reconciliation."[38]

The current focus on justice and anti-oppression work seems to me a natural evolution in archival thought that began in the 1960s and 1970s, but did not appropriately accelerate until the turn of the twenty-first century, when writers began to apply scholarly thinking from outside the profession to the questions of archival theory and practice. This process sped up in the 2010s, leading to fresh notions of what constitutes archives, challenges to the ideas of objectivity and neutrality, and the still-developing instantiation of justice as normative archival theory. The bottom-up collecting of the 1970s has not been replaced; it has been altered and joined by a revitalized community archives movement in which archivists often partner with or play an advisory role in the work of communities to recover their history, fill silences in the record, actively document the present, or use records to inform political activism.[39] The politics of community archives addresses the very questions we have raised. Whose voices are included in the archival record? How do we give voice to those who have been silenced? Who gets to determine what is remembered and what is forgotten?

Archival Justice

Forgetting in biblical texts is equated with losing one's moral and ritual bearings and has no useful purpose. Moral and ritual activities are associated with the concept of justice. (Here, I define *ritual* as the trappings of cultural and social identity and thus the basis for group narrative.) If I stray from the moral path, I fail to engage in acts of justice. The prophet commands: "Justice, justice shall you pursue."[40] The repetition of *justice* suggests that both the ends and the means to justice must be just, while *pursue* carries the implication of effort and eagerness in its pursuit.[41]

So, what are we to make of archival forgetting? Yerushalmi provides an edifying answer in writing about the Nazi war crimes trial of Klaus Barbie. During the trial, the editors of the French newspaper *Le Monde* asked their readers, "Of the two following words, *forgetting* or *justice*, which is the one that best characterizes your attitude toward the events of this period of the war and the Occupation?" Yerushalmi muses, "Can it be that the journalists have stumbled across something more important than they perhaps realized? Is it possible that the antonym of 'forgetting' is not 'remembering,' but justice?"[42] The answer is *yes,* when we give consideration to justice in our archival decision making and we are attuned to what can productively be forgotten and what must morally be remembered.

Justice is ineradicably entwined with archival remembering and forgetting. In reading the extensive archival literature on South Africa and the rest of the colonized world, the Tuskegee Airmen syphilis case, the treatment of First Nations, and myriad other works about silenced populations and marginalized peoples,[43] it is easy to understand why archivists should be attuned to remembering and forgetting. These are large, clearly drawn issues of political, economic, and cultural justice whose vocabulary encompasses whistleblowing, redress, truth, correction, empowerment, and reconciliation. Realistically, most archivists do not encounter these types of issues in their daily work on as large a scale or stage. Nevertheless, our daily work of remembering and forgetting is the work of justice.

Like the biblical prophets, Harris argues that archivists must attend to the demand for justice. Justice is wrapped in questions of our relationship to *the other* and the nature of our politics. Yet Harris believes, as do several authors of recent studies, that justice as a process is always coming, but never arrives fully formed.[44] I concur with this assessment, but suggest that the striving for justice requires an expansion of Harris's formulation. Indeed, we should listen for and hear "the call of justice," and in response we must answer by accepting "the call to justice."[45]

Justice is certainly encountered in the judgments of courts, the findings of truth and reconciliation commissions, the repatriation of sacred objects, the new-found voices of previously silenced peoples, and govern-ments held accountable. Justice is all that, but it is also far more. Justice is fashioned from the complex interactions of our individual and col-lective sense of rights and freedom with our summons to duty and obli-gation. Justice asks questions about how individuals treat one another, how groups of individuals interact, what our laws should be and do, and how society should be organized. It is nurtured by a society's ability to remember productively and to forget only those things that can be for-gotten without social or political damage to the dignity of groups in soci-ety. Justice is, no less, about our core values, ethics, archival virtues, and moral compass; our faith in the future; and our genuine encounter with our neighbors. Harris argues that justice is based in hospitality toward *the other*. It requires being open to what is "outside the boundary" and resisting the "insularities" of our particular situations in order to achieve the possible in the struggle for justice. We act with justice when we rec-ognize ourselves in the face of *the other*.[46]

Verne Harris, Rand Jimerson, David Wallace, Terry Cook, Joan Schwartz and others for more than two decades have focused our atten-tion, explicitly or implicitly, on the archival concerns of power and jus-tice. In recent years a new generation of archival theorists—including Michelle Caswell, Marika Cifor, Ricardo Punzalan, Jennifer O'Neal, Lae'l Hughes-Watkins, among many others—has introduced a staggering body of justice and human rights theory to archival thinking and prac-tice, including feminist theory of care, radical empathy, affect theory, and critical race theory, among others.[47] The subtext is that archivists should be activists who embrace—or at least understand—these theories in order to perform archival work as facilitators, if not crusaders, for justice.

Archives can and should promote justice. At the very least, the archivist as a good archival citizen needs to apprehend and welcome the complexity of the issue of justice in society. So, the initial question about justice needs to be reframed: What, then, do we mean when we talk about archival justice? A reductionist answer simplifies it to three propo-sitions. In all of our work, our concerns should encompass (1) not forget-ting that which should be remembered, (2) remembering that which has been forgotten, and (3) forging a conception of (and supporting others in striving for) the common good.

Norwegian archival educator Gudmund Valderhaug, writing about Norway's war children, maintains that building relationships is a challenge that archivists must confront if justice is to exist in the archives. He suggests that archivists are not judges or social workers, nor can we make claims about whether information in our archives is sufficient to ensure justice will be served. Valderhaug sums up his position by cautioning, "The archivist's role in the documentation of personal rights is to be an archivist. . . . Our role, then, is to supply documentation and put this into the societal and administrative context. And this role is indeed difficult and challenging."[48] Individuals seeking information, especially those who have been victims, are often unfamiliar and even intimidated by the archives, how to use its systems, search its records, and decipher the language of bureaucracy. The archivist must build trust, build relationship. Valderhaug continues: "A living democracy depends on every citizen's right to access, understand and use public information, including current and archival records, for their own individual—or collective—purposes. This right must form an integral part of what might be called an archival justice."[49]

Valderhaug's archival justice is traditional in the sense that it is institution-centric. We might add the role of advisor to his argument and move it outside of the bureaucratic, structural confines of the archives. Stacie Williams and Jarrett Drake note that in assisting with the establishment of A People's Archive of Police Violence in Cleveland, an independent community archives, the role of "professional archivists" is to be "advisory archivists"; and the community members who lead the effort are "citizen archivists."[50] This division of labor in community archives is not really a division at all; it is a relationship that I would describe as covenantal. It is justice in relationship and relationship as justice.

From a justice perspective, siting archives in their societal and administrative context is politically fraught. Verne Harris and Wendy Duff point to the problem of archives as the purview of the privileged: "Some voices have been silenced in archives, but our descriptions should strive to respect the rights of all voices. However, if we try to give voice to the marginalized, will we misrepresent, will we negatively bias the inter-pretation of the records, and will our own biases do more damage than good? Can the mainstream ever accurately represent the marginal?"[51] It is precisely here that archivists and archives are served by a justice whose foundation is relationship built of covenant, sacred obligation, hospital-ity, care, trust, and fairness. And to argue that we are serving justice in the archives, it is necessary to employ the broadest definition of archives and move it outside of our institutions and discussions of traditional practice.

David Wallace's definition of contemporary justice, "the demand of respect for the other," leads him to ask a series of important questions:

> What type of justice is possible in the contemporary realm? What types of restorative possibilities exist and can exist? What beyond the cultural authority and concrete outcomes of the law can be seen as having a justice dimension? What is lost when we view contemporary justice through a predominantly legal lens? What . . . other forms of thinking of justice should we be concerning ourselves with?[52]

Wallace's questions move us along a path that suggests justice is ulti-mately about our quality and way of life.

American ideas about justice are tied too closely to the language of individualism and concepts of freedom structured around personal will and consent. Michael Sandel argues that society must be built on a foundation of responsible citizenship that fosters *the good life* for all. He maintains that claims of solidarity, patriotism, family, fraternal and filial loyalties, and more possess moral force and encumber us with duties and obligations that are "bound up with the narratives by which we interpret our lives and the communities we inhabit."[53] Kwame Gyekye's communi-tarian ethics takes Sandel's position a step further in suggesting that if the common good is achieved, it is in community and thereby the individual good is also achieved.[54] If justice is not primarily about free will, personal choice, and individual freedom, then we are obliged to consider that it is about community welfare, and moral and ethical determinations of what constitutes the common good. We are, then, compelled by moral agency to shape a just society that supports the common good and in which justice cannot be dispassionate. The social, cultural, and political narratives that bind us together and draw us to consider the common good are inextricably linked to what we have chosen to remember and what we have consigned to forgetting. It may not be possible, or even desirable, to deliberate about justice without deliberating about the good life.

Sandel holds a deep conviction that justice involves virtue, and he argues that thinking about justice means thinking about the best way to live. He makes a compelling case that achieving justice and forming a just society requires that we all "reason together about the meaning of *the good life.*" This entails cultivating civic virtue and creating a public culture hospitable to confronting our moral disagreements. Sandel concludes that "justice is not only about the right way to distribute things. It is also about the right way to value things."[55]

Justice, then, is acting on moral values within the political and social context of civic responsibility—for our profession, it is a manner of *archival being*, both individually and collectively. Wallace, in arguing that justice should be at the heart of the archivists' code of ethics, suggests that a code "has to be based more affirmatively on human morality as our core professional value."[56] Archival justice, like O'Toole's moral theology of archives, is not situational; it is concerned "with the norms that govern (or should govern) human behavior."[57] In this sense, justice strives toward four goals that should constitute these norms: full human recognition, fair and just (re-)distribution, full and equal participation, and acknowledgment and remediation of historical inequalities.[58] While archival work can support these goals and the correctives and redress of grievances necessary in society, there is an equally valuable role for archives to play in cultivating justice through civic and archival virtue and the nurturing of genuine relationship. This conception of archival justice must be based on an archival *will to connect.*

The Will to Connect

The archival art movement of the past several decades focuses, at least in part, on installations of found objects, historical information, "spontaneous" monuments, and the imaginary.[59] Such works include spontaneous shrines and art works based on those shrines that cry out for preservation in some form. Examples include the spontaneous street art, flowers, photos, documents, and other ephemera at the spot in Minneapolis (and around the nation) where George Floyd was murdered; the commemorative materials left near Ground Zero following 9/11; and roadside memorials for victims of traffic accidents. These have been described as "just monuments" because they are grassroots or created from "below."[60]

Art critic Hal Foster, writing about the archival impulse in modern art, suggests it seeks to associate the past with the present, that it is "the will to connect what cannot be connected....a will to relate." This work queries a lost or misplaced past by attempting to discover what might have endured that can inform the present. The will to connect, he argues, turns "excavation sites" into "construction sites" by shifting historical thinking away from a view of "the historical as little more than the traumatic." In doing so, Foster allows that archival art makes room for and even "calls out for a practice of counter-memory."[61] The contesting of narratives can result in a battle between stories in the memory marketplace. The archival will to connect, however, opens this marketplace to all narratives and allows the integration of multiple memories that can exist side by side in a larger conception of memory.

The will to connect is an archival virtue, one that depends on memory that is more than simply metaphor. This idea is embodied in feminist memory work, a methodology that involves "any activity that deliberately tries to understand how historical memories can influence contemporary life and future possibilities."[62] Feminist memory work "is based on the premise that remembered narratives provide a window into, or a bridge between, the personal and political. Irrespective of participants' gender identity, gender analyses are central and are conducted not only with individuals in mind but also with social groups."[63] It is a qualitative approach to research based in group memory that entails interviewing respondents in small group settings. It is a justice-sensitive methodology that promotes equality through an awareness of the processes of socialization, and the study and understanding of the contextual. In selected situations, this memory work could provide a useful approach to appraisal, archival representation, and outreach, even perhaps in exploring a compassionate, caring user experience in the reading room.

Truth and Mist

The records that archivists acquire and manage can be used fruitfully by citizens to fulfill their duties and obligations, and nourish justice through civic engagement and discourse. They are tools to support and foster public interactions and discussions of civic issues that affect our way of life and the common good. Archivists cannot guarantee that contending individuals or groups will conduct themselves in a civil manner. But we can engage our work in just such a manner while providing equal access to the records that allow reasoned discourse on thorny issues. Archivists must support better civic engagement through policies and actions in collection development, appraisal, acquisition, descriptive practices, digital preservation, open access, and outreach. When records are used to give voice to once-silenced history, to promote better understanding between political or cultural communities, to explicate legal and legislative intent, and to nurture dialogue in the public sphere, they become tools of civics as justice.

These are not new ideas regarding the use of records, but when framed in Sandel's conception of justice, archival work takes on a compelling and perhaps transformative power. Records are deemed to have enduring value, or conversely to have no long-term value, for many reasons; I am not in any way making a case that appraisal decisions based on those reasons are not legitimate. Rather, I am arguing that archivists attune their thinking about records to considerations of justice as a vital element of the archival endeavor. Notions of justice—as a way of living, as the common good—must be reflected in our decision procedures concerning what of our documentary heritage is remembered and what of the record of human activity is forgotten.

Margaret Hedstrom, in her discussion of archives and collective memory, argues that "archival documents are not representations of collective memory and archival institutions are not storehouses of collective memory. Rather, archives are sources for the potential discovery or recovery of memories that have been lost."[64] In that sense, archives—as places of discovery or recovery—are also sites of inspiration, especially in the word's original Latin meaning of *breathing into*; a significant responsibility of the archives is to breathe the truth into the argument that is history. David Wallace makes this point eloquently:

> Responsibility here is to help "tell the truth about what actually happened in the past." While the notion of "truth" is easily problematized, it must be recognized as a feature of the past that is distinct from historical evasion and manipulative erasure of discomforting episodes. "Truth" as used here as a frame for analyzing the politics of memory, is merely the recovery of that which happened but was consciously or subconsciously submerged and forgotten due to political and other power contingencies.[65]

Our job is ensuring there are historical records available that can be mined for this truth, whether the work is accomplished by good archival citizens or citizen archivists. While archivists engage in substantial forgetting, hopefully of a positive nature, we need to be particularly vigilant in appraisal, selection, description, and access to ensure that we are not forgetting records that would serve the public good. Remembering and forgetting necessitate an eye toward justice—justice writ large and small. Our decisions about remembering and forgetting must be informed by an understanding of, and obligation to, civic virtue; personal, professional, and community values; and moral and ethical action.

Remembering and forgetting are both necessary functions of the archival profession, and we need to be mindful to foster forgetting of that which can be productively forgotten and remembering that which extends justice. This is a heady challenge—to understand the value we bring to creating a moral society; to ensure that our slice, our trace, has meaning for all citizens; and that our work and actions promote the common good and the good life.

We return to the poetry of Yehuda Amichai whose intensely personal work translates to our collective experiences. In the final stanza of *Letter*, a poem of remembrance of lost love, he sums up our concern about forgetting with moral intent and remembering with value:

> And to finish: I remember only
> that there was mist. And whoever
> remembers only mist—
> what does he remember?[66]

> *The way to right wrongs is to turn*
> *the light of truth upon them.*
>
> — IDA B. WELLS

CHAPTER FIVE

Archival Validity

Ernest Hemingway wrote in *A Moveable Feast*, his episodic memoir of life in 1920s Paris, "I was learning something from the painting of Cézanne that made writing simple true sentences far from enough to make the stories have the dimensions that I was trying to put in them. I was learning very much from him but I was not articulate enough to explain it to anyone. Besides it was a secret."[1] Hemingway is suggesting that truth is a central value in—and even a catalyst for—art, and that it can be imparted through story. He believed in a kind of truth that was simple, yet elemental to literary being. He described the process he used when confronting writer's block: "All you have to do is write one true sentence. Write the truest sentence that you know. So finally I would write one true sentence, and then go on from there. It was easy then because there was always one true sentence that I knew or had seen or had heard someone say."[2] Despite this self-proclaimed ability to construct true sentences, Hemingway's confrontation with Cézanne's art frustrated the writer by introducing a mode of truth that he could not yet decipher.

Truth, which is hard enough to define in any objective way, may be measurable only through cultural myth—which suggests multiple truths—and the construction of stories that can illustrate both meaning and value. But discerning truth, let alone measuring it, is difficult to do with any sense of clarity. This is what Hemingway meant by his admission that what Cézanne had to teach was, to him at least, a secret. For archivists, that secret is discoverable, not solely in framing stories nor with brush strokes creating a moment in time where sense and touch converge,[3] but via archival listening—listening that, if done well, illuminates the archival record and exposes the listener to a kind of truth present in the best of Cézanne's work. And although I have expressed my unease with the concept of truth, I believe that truth is an archival virtue, indeed, an ideal toward which archives and archivists strive—not *the truth*, but rather the *multiplicity of truths* that animate the diverse communities that create, use, and benefit from archives.

Archivists, as they should be, are obsessed with the value of archives. We rightly spend countless hours contriving arguments for our resource allocators that will convey the value of the records we have chosen to preserve. In recent years, archivists have begun to talk about demonstrating the "value proposition" of archives. The phrase is a product of the business world, specifically from marketing, and is now used in many arenas including our own. Much solid and necessary research has been directed to devising metrics that illustrate value, whether through use or financial impacts, in an attempt to move away from solely relying on anecdotal stories of money saved, justice served, identities found, and cultures honored. This work has given us useful templates and methodologies for measuring elements of the archival endeavor that can aid archivists in drawing conclusions about the value of archives.[4] Presumably all archivists use metrics (such as use statistics or processing data) for internal advocacy in justifying program development, enhancement, and budgeting. But that valuing, as important to some aspects of our work as it might be, can and often does take the form of commodification of archives and, as a growing body of literature argues, language around cost efficiency and monetizing value both devalues archival labor and moves the focus of archives away from valuing community.[5] My concern is with the value and values that likely are not measurable quantitatively, but rather must be evaluated qualitatively.

Archival value derives a great deal of its authority from the relationship of the archivist to the archival record and those to whom the record matters. When we talk about measuring the value of archives, we are also talking about measuring the value of archivists. To some degree, this is done via the stories they tell, but more important the stories they carefully listen to and how they listen to them. There are two broad ideas that form the foundation of this conception of value: *archival validity* and the virtue of *archival wisdom*. Archival validity correlates to how well archivists listen to and report out the stories that comprise the historical record. Archival wisdom concerns how we view and live in a professional world that turns on the questions of archival validity and whether we can achieve it.

Archival Validity

Validity, in the simplest terms, is the quality of being logically or factually sound. But nothing is ever quite so simple. Validity is defined and methodologically employed in different ways in the fields of psychometrics, logic, philosophy, education, the natural sciences, and a host of other disciplines. In the archival sphere one might argue—and I think rightly—that validity is swaddled in the blankets of integrity and authenticity, in professional and technical knowledge and skill, and in ethical and moral action. Just as Hemingway drew on another art form in his search for what is true, we will look to another profession to construct a better understanding of what archival validity might be—and perhaps get a better understanding of what Hemingway meant when he talked about truth.

The American Evaluation Association (AEA) stipulates that "Evaluation involves assessing the strengths and weaknesses of programs, policies, personnel, products, and organizations to improve their effectiveness." AEA's statement of values notes, "We value high quality, ethically defensible, culturally responsive evaluation practices that lead to effective and humane organizations and ultimately to the enhancement of the public good."[6] The statement of core professional values of the Society of American Archivists is not dissimilar in making its claim for furthering the public good. In its introductory paragraphs, the 2011 version of the Core Values of Archivists notes: "Since ancient times, archives have afforded a fundamental power to those who control them. In a democratic society such power should benefit all members of the community. The values shared and embraced by archivists enable them to meet these obligations and to provide vital services on behalf of all groups and individuals in society."[7]

Michael Scriven, a polymath who has held university appointments in philosophy, history, mathematics, and psychology, and has been among the most important theorists in the evaluation field, suggests that valid evaluations "are ones that take into account all relevant factors, given the whole context of the evaluation (particularly including the client's needs) and weight them appropriately in the synthesis process."[8] Most archival functions require some level of evaluation. An obvious direct archival analog is appraisal, which is an evaluation of record value based on acquired knowledge of the vast context of the record. Similarly, representation involves the evaluation of record content and context. But there is a more expansive and expressive theory of validity that, I believe, aligns more closely with archival work.

Ernie House, professor emeritus of education at the University of Colorado, has been one of the most influential evaluation theorists for over four decades. House notes, in his enduring 1980 book *Evaluating with Validity*, that the standard definition of validity is "the quality of being well-founded on fact, or established on sound principles, and thoroughly applicable to the case or circumstances. . . . In a broad sense, I take validity to mean something like 'worthiness of being recognized.'" He further suggests that "evaluation is properly seen as a social decision procedure" and that validity should be understood in the sense of argumentation.[9] House implies there is a moral imperative when conducting

an evaluation to take seriously the opinions of others, to engage in meaningful discourse, and to listen to all voices, even as one must pay attention to the practical demands of making persuasive arguments based on
the way things are.[10]

It is easy, then, to recognize a kindred relationship between evaluation and archives. After all, appraisal is an argument about the value and
hence the importance of records that is served well by the inclusion of all
voices that are a party to the creation and use of the records; and representation is an argument about what the records are, what they say, how they
have been used, and how they might be used in the future. House takes
us down the road of what makes the arguments valid, claiming that there
are three dimensions that make an argument valid—*truth*, *beauty*, and
justice—and that all three must be present to ensure validity. For House,
"the validity of an evaluation depends upon whether the evaluation is
true, credible, and normatively correct."[11] Thirty years after the publication of *Evaluating with Validity*, House revisited his work and affirmed
his key theoretical point: "Truth is the attainment of arguments soundly
made, beauty is the attainment of coherence well wrought, and justice is
the attainment of politics fairly done. . . . If an evaluation is untrue, or
incoherent, or unjust, it is invalid. In other words, an evaluation must be
true, coherent, and just. All three criteria are necessary."[12] But his statement provokes questions. What does House really mean by these three
highly charged terms? How are they applied in evaluative thinking? And,
for our purposes, what might they look like in the archival setting?

Truth

James C. Griffith and Bianca Montrosse-Moorehead, in introducing a special issue of the AEA journal *New Directions for Evaluation* dedicated to a
reappraisal of House's theoretical model, point out that the goal of evaluation "is to achieve credibility and to persuade rationally." Credibility is
what is meant by the concept of truth, and truth can only be attained
by engaging all parties to an evaluation in serious dialogue, gaining an

understanding of the context of the evaluation, and getting the facts and the basis for those facts correct. That is what House means by the phrase "arguments soundly made." Griffith and Montrosse-Moorehead, who are both academics and evaluators, note that other evaluation theorists argue that one must modify validity with the term *approximately* because we can never know precisely what is true. "At best, one can know what has not yet been ruled out as false."[13] Thus, in line with postmodern thinking, truth is not an objective matter; rather it is the hard work of developing rational, sound evaluative arguments. This entails asking the right questions, gathering and presenting defensible evidence, appropriately analyzing, and developing valid conclusions.[14]

Archival appraisal is the most obvious (though not the only) function in which the archivist acts as evaluator and in which a truth argument is generated. Appraisal, as an intellectual process, requires evaluation of the content of records, supposition about future use based on knowledge and judgment about research, and a clear assessment of the context surrounding creation, and past and contemporary use.[15] To be done well, the appraisal archivist embraces the evaluator's penchant for truth—developing the set of right questions; engaging with the appropriate individuals associated with the record or with community members who are, as a defined community, subjects of the record; making a defensible case based on gathered and analyzed evidence; and using archival knowledge and the archival way of thinking to make a sound argument. As important are the twin ideas of expanding what constitutes records that document society in an inclusive manner, and the recognition that—in social and cultural terms—truth must be considered plural. When these factor into an appraisal decision, we can assert that it is constructively correct. Truth, in the evaluative sense, is not the Jenkinsonian positivist, objective, capitalized Truth, but rather it is the socially and culturally contingent argumentation that points toward justice in its many forms.

Beauty

Beauty, in evaluation, refers to whether the story told is coherent. Better stated by evaluator Jane Davidson, "Beauty is about the aesthetics of evaluation . . . and how well it presents a compelling and persuasive argument that is credible to all the various stakeholder audiences."[16] Thus, beauty is best thought of as the coherence required to present the credible (truth) argument of an evaluation. Coherence and credibility are about presenting evidence in a manner that is relevant to and has meaning for one's audience. It requires understanding the contexts that affect an audience and privileges—or at least takes into account—their values when framing an evaluation. In other words, credibility, in this understanding, is the attempt to account for the breadth of contexts that shape the evaluation's audience; coherence is about how the facts and arguments are organized, how the evaluative problem is represented, and how convincingly the evaluation story is framed.[17] Beauty is about expressing meaning with clarity.

The concept of framing plays a vital role in the pursuit of credibility and coherence. Framing in the pursuit of beauty is the admission that context matters. As Griffith and Montrosse-Moorehead argue, "we need the framing for the facts to be coherent. Facts without context are virtually meaningless."[18] Framing is making sense of context. But more than that, as House emphatically states, "Frames enable us to interpret events coherently and meaningfully. That's how our minds are structured. At the same time, inappropriate framing is a major source of cognitive bias. . . . The wrong frame has evaluators looking for the wrong things."[19] A careful and well-crafted frame, according to Davidson, is more than aesthetics (as it is to House, also); "It is a critically important route to achieving the clarity and coherence of thinking needed to get the evaluation right."[20]

The ideas of beauty and the framing required to present coherently are certainly archival concerns. If framing is about structuring and understanding context in all its multiplicity, and beauty is the coherent and credible expression of argument based on contextuality, then beauty can reasonably be seen as the translation or interpretation of context. And getting context wrong will negatively impact the ability to understand and find meaning in the record, not to mention potentially making it either of little use or, at worst, harmful.

Beauty is the most physically visible of the three criteria, whether in evaluation or the archives. Even in its simplest understanding, beauty is a major concern in archival work. Again, appraisal is an argument, among other things, about what the records are, what they say, what they were used for, and ultimately what they mean. The archivist is obliged to frame the argument and translate the context properly in the effort to avoid cognitive bias and prejudgment. The appraisal report must be clear and comprehensible to have value; when the report is credible and coherent, it exhibits beauty. An archivist's goal should be striving for elegance and making the complex as easy to understand as possible without confining the complex to the simplistic.

Davidson makes the case that if evaluators get the truth and beauty criteria right, "then evaluation has a good chance of not just producing valid and credible findings, but of fulfilling its social justice obligations. By this I mean we become a positive force for change by delivering value-infused, justice-oriented insights in a persuasive form that allows clients to understand what really matters and take action for social betterment." She goes on to make the all-important observation: "Beauty is not just about making evaluation pretty and palatable; beauty is the clarity of thinking that is essential for getting both the justice/values and truth/validity aspects right."[21] Thus beauty, the coherence of the argument well made, is necessary to achieve or at least to gravitate toward justice, whether in evaluation or in the archival endeavor.

Justice

House, more than any other practitioner/theorist, is responsible for the now common notion that evaluation has a justice imperative. He developed his theory of justice in evaluation after reading John Rawls' *A Theory of Justice*, in which Rawls proposed the notion of "justice as fairness" or perhaps better stated, justice as equity.[22] Rodney Hopson suggests that for House, justice in evaluation is about ensuring that all stakeholder voices are heard. It is concerned with the dual issues of "voice and representation—whose voices are heard and how are they represented?" It is about how disparate opinions are expressed; it is concerned with equity and the inclusion of "diverse, authentic interests through reasoned discussions, evidence, argument, and deliberation." Justice, in other words, requires the democratization of the evaluation process.[23] House recognizes that our conception of justice has shifted since Rawls laid out his framework in which "impartial experts judge what is just based on fundamental principles." The general ideal of impartiality has been challenged, especially in feminist theory and critical theory. House goes on to declare, "The idea that participants can express their own views, values, and interests has supplemented, and in some cases supplanted, the idea of impartial judges. Hence, we have participatory evaluations, including deliberative democratic evaluations. Again, justice applies as a criterion, but what we mean by justice has shifted."[24]

Responding to House, Montrosse-Moorehead, Griffith, and Pamela Pokorny write what could easily be included in archival journals today. They note that "justice also contributes to credibility. That is, when stakeholder voices are omitted, particularly those who have been historically underrepresented or excluded altogether, this also impinges upon credibility."[25] Using this model, archival justice in appraisal is concerned with the inclusion and pluralization of the records in our collections and the inclusion of voices that traditionally have not been heard in our stacks. And justice-oriented representation aims at archival hospitality in the reading room and in the community for those who historically have not been welcomed. This accommodation of justice is the recognition of multiple truths in the archival multiverse.[26]

House notes that when he first wrote about justice and evaluation in 1975, he was confronted with incredulity from colleagues. The response was: "What could justice possibly have to do with evaluation?" Today, that response is difficult to imagine because "justice is so much a part of the discipline's identity."[27] The drive to include justice as an integral element in archival theory is powerful and ascendant. One still hears claims that objectivity and neutrality are archival values, but there is growing recognition that the latter is impossible and the former, at best, is an ideal toward which archivists might strive, but will never attain. Understanding what justice, in all its complexities, might look like in an archival setting is crucial. When archivists strive for fairness, we embrace Rawlsian justice; when we hope to provide users with what they need, we engage (to some extent) with Aristotelian justice; when we build authentic relationship, we embrace justice as covenant and care. Justice, as an element of archival validity, also relates to how we attend to our values—not just our professional values, but also our personal values.

Intersection of Truth, Beauty, and Justice

Truth, beauty, and justice are necessary components of archival validity. Whether one criterion is privileged over another may depend on institutional circumstance or may vary at different times within a single institution. In evaluation, truth is sometimes given priority, but as Griffith and Montrosse-Moorehead suggest, "it must be a truth that is both scientifically and culturally humble" to ensure that it intersects with beauty/ coherence to provide arguments that are credible (true) and above all meaningful to its audience. Attending to the truth criterion and presenting findings coherently ensures that justice is present and authenticity confirmed. If one assiduously and genuinely examines and grapples with context as understood by the relevant parties and enters into that examination with a sense of cultural humility, then evaluations, decisions, and actions can be considered normatively correct.[28]

Admittedly, this primer obscures the complexity of House's paradigm and the brief archival examples do not explore the breadth or depth of its application to archives. The important point is that truth, beauty, and justice are necessary elements in archival work for all archival functions to ensure validity and meaning. The quest to imbue the archival endeavor with truth, beauty, and justice is a journey toward ideals. The importance of instantiating ideals in our value system runs up against the recognition of the impossibility of fully realizing those ideals. House makes the similar observation, "Of course, these criteria [truth, beauty, and justice] are ideals. We can never have a perfectly true, coherent, or just evaluation. Attainment is a matter of degree."[29] What we can do is employ our best "good judgment" through deliberation, care, and listening to diverse points of view to make the most reasonable decisions within our abilities.[30] The ideal of validity in archival work may be impossible to wholly achieve, but the attempt to realize it still requires us to commit to unravelling context, establishing a reasonable frame for crafting the stories that explain the value of archival work, carrying out that work with integrity, and understanding the profound difficulty involved in making real life choices. Even as the ideals of truth, beauty, and justice may be impossible to perfectly achieve, they are integral in the pursuit for archival validity.

In the archives, we need to be cognizant of how we represent our work, how we relate it to our various audiences, whether we are justifying appraisal decisions, crafting finding aids, designing exhibits, undertaking educational outreach, providing reference services, or advising community partners. Archivists have stories to tell and must be critically concerned with how these are framed. What language, tone, and images are used to convey meaning? And is the frame devised appropriate to the situation? Whose voices are being heard? The ability to conduct our work so that our outcomes contain the elements of truth, beauty, and justice requires that we make a wide range of decisions at every stage of our work. Throughout this book I have made the case that archivists are oriented toward others and that an element of our work is making our best judgment in innumerable actions and relationships. Attending to and successfully incorporating the ideals of truth, beauty, and justice into archival work in the pursuit of good judgment requires the employment of what I will call *archival wisdom*.

Archival Wisdom

Let's pivot for a moment to talk about hairdressers. Professors Barry Schwartz and Kenneth Sharpe, reporting on a study of skill and knowledge in that industry, observed:

> These hairdressers had the skill to help the clients figure out what they really wanted. They knew how to listen to the client, hear what the client was thinking and feeling. They knew how to ask questions to help the client decide if what she wanted was more "sassy" or more "demure." The conversations were a delicate interplay of talking and listening, of subtle interpretations—almost an improvised dance by which each steered the other in the right direction. Being a good hair stylist demands the wisdom to be a good counselor.[31]

To pursue a craft that serves others and to do it well, one needs to demonstrate wisdom, just as these hairdressers do. But what is wisdom? The term is used from time to time in archival literature, but like many value terms, it is never defined. Wisdom, as used by archival writers, usually relates to knowledge garnered from experience and handed down from senior archivists to younger, rising generations. However, while knowledge and experience are integral to developing wisdom, they alone are not enough to produce wisdom. Wisdom is the good judgment to consider how choices today may determine how we confront the future. Wisdom differentiates action from impulse. It is the good sense to eat oatmeal rather than donuts for breakfast in order to avoid high cholesterol and potential heart disease later. It is knowing to build relationships today that could be beneficial in the future. But wisdom is also more than good judgment and good sense. Wisdom is a virtue, and we should define it as an archival virtue. There are two types of wisdom that are required in archival work—practical wisdom and moral wisdom—and both are necessary in making difficult archival choices.

Archival actions are determined by senses and intuitions, as well as the ability to reason. If an archivist can be said to have achieved wisdom, it would be in our nature to claim it is practical wisdom. Practical wisdom is concerned with what is contingent in life, with situations that can be changed to make things better. Practical wisdom is a primary human virtue derived by obtaining the necessary knowledge to succeed and flourish at what we do; it means being guided by the goals and aims of a practice and translating those to concrete decisions and actions. It is knowing, understanding, and communicating what your purpose is and doing the sound, professional thing because it is what being a good archivist demands. But aspiring to the right thing is not enough. Practitioners, whether doctors, electricians, teachers (and, we might add, archivists), "need to imagine the consequences of what we do. They need to figure out what's possible and not just what's ideal."[32]

Schwartz and Sharpe identify six key characteristics of practical wisdom that easily map to archival work and wisdom.

1. Knowledge and desire. One must understand what constitutes proper action in an activity, have the desire to do the right thing to achieve results, and recognize there is an obligation both to obtain the knowledge necessary to address the need and then to actively do so. This is sacred obligation, an intrinsic element of archival covenant—turning what would be a transactional encounter into a relationship.

2. Flexibility. This entails the ability to think quickly on one's feet and improvise, and the recognition that we are often confronted by conflicting aims that must be brought into conversation. This is the understanding that no two situations (or sets of evolving situations) are the same. For example, no two appraisals are the same; they require separate analyses and different decision agendas.

3. Perceptivity. The wise person knows how to perceive social context, is able to see beyond simple (and unrealistic) answers, and understands that many areas of archival work are bathed in gray. This is the ability to recognize and to hold complexity, the ability to be unsettled without being paralyzed during decision making processes.

4. Seeing situations through the eyes of *the other*. This is the characteristic required to serve truth, beauty, and justice; it is what allows us to feel compassion and empathy and make decisions in the service of nurturing relationships.

5. Relying on emotion. Compassion and empathy are legitimate influences in decision making. A wise person should be able to rely on emotion and put it in dialogue with reason when confronting a situation. Emotion enables one to act quickly when necessary, rather than being bogged down in working through a decision tree. But one must be sure that "his emotions and intuitions are well educated."

6. Experience. Experience in this case is not a function of age; simply having a breadth of experiences is not sufficient. It is necessary to cultivate a disposition that ensures the lessons inherent in those experiences are learned—the virtues of intention and radical self-understanding are in play. Wisdom is a craft to be learned and nurtured. Similarly, virtues are not inherent; they must be learned and practiced.[33]

Making correct choices requires a good deal of wisdom. Our most difficult choices are not always between right and wrong, but more likely "choices among right things that clash, or between better and best, or sometimes between bad and worse."[34] Choice in the archival setting entails navigating ambiguity when confronted by opposing propositions. Should we employ MPLP? And, if so, how? How detailed do we make our finding aids? How much time do we spend on preservation and conservation concerns? How much and what do we digitize? What are reasonable and equitable uses of our resources? How do we balance custodial and postcustodial concerns? These questions are generally practical and relate to time and resources. But there are also the much larger societal issues related to appraisal and selection, representation, and access. What role can we (and our institutions) play vis-a-vis community archives? How do we support inclusion of marginalized or historically underrepresented populations in our records and our reading rooms? Should we advocate on behalf of political, social, economic, and cultural issues? What does justice mean in my particular archival setting? Is it even a concern? Values-laden questions demand the wisdom to negotiate the power structures of the institutions that administer archival programs. Wisdom is not about weighing pros and cons or laying out options; it is about deliberation and discernment. It is about framing and articulating the story of the situation which is critical to determining what action to take.[35]

Practical wisdom includes the ability to balance conflicting aims; being cognizant of the particularities of each context; understanding the perspective of *the other*; feeling empathy; and, in the case of the hairdressers (and archivists), making decisions that serve the client. But we may find ourselves faced with the possibility that a decision emanating from the application of practical wisdom might not be the "right" thing to do. Empathy, attention to the perspectives of others, and the obligation to serve the client necessarily require moral imagination. According to Schwartz and Sharpe, "Moral imagination—the ability to see how various options will play themselves out and the ability to evaluate them—is thus critical to perception."[36] Here, we are crossing the boundary into the realm of moral wisdom.

A branch of moral philosophy believes people do the right thing because it is the right thing to do.[37] The question of what is the right thing is complex and often perplexing. Questions that are tied to reward and incentive almost never have the answer "be more caring." Yet, when trying to perceive or imagine the needs of our stakeholders, compassion and empathy—in concert with cognitive skill—are precisely the emotions to employ in the hope of choosing the right thing.

Although an objective of wisdom is to be perceptive about others, it is also vital to develop the "capacity to perceive oneself—to assess what our own motives are, to admit our failures, to figure out what has worked or not and why."[38] This gives rise to questions of moral purpose and the necessary faculty to reflect on it. Moral wisdom also is concerned with contingency, but perhaps more importantly, with necessity. Although

I have free will, my identity, sense of integrity, and empathy—in other words, my being—influence me to act in a certain way.[39] Being cognizant of this is integral to understanding one's own context, biases, and prejudices.

Philosopher John Kekes argues that "Moral wisdom is . . . the virtue of reflection" aimed at attaining the good life. But to do that one must acquire the knowledge of what in life and work is worth valuing and what actions are worth taking to attain what we rightly value. The necessary requirement of all good lives is possessing certain goods: the ability to satisfy personal needs, the actuality of forming personal relationships, and living in a society where possession of these goods is valued. In life, and in the archival workplace, these are the goods of radical self-understanding, genuine encounter, and sacred obligation. They are the goods of responsive relationship. When we have a conception of the good life and the common good, "we know how to evaluate and judge complex situations. And then the exercise of courage in pursuit of justice becomes a matter of applying our knowledge to make the right effort, in the right circumstances, in the right way. We know then what dangers we ought to face, what desires we ought to control, and what we owe to other people."[40] This idea of the good life puts moral imagination, emotion, character, and virtue at the center of choice because they provide the capacity to understand what needs to be understood. And archival work, which is about navigating a series of relationships, is more productive when those goods are in play.

Moral wisdom, according to Kekes, is the "'capacity' to judge, but the mere capacity is not sufficient because judgment needs to be 'right,' 'sound,' or 'just'" when dealing with the existential dilemmas of the human species.[41] Although wisdom is considered a virtue, it is more; it is a regulator of virtue—of the virtues of prudence, mercy, tolerance, love, etc. Wisdom-generated deliberation, decisions, and actions channel the other virtues toward justice and the common good. Wisdom seeks to do for our future what memory does for our past.[42] Practical wisdom and moral wisdom cannot be separated, even when they might be contradictory. Basing one's decisions and actions on one's moral wisdom unquestionably can put the archivist at odds with the power structure in which she is employed, or even at odds with decisions and actions she might take based on practical wisdom. This is the constant tension between professional values and deep personal values. We need to be able to discern and deliberate about choices in the practical displays of our work, but at the same time perceive what is morally relevant or necessary in making choices and judgments.

There can be little question that wisdom in the pursuit of the archival endeavor is a good thing and that the capacity to judge is an important methodological skill. Archival judgments should reflect truth, beauty, and justice; these are fundamental moral exemplars. I believe we all are guided by an internal desire for moral order, and that we carry—and should carry—this virtue into our workplace. A personal moral compass is essential for meaningful archival practice and discourse.

Listening

Discernment, deliberation, and judgment regulate our values and direct or guide them toward the good. Wisdom, then, is a process to be employed in considering options. It is exercised in framing evaluative situations and telling the stories that are appropriate for our audiences. Cultivating archival wisdom is a life practice; it can be learned through lived experience and the accumulation of knowledge. And one of its most important expressions is listening.

In performing our work, it is all well and good for us to exercise the necessary framing elements—imagery, plot, metaphor—to tell a good story, but to really achieve coherence and credibility, we need to develop a deep understanding of the self and others. As Schwartz and Sharpe note when talking about medical care providers, one can approach understanding and meaning only by being an expert listener, but listening is not a simple task. Listening can demand interrupting, but it must be followed by encouraging the speaker to move back on track. We must learn how to interrupt without cutting off what the real issues are or what the speaker is really trying to convey. Listening is a "window into empathy."[43] As I argued in relation to archivists' sacred obligation to others, we have a drive for relationship in common with medical care providers. Indeed, if we approach archives work from the frame of a feminist ethics of care, "archivists are seen as caregivers" bound to others "through a web of mutual affective responsibility."[44] Listening, then, is a necessary archival function.

Based on his career-long work with Holocaust survivors, psychologist Henry Greenspan contends that single event testimonies (oral histories) do not produce coherent stories. They are one-time narrations affected more by the context of the interview moment than the experience of the past. In a cultural sense, stories typically are mechanisms for understanding. However, as Abe, one of Greenspan's respondents, suggests, most Holocaust testimony does not elicit real understanding because most survivors provide the information they believe the interviewer wants in a particular circumstance. He continues: "They can't understand, they can't relate to, the terror, the smell, the chaos, the dead bodies all around. How can they relate to that?"[45] Greenspan argues that Holocaust testimonies lead to ritualized relationships with survivors "with more and more talk about survivors but not necessarily more sustained talk with them."[46] Similarly, archivists must be careful not to create a ritualized relationship with their records. That is, they should not presume that records are static and tell just one "sacred" story. Just as Abe told his story differently each time—sometimes with vastly different meaning to the listener—records tell disparate stories depending on the context of the listener or the desired use of the material. If archivists do not recognize the multiplicity of stories the record tells, we are not engaging in productive listening.

Greenspan engages Holocaust survivors in sustained dialogue over the course of many years. This allows him to gather deeper, more comprehensive stories as present context, mood, and physical comfort change and shape the multiple tellings into a coherent story over time.[47] Greenspan acknowledges the many seemingly good reasons for interviewing survivors (thwarting Holocaust deniers, teaching tolerance, honoring survivors, among others), but claims that these are products of the ritual. He believes "the sufficient reason to listen to survivors is to listen to survivors. No other purpose is required."[48] Each listening educes new information and illuminates greater nuance and complexity.

David Levy argues that documents are "talking things" that are imbued with social meaning and value; and if they survive, they speak to us over and over again.[49] The meaning and value of the document resonates in the world only when we listen to it, and listen in an active manner. John Fleckner also expresses this idea of active listening: "The records could speak to me in whatever voices my curious ears could hear, with whatever messages I could understand. It was my job, I knew, to be imaginative in listening to these records."[50]

Likewise, there are many good reasons to listen to a record's "original" story. The archival mantra—evidence, accountability, identities found, rights protected—steers us toward powerful, ritualized story. But there must also be a recognition that archives ultimately are a cultural phenomenon in the broadest understanding of that term. Richard Cox and James O'Toole speak to the transcendent nature of records, noting that "archivists are surrounded by the real stuff of real life. The records in their custody are genuine; they are carriers of information that speak, from one person to another, across the barriers of time, distance, and experience."[51] Listening to the record (and to the creator and the user) enlarges our appreciation of the contextual complexity of meaning in the record.

This meaning and value of the record is a multiplicity. Jennifer Douglas, calling for more honest descriptive practice, illustrates how archival aggregations are shaped by records creators, archivists, and "by other interested parties."[52] The record is constantly changed or remade by a variety of forces: our own arrangement and description, by its use, by additional related records or accumulations that can alter contextual understanding, and by external social, cultural, and political influences that impact the archival ecology.[53] The traditional finding aid—if written but not revisited—is much like Greenspan's view of Holocaust testimony: it is ritualized, incomplete, devoid of contextual clarity. We need to listen to all of these activations of the record, each a story within a story. It is our responsibility to listen to, capture, and make sense of the evolving record.

Hugh Taylor argues that this all "requires a deal of wisdom if we are not to fall into the trap of a crass and arrogant subjectivity and will require a high level of self-knowledge."[54] Just as we cannot fully understand the Holocaust experience (even using Greenspan's sustained discourse), we cannot wholly understand the meaning (and thus the value) of archives because we can never know the totality, complexity, and nuance of the record context. But by exercising archival wisdom in the pursuit of archival validity, we can certainly make the honest and fair effort. Just as Greenspan reminds us that the beginning and the end is the listening itself,[55] we can engage in both unfettered listening to and sustained discourse with the archival record. This is the quest for truth, beauty, and justice; it is context as story and story as context.

PART THREE

Archival Spirituality

66

*Never forget that justice is
what love looks like in public.*
— CORNEL WEST

*People who deny the existence of dragons
are often eaten by dragons. From within.*
— URSULA K. LE GUIN

*I am a strong advocate of the general
argument that "truth" as preached by
scientists often turns out to be no more
than prejudice inspired by prevailing
social and political beliefs.*
— STEPHEN JAY GOULD

66

The real question is not where do
ideas come from but where do they go.

— Paul Beatty

CHAPTER SIX

Archival Transcendence

In *The Heart of Understanding*, the great Vietnamese Buddhist teacher
Thich Nhat Hanh writes:

> If you are a poet, you will see clearly that there is a cloud
> floating in this sheet of paper. Without a cloud, there will be
> no rain; without rain, the trees cannot grow; and without trees,
> we cannot make paper. The cloud is essential for the paper to
> exist. If the cloud is not here, the sheet of paper cannot be here
> either. So, we can say that the cloud and the paper inter-are.
> "Interbeing" is a word that is not in the dictionary yet, but if we
> combine the prefix "inter-" with the verb "to be," we have a new
> verb, inter-be. Without a cloud, we cannot have paper, so we
> can say that the cloud and the sheet of paper inter-are.

Nhat Hanh then enumerates everything else that is embodied in the
paper including sunshine, the forest, the logger, the paper mill, wheat,
bread, the logger's father and mother, ourselves, our minds, space, the
earth, rain, minerals, soil, river, heat.

Everything coexists with this sheet of paper. That is why I think the word interbe should be in the dictionary. . . . To be is to inter-be. You cannot just be by yourself alone. You have to inter-be with every other thing. The sheet of paper is, because everything else is. . . . As thin as this sheet of paper is, it contains everything in the universe in it.[1]

Nhat Hanh asserts the ineffaceable relationship of all things, not dissimilar to Hugh Taylor's musing on sacred texts in which he writes "The creation moment, becomes the ultimate context of all matter as it moves down through the galaxies, nebulae, planets, and stars to life in all its forms on our own planet; all creation is connected in various ways in a marvelous spatial balance." Taylor then concludes that "all life is seen as emergent and interconnected."[2]

Similarly, Martin Luther King Jr., while incarcerated in the Birmingham jail, wrote: "We are caught in an inescapable network of mutuality, tied to a single garment of destiny. Whatever affects one directly, affects all indirectly."[3] King never read *The Heart of Understanding*, which was published twenty years after his death; Taylor's article appeared ten years after Nhat Hanh's book.[4] In their own ways, these three men were writing about the interconnectedness of all life; they expressed that an understanding of that relationship is a prerequisite for meaningful human existence in which love, obligation, covenant, and justice can flourish. These activist leaders understood that this "network of mutuality" is greater than the sum of its parts, that it transcends the particular. And, to fully understand and engage in that transcendent network, the individual must embrace the work of transcending the self.

There is transcendence in the archival endeavor, and the capacity for self-transcendence—going beyond the self—in archivists. So far, much of this book has pointed toward King's "network of mutuality" and Nhat Hanh's concept of interbeing. The exploration of these ideas and teachings leads me to reframe a key passage from Nhat Hanh's text. In my imagination it reads: "The archives is, because everything else is."

Transcendence

Transcendence is most often expressed in theological terms and associated with a being or power or majesty that is outside human control and completely independent of our worldly experience. Normative religious orthodoxy points to ethereal beings such as angels, demons, and ultimately, one's God,[5] but it also considers the notion of hidden miracles and a sense of wonder regarding creation. Abraham Joshua Heschel, for example, writes about a deity who is beyond all things and can be apprehended only through "a sense for the allusiveness of reality to a super-rational meaning." On the other hand, he also couples that idea with the notion of self-transcendence: "Faith is an act of man who transcending himself responds to Him who transcends the world."[6] These passages are central to Heschel's religious faith; nevertheless we can apply some of these sentiments in a secular manner to the archival endeavor. In the following pages I will continually return to archival faith, discussed at length in chapter one, as a focal virtue in our profession. Self-transcendence and the idea of transcending the world, which are elements of that faith, should be defined as extending beyond the limits of ordinary experience.

Contemporary with Heschel, philosopher Jean-Paul Sartre equates transcendence with existential freedom. He links transcendence to what he defines as its opposite—facticity, the givens of reality or, simply put, what is. Humans exhibit certain characteristics, such as height or skin tone, and are bound to particular (but changeable) realities, such as residential location or occupation. These represent facticity. Transcendence relates to how a person *is* while living those realities; thus, it is a dimension of *being*. Sartre claims that transcendence is expressed through freedom and the responsibility that is coterminous with it.[7] Self-transcendence, whether expressed as religious or secular, depends on self-examination and radical self-understanding.

Adding clarity to this understanding, Susan Neiman argues that humans have a need to reach beyond mere experience; we want to determine our own time in the world, we want to be explorers, rather than simply observers. "We are born and we die as part of nature, but we feel most alive when we go beyond it," Neiman maintains; and echoing Sartre she claims, "To be human is to refuse to accept the given as given." Neiman asserts humans have a need for transcendence and that need is expressed by two desires: "One is to criticize the present in the name of the future, to keep longing alive for ideas the world has yet to see. The other is to prove our freedom, and dignity, by having a hand in bringing those ideals about through some form of human creativity."[8]

The existential freedom that Sartre articulates generally refers to the inevitability of and responsibility for making the difficult choices that occur at every turn of one's life. The existentialists comprehended this as a disquieting fact; I regard it as a gift of archival being. The notion of freedom and its coupling with the acquisition of ideals vibrates with an archival intensity. The archival endeavor is about freedom and responsibility, dignity and human creativity, character and conduct, caring and doing. These trenchant themes point to the transcendent in our work.

The archival endeavor contains within it elements that, simultaneously, go beyond it. If we scrutinize our work and ourselves closely, we will experience the character of that work extending or lying beyond the limits of ordinary praxis. That is to say there is transcendence in the archives. To make this case, let us consider a thesis proposed by sociologist Peter Berger. Berger, in a brief and beautiful work titled *A Rumor of Angels*, challenges theology and theologians to seek out what he calls signals of transcendence in our lives. He identifies five prototypical human gestures that constitute such signals: a propensity for order, the suspension of time through play, the futurity of hope, the outrage of damnation, and the phenomenon of humor. To be sure, Berger, a devout Christian, is not talking about the philosophical, and certainly not about archives. He clearly is positing in theological terms an argument for the reintroduction of the supernatural in religious life when he writes: "I am not using transcendence here in a technical philosophical sense but literally, as the transcending of the normal everyday world that I earlier identified with the notion of the supernatural."[9] But, again, as with Heschel and the other theologians cited in this book, Berger's deeply held religious conception of transcendence can be productively translated to the secular realm in an appropriate and sensitive manner.[10] If we consider Berger's schema in secular terms, it appears applicable to archival concerns. The following illustrates how these human gestures, which Berger casts as arguments, communicate a powerful and deeply spiritual dimension in archival work.

The Argument from Order

In his *Argument from Order*, Berger seems to suggest that the fundamental state of nature is chaos and that the greatest human fear is the terror engendered by that chaos. The role of cultures, communities, and societies is to create social cohesion and bring order to our lives. Within the boundaries and norms of this order, one can make sense and meaning out of life—both the life of the group and of the individual. In the face of the terror of chaos, one can "proceed from the faith that is rooted in experience to the act of faith that transcends the empirical sphere." Humans have a powerful tendency to impose order on reality. Erecting monuments, creating historical societies, and celebrating common defining events is the attempt to order a community's history, to choose what is remembered and what is forgotten as a way to situate cultural identity and exact meaning from both individual and group experience.[11]

This sense of ordering is not restricted to the large gestures of community building. Berger finds the argument from order in the ordinary. His best example of fashioning order is the role of parents whose *raison d'etre*, as parents, is enveloping their child in what he calls "a protective structure of meaning"—an ordered universe. Parents take on the role of world-maker for their children and create the boundaries and explanations for that world. Berger believes this ordering of reality demonstrates "an intrinsic impulse to give cosmic scope to this order, an impulse that implies not only that human order in some way corresponds to an order that transcends it, but that this transcendent order is of such character that man can trust himself and his destiny to it."[12]

The propensity for order pervades the archives profession from the simplest tasks to the most profound philosophical musings on the meaning of what we do. Brien Brothman argues that archivists impose order; they try to ensure both physical and intellectual space is ordered and "that things are in their proper *place*." He goes on to state, "For archivists, the principal aim is to achieve a condition of positive order in their domain."[13] This is no small task. After all, records themselves are imbued with power and are created to establish order, thus in some sense setting up a struggle with the archivist. Joan Schwartz and Terry Cook make this case in pointing out that records are created by institutions and individuals in society, in great measure, to wield and maintain power. "Records are also about power. They are about imposing control and order on transactions, events, people, and societies through the legal, symbolic, structural, and operational power of recorded communications."[14]

To be clear, the type of order Berger discusses and Schwartz and Cook are suggesting is not that of domination and control in which records are used to consolidate state power, and exclude and silence non-privileged groups. Rather, order should be seen as part of the process of finding meaning in our lives.[15] The archivist's role, ideally, is no less than helping to create order by trying to make sense of the past, and to weave a fabric of memory that can be a protective structure of meaning for future generations. This is not suggested with irony, archival mythologizing, or false idealism. Everything we do is infused with a demand for order and executed from a seat of archival power that we must take seriously. If we apply Berger's notion of chaos in an archival frame, then we must confront a kind of brokenness that needs repair. Lae'l Hughes-Watkins, noting that the definition of repair is to put something in proper order, interjects the wonderfully evocative term *reparative archive* into the archival vocabulary.[16]

Canadian archivist Tom Nesmith, recognizing the interaction of the demand for order and the power placed in the hands of the archivist decision maker, shapes what can be known in the future, at least in the archives space, and what meaning we extract from records contexts:

> When a record is designated archival, it is assigned a special status. It is circled, framed, or privileged for a particular type of viewing, and often becomes a symbol of community aspirations or cherished values. . . . This very act of placing certain records on the pedestal of national progress, sacred memory, civilization, history, culture, democracy, or societal necessity often raises records which were once thought quite ordinary to this new special status as *archives* or, for some records, even higher yet, as archival *treasures*.[17]

This privileging and elevation of the record is, of course, what we do. It is part of the ordering of our documentary world. Seen and acted on in a positive light, the identification and ordering of records that become sacred memory and symbols of community aspiration is the act of creating a protective structure of meaning.

Obviously, this is a far more complex notion than presented here. Order necessitates contextualization and to contextualize requires understanding. Philosopher Hans-Georg Gadamer could have been writing about archival context in arguing that historical understanding knows no present, "but rather constantly changing horizons of future and past."[18] A critical element of these changing horizons is each individual's own context and the effect it has on historical thinking and understanding. Here Gadamer discusses prejudice in the Latin sense of prejudgment which he argues is a positive disposition that opens us up to understanding through the confrontation and questioning of our biases. Gadamer's image of changing horizons mirrors Terry Cook's formulation of the record as a "mediated and ever-changing construction."[19] All actions on and uses of the record remake it in an endless process requiring continual recontextualization by the archivist. Eric Ketelaar describes this as adding a branch to the semantic genealogy of the archive.[20] Just as a family tree lends order to family history, the semantic genealogy—the reconstruction and branching of context—is an ordering process in the archives.

The Argument from Play

Berger's second signal is the *Argument from Play*. Play, by its very nature, suspends time and reality and constructs a reserve—an enclave, if you will—that shelters the participant, at least momentarily, from the chaos and the ordinary time structures of life. Berger calls this "a separate universe of discourse with its own rules," arguing that it removes one from the "serious" world. He notes that the intention of play is joy, and that in all experiences of joy time becomes eternity. When one steps into play, it is a conscious movement from the real and ordinary into a time lock in which, for the duration of the play, the outside world no longer exists. "When adults play with genuine joy, they momentarily regain the deathlessness of childhood."[21]

Gadamer observed much the same thing about play, noting that it has a special relationship to the serious business of the world. Like Berger, Gadamer suggests that existence does not simply disappear during play; it is suspended. Yet, he argues that "play itself contains its own, even sacred, seriousness." And while there is an ease and sense of relaxation to play, it is characterized by a structure or order that absorbs all who are engaged in the activity.[22] As Berger notes of children playing hopscotch, "They are completely intent on their game, closed to the world outside it, happy in their concentration. . . . And, by implication . . . pain and death, which are the law of that world, have also ceased to exist."[23] Time is no longer a reality when we engage in joyful play. Play points beyond time and beyond the temporal boundaries of our lives.

I am not making a case that archives is play; indeed, it is very serious business. Nevertheless, some (most?) archivists may define their feelings while immersed in archival work as a sense of joy, and in that way, it is linked to play. Archives, too, is often marked by a suspension of real time. Especially when working with older materials, it is possible for the archivist to get lost in the joy, in the play of exploring contextual understanding—the joy of order and meaning. Time not only stands still, it may even reverse for some period of time. Archives points beyond time and our reverie propels us beyond the confines of daily living. Still, joyful play, though deathless and eternal, is always ordered, bound by some standards and rule-making. Two-and-a-half decades ago, Maygene Daniels evoked this notion in her Society of American Archivists presidential address, noting that archivists seek "an underlying pattern, order, and explanation" and further suggesting that direct contact with the legacy of human activity is a source of great delight and joy.[24] John Fleckner also gave voice to this idea:

> Well then, this is my joy in doing archives. To be, at once, a master practitioner—with esoteric knowledge and uncommon skills—and a participant in the most profoundly and universally human of all undertakings: to understand and preserve the past on behalf of the future.[25]

In 2015–2016, the Society of American Archivists sponsored an ongoing conversation with members called "A Year of Living Dangerously for Archives." It should not be surprising that the nearly two hundred member responses to SAA's question—"Why am I an archivist?"—are infused with the sense of joy that archivists have in moments of discovery and service to the public.[26] Ketelaar echoes this in discussing one's absorption in reading a book, browsing a photo album, and rereading a diary or old letters. "Such attention and affection for an object creates a state of flow in someone: [one] is completely taken with the object, losing any conception of time and finding great satisfaction in interacting with the object."[27] Being lost in time is a product of love, joy, and play.

The Argument from Hope

The *Argument from Hope* is Berger's third signal of transcendence. He maintains that it is through "an unconquerable propensity to hope" in the face of all the terrible things that happen in the world that we overcome the difficulties of the here and now. He cites philosopher Ernst Bloch who "emphasizes that man's Being cannot be adequately understood except in connection with man's unconquerable propensity to hope for the future." Thus Berger argues, "An essential dimension of this futurity of man is hope. . . . And it is through hope that men find meaning in the face of extreme suffering."[28] This hope-based, future-centered outlook fortifies humans with a courage that Berger links "to hopes for human creation, justice, or compassion."[29]

Berger argues that "human existence is always oriented toward the future." Whether consciously or subconsciously, everything we do is based on extending our lives into an unknown future. This movement forward might be related to the ordinary moments of life or the projects fostering human dignity or through the pain and anguish of degradation and war. What seems clear to Berger is that even in our darkest hours, we cling to hope, which he couples with the virtue of courage, as a manifestation of our defiance of death.[30]

Here, I will modify Berger's signal of hope and suggest that a more suitable term, especially for archivists, is faith. As argued earlier, faith is central to archival identity, to archival being. Again, this is not to be confused with (but not necessarily separate from) religious faith; rather it is a secular faith in the future of humanity. Terry Cook offers this eloquent conception of archival faith: "Are not these archival impulses to remember profoundly spiritual, a de facto witness to transcendent faith in humankind and its continued shared existence on this planet?[31] As suggested in chapter one, from a rational view of the twentieth and twenty-first centuries, faith may make little sense. As Kierkegaard writes, "Faith therefore is not an aesthetic emotion but something far higher, precisely because it has resignation as its presupposition; it is not an immediate instinct of the heart, but is the paradox of life and existence."[32] Faith, then, is (as Berger argues about hope) also about courage. It is an argument about continuity and constancy, and about devotion and fidelity between the past and the future.

From the practical, archival perspective, Cook observes that "without continuity with the past, future directions lack legitimacy." Ultimately, he is arguing that we must learn from struggles, mistakes, and foibles of previous generations, and worse, from the concerted (and sometimes unconscious) efforts to eliminate *the other* from the historical record. Archivists must understand and learn from their own history so they do not repeat or perpetuate past errors and injustices. As Cook asserts, "From the contextual principles of the archival past, the guiding prologue to the archival future emerges."[33] Berger's discussion of hope encompasses what he calls the dimension of futurity. For archivists, it is a dimension characterized by archival faith, a consuming faith in our future. That futurity, however, must be informed by a profound understanding of our past, otherwise, our work in remembrance for the benefit of our unknowable future may be found wanting.

The Argument from Damnation

The most difficult of Berger's signals of transcendence is the *Argument from Damnation*. He asserts that we are outraged by acts that go beyond what is humanly permissible, acts whose only response can be "a curse of supernatural dimension." In making this argument, he notes that some "moralities are socio-historical products which are relative in time and space." But he emphatically declares that certain violations are not subject to relativist analysis. He points to the evils of Adolf Eichmann whose actions cannot be observed with detachment, nor can they be considered actions merely relevant to time and space. They lead us to certain and absolute condemnation that obtains "the status of a necessary and universal truth." As he concludes, "Deeds that cry out to heaven also cry out to hell."[34] Berger is talking about moral evil, a problem that Susan Neiman says "is fundamentally . . . about the intelligibility of the world as a whole."[35]

Berger is correct in his assessment that there are acts so beyond the pale that there can be no equivocation or relativist argument to constrain one from crying damnation. But for the archival setting, we can reframe this sense of outrage and condemnation to that of a more positive embrace of the ideal of justice. As memory institutions, archives cannot escape the idea that memory, especially cultural and political memory, is closely tied to the virtue of justice. The archivist's job is, in part, to determine what in his or her documentary universe is forgotten and what is remembered, an existentially fraught choice laden with questions about the nature of justice. Admittedly, my focus on justice in archival space is not to argue that it means people must receive equally what they deserve (although I believe this), but rather that they should receive what they need to live the good life in the context of the common good. However, Berger's argument from damnation demands a different response.

Berger purposely refrains from using the term *justice* because, he argues, it conveys a positive sense that he deems inappropriate for the discussion of monstrous evil. The substance of Berger's damnation rings throughout the writings of Verne Harris about his experiences in apartheid South Africa. Harris does not explicitly cry out in damnation, but rather he demands that we open our hearts and minds to the call of justice heard throughout the archives. Heeding the call is necessary for archivists and their institutions to implement the virtue-goals of archival obligation, duty, and hospitality.[36] Most of us do not work with records of evil that rise to the level of the Holocaust, apartheid, or slavery. But, no doubt, most of us confront records that document events and actions (or inactions) so morally or ethically egregious that we hear the deafening call of justice in our stacks. When we theorize about accountability and transparency, about human rights, about reparative justice, are we not condemning the immoral, unethical, the unjust? Is this not, perhaps, pre-emptive damnation? The demand for justice is a signal of transcendence, perhaps the most obvious of human gestures. Attuning oneself to hearing, listening, seeing, and being cognizant of the call is to be awake to the world. In Harris's words, "It is open to the future and to every 'other.' It respects—gives space to, looks again at—'radical otherness.' In the powerful formulation of Levinas: 'the relation to the other, i.e., justice.'"[37]

The Argument from Humor

Finally, Berger moves to the *Argument from Humor*, the gesture that he argues is redemptive. Theories about humor are broad and wide ranging, but they share at least one common assumption—humor is derived from the discrepancy between what is and what ought to be. And the most fundamental discrepancy is between humans and a universe which ultimately describes the comic event as reflecting "the imprisonment of the human spirit in the world."[38] Humor, like tragedy, is commentary on human finitude; it is perhaps also an antidote to that finitude. Mortality is an objective matter; that is, we are all going to die. Thus, humor is not a subjective or psychological response to reality, but rather an objective human trait. The power of humor is that it can bracket tragedy (at least for the duration of the comic event) and thereby suggest that the imprisonment of the human spirit is not a final condition but is subject to being overcome. Similar to the deathlessness of play, humor and the comic event are vindications of joy.[39]

There is humor in the archives. There are, of course, the inevitable clever titles of articles in the archival literature, especially homages to Shakespeare: "Much Ado about Paperclips" and "Et tu Schellenberg? Thoughts on the Dagger of American Appraisal Theory."[40] I am still amused by Andrea Hinding's 1993 article title, "Of Archivists and Other Termites," and her introduction to envisioning goals and objectives for SAA: "My third observation concerns planning and vegetables."[41]

Of course, puns in the profession are not what we are discussing here, just as Berger was not talking solely about telling jokes. Philosopher Andre Comte-Sponville, echoing Berger's argument, maintains that humor undermines serious-mindedness and deflates arrogance; it cancels self-deception and self-satisfaction; and it turns despair into delight.[42] Humor mocks the serious business of the world. Again, this is not to say that archives is not serious business. But archives exhibits humor in the same way it apprehends play. Archives is humor; it is a practical joke played on finitude. Humor and play are inextricably associated with time, both in the suspension of time and time's relation to our mortality. Recognizing our finitude emphasizes the preciousness of time, it gives every moment value, and it underscores the importance of redemptive humor.

The intention of archival humor, as it is for play, is pure joy, as Hinding suggests when discussing memory and mortality:

> Seeing archives as part of a larger phenomenon gives us another way to find meaning and value in our work. Acts of memory as I define them, stem from an individual and collective sense of time which is ultimately a sense of our own mortality, that most profound biological and existential fact of human existence. We express our sense of time and mortality in our children, simply by having them and seeing in them a connection with the future . . . Our individual and collective acts of memory are another expression of mortality—and of solidarity with our species in time.[43]

Yes, we are mortal; we will die. But our work done well will not. We continually dip our hands into immortality by assisting the dead in communicating with the present and future. We transcend our world, and in doing so, we bracket—perhaps even defeat—our mortality. This, perhaps, is what we can call archival salvation.

Hinding was a tireless advocate of humor, both in the joking sense and as an exercise in humility. "My final observation," she writes, "is that we need to laugh a bit more, for humor is the ultimate expression of a healthy sense of proportion. The items on the agenda of the Society and the profession must be taken seriously, but we should not be unduly grim. . . . We should recognize our deficiencies as a Society and profession in not planning or in not interpreting our work effectively, but we should not forget that we have performed good works together."[44]

Transcendence as Archival Theory

Berger's short treatise is a stand against the powerful attraction and appeal of vacuous relativism in Western thought. Although it is true that his intention is the rejuvenation or rediscovery of the supernatural in the religious life of modern society, he is not arguing for a human nature that is somehow outside of history. Indeed, Berger has identified five key signals of transcendence that are part of the human experience and that significantly embody a highly emotional response to our lived reality. In this respect, archival transcendence reveals similarities to affect in the archives and "the reality that there are times, places, and spaces where lives are explicitly lived through affects (love, pain, pleasure, hope)."[45]

Establishing a foundation for affect theory in the archives, Marika Cifor and Anne Gilliland point to psychologist Robert Plutchik's classification of eight primary emotions.[46] With some scholarly license, it is possible to relate these emotions to Berger's signals of transcendence. Additional links of affect and transcendence are witnessed in studies of community archives in which community members conceive of their records carrying the "voices of past lives" and enabling a community "to envision its future."[47]

Transcendence and Emotion

Berger's signals	Plutchik's emotions
Order	Fear
Play	Joy
Hope	Anticipation, trust
Damnation	Anger, disgust
Humor	Surprise

Berger's signals of transcendence can be placed squarely in the archivist's everyday encounter of records, work, and community. And just as we are rooted in the everyday, in a certain time and space, at the same moment we can find ourselves transcending our place. Archivists should easily recognize this phenomenon. This transcendence plays out in our experience of history and culture whether in the archives or our sister memory professions. It is probably a tautology to say history happens sequentially; it has to, there is no other option. However, our personal experience with history can be surprisingly nonlinear. While we might look back on events and try to construct a sequential accounting, our understanding of myriad historical movements and meanings drawn from those events is less tidy. And when we superimpose memory on "fact" to create cultural myth and community narrative, the whole business becomes quite messy and meaningful. We need only to think about Richard White's encounter with Sara Walsh's memories introduced in chapter four.

My personal experience with the nonlinear began in 1979 with a visit to the Israeli kibbutz where my wife volunteered in 1973–1974. At Friday night dinner in the communal dining hall, a kindly looking, grey-haired man pushed a cart of chicken by our table and served us. I learned from my wife that this was Abba Kovner, a renowned Israeli poet and the leader of the Jewish partisans who mounted a resistance movement in the Vilna ghetto and later fled to the Lithuanian forests to fight the Nazis during World War II.[48] In 1979, he looked like someone's benevolent grandfather—and, no doubt, he was. Thirty years later, in late May of 2009, I was viewing the exhibits at Yad Vashem, the Holocaust memorial in Jerusalem, and came upon a video that mesmerized me. It was an audio-visual recording of a forty-three-year-old Abba Kovner reading the 1942 manifesto he wrote to persuade Vilna Jews to join the resistance; he was reading it at the 1961 trial of Nazi war criminal Adolf Eichmann. I watched the video six times, captivated by the power and intensity, especially in the eyes, of the soft-spoken poet/warrior.

Today, among the many things that strike me about these encounters is the nonlinear juxtaposition of a sequence of events in time and space. Kovner formed the United Partisan Organization in 1942 (and later was an officer in the 1948 Israel War of Independence); he served me a piece of chicken in 1979; he testified at the Eichmann trial in 1961, giving testimony about events in 1942–1945; I witnessed the testimony on video in 2009. This experience with and of Kovner has led me to consider professional questions among the human gestures that signal transcendence in my work life. In some measure, archivists are time travelers; we often live in the past, yet we talk in the future tense. We visit the lives—whether individual or institutional—of those who have gone before us with the hope of understanding some portion of their lives, their passions, their commitments, their dreams. And we are committed to transmitting that obtained knowledge, in some ordered way, to the future; or as I suggested to my students, we assist the long dead to speak to the as yet unborn. We do this, as well, to understand our own lives.

The events of history may hopscotch about in our experience and understanding, but they also have a powerful quality of rootedness.

Gadamer, writing about history and historians, gives us a frame for understanding the transcendence of time:

> Time is no longer primarily a gulf to be bridged because it separates; it is actually the supportive ground of the course of events in which the present is rooted. Hence temporal distance is not something that must be overcome. This was, rather, the naive assumption of historicism, namely that we must transpose ourselves into the spirit of the age, think with its ideas and its thoughts, not with our own, and thus advance toward historical objectivity. In fact, the important thing is to recognize temporal distance as a positive and productive condition enabling understanding. It is not a yawning abyss but is filled with the continuity of custom and tradition, in the light of which everything handed down presents itself to us. Here it is not too much to speak of the genuine productivity of the course of events.[49]

Despite his language of "temporal distance," Gadamer recognizes (and I believe archivists should think this way) that distance is also proximity. The investigation of an object is undertaken "through the intelligibility and familiarity of the moral world," a practice that fully integrates the historian with the object being studied.[50] If we superimpose an archival perspective, Gadamer is talking about the contextualization of the record *and* the archivist, and the relationship both contexts have in understanding the object. Tom Nesmith, without invoking the term, elevates context to the plane of transcendence. "To the extent that an object (or record) can be known at all," he writes, "it can only be known over time, as it goes through these processes of contextualization and recontextualization, and more of its relationships with other records and actions are understood."[51] The recontextualizations, activations, or remaking of the record through time is transcendence.

Berger recognizes that some values such as truth and morality may have different meanings for different societies or cultures. Excepting his argument from damnation, then, Berger is enough of a postmodernist to realize that objectivity—even when defined as the pursuit for honesty and fairness—is an elusive ideal. Archival scholars make the same argument about archival work and also add that there are no neutral documents. Nor are there neutral experiences. Nor are there neutral archivists. Records are created out of human experience, by human hands; decisions about retention are human decisions, as are decisions about archival description; and certainly, how archives are interpreted by researchers is open to their own human subjectivity. This notion puts greater pressure on archivists to be cognizant of our own biases, assumptions, and politics; and to take great care in the use of power in appraisal, description, and reference. My knowledge of and experience with Abba Kovner is measured by memory, history, romance, myth, and joy—all of these affect my ability to represent that experience. Recognizing and managing those forces and emotions, and others that come into play day in and day out, hopefully informs our work. Our engagement with order, play, hope, damnation, and humor—with the signals of transcendence—creates a blanket of responsibility to represent our work with ethical attachment.

Archival Angels

This movement across space and time is an archival signal of transcendence. Yet, movement and transcendence occur while we are firmly rooted in the everydayness of our lives. If we succumb to simple observation of everyday experience rather than exploring its meaning, we will fail to recognize and savor transcendence. Susan Neiman suggests this when she writes, "Even your ability to ask why something happened one way rather than another depends on principles that are never known from experience. . . . Human life gains meaning in opposition to experience."[52] It is an essential human task to engage in self-examination—to look inward in order to be able to look outward. The key is not getting distracted or lost while looking inward and not finding the way out, because it is outside of our centricity that life really happens.

Berger notes that angels in Western religion are messengers who signal divine concern for the world. I am not going to suggest that archivists are the equivalent of angels; that would be an overwrought expression of vocational awe. Rather, Berger's angels are his signals of transcendence—order, play, hope, damnation, and humor. And I suggest it is not unwarranted for us to describe these human gestures as archival angels. Human grappling with these gestures is an essential activity in realizing meaning in our lives, both personal and professional. The goal of this self-examination should be a commitment to self-transcendence, the process of overcoming self-absorption and devoting the professional self to doing for others. The recognition of archival transcendence and spirituality supports that self-examination and an orientation to *the other*. As Hugh Taylor suggests, "Being grounded in a reality beyond the fragmented, contingent hustle of our lives may well radicalize us out of previously accepted social norms, and perhaps the norms of our profession."[53] Self-transcendence, then, is a critical component of archival being and serving our communities in the spirit of good archival citizenship.

It is totally appropriate—and necessary—that we engage Berger's human gestures in our everyday work lives. Berger's transcendence "arguments" are nothing less than the recognition that we are mortal and should use our time on earth wisely and compassionately. In arguing that we need to laugh and play, Berger still cautions, "This in no way implies a remoteness from the moral challenges of the moment, but rather the most careful attention to each human gesture that we encounter or that we may be called upon to perform in the everyday drama of human life—literally, an 'infinite care' in the affairs of [humanity]."[54] A significant, even critical, element of the archival mission is to make the human spirit at home in the world and to participate in creating protective structures of meaning in our communities.

Understanding our human gestures and the idea of archival transcendence opens the doors of possibility for embracing the spiritual nature of the archives. Spirituality runs deeply through *archival being*—the way that we are as archivists, and as members of the human family. Archival work, then, cannot be a passive endeavor. We are obligated to be active poets, to see the cloud in the paper, and to be willing to hear and listen to our own rumors of angels.

> 66
>
> *I tell my students, "When you get these jobs that you have*
> *been so brilliantly trained for, just remember that your*
> *real job is that if you are free, you need to free somebody*
> *else. If you have some power, then your job is to empower*
> *somebody else. This is not just a grab-bag candy game."*
>
> — TONI MORRISON

CHAPTER SEVEN

Spirituality and Archival Culture

Peter Berger's framework of human gestures—his signals of transcendence—opens the archivist to vistas of meaning that are ultimately spiritual in nature. Archival meaning and our personal meanings as archivists depend, in no small measure, on our serious acknowledgment that the archival endeavor involves a kind of journey through our individual and collective identities that makes room for *archival being* and *archival spirituality* at its core.

Hugh Taylor is the archivist who speaks of spirituality most often and in an unselfconscious manner. Taylor's spiritual bearing is the product of his personal context. An Anglican by religious persuasion, he exhibited an environmental consciousness that concerned the nature of bioregions, but also imposed an ecological imperative on the management of records. Importantly, he did not view these as separate intellectual or existential spheres. He situated twenty-first-century archives in an organic and moral framework that was expressed through the language of spirituality and transcendence. Employing the prose of self-transcendence, he writes:

> Reliance on reason alone may be insufficient for our approach to the management of records in the next millennium. A fully holistic view of our responsibility for documentary heritage cannot be achieved without a spiritual dimension beyond the teeming thoughts generated in the mind by the ego. . . . A spiritual grounding in our lives may help to radicalize us as a profession within the structure of our institutions.[1]

Taylor calls for a "return to a lost spirituality" and a grounded self-aware reality that transcends ego.[2] His argument encompasses radical self-understanding and self-transcendence, and is core to the existential bearing required for living as an integrated being in the world.

Taylor's expansive approach to incorporating moral authority in archival thinking and practice argues that in imagining responses to our rapidly changing information ecology as well as achieving an honest understanding of diverse cultures, "the use of pure mind will not be enough without a spiritual awareness which stems from the ground of our being."[3] Adequate documentation of our world necessitates a spiritual connectedness in our relationships to each other, society, other living systems, the planet, and the multiplicity of records and record forms we encounter.[4] Although Taylor's Anglican beliefs shade his remarks in religious tones, he couches much of his argument as "inner work" focused on attaining clarity in the process of taming the ego and moving beyond the chaotic "hustle of our lives" in an attempt to shake free of social and professional norms that might constrain archivists from addressing the needs of the future.[5] Looking beyond the workplace, with a conviction that all of life is intertwined, Taylor stresses the need to build organic communities that "share the warmth, passion, wise strength, and forms of spiritual growth already evident in hundreds of micro-gatherings of people determined to effect profound change."[6]

Taylor is speaking about bringing a spiritual and covenantal consciousness to the archival table. Yet, he does not define precisely what he means by the term *spiritual*. As noted, his language runs the gamut from religious insinuation to a perilously close encounter with new age metaphysics. Still, his assumption that archivists need to embrace the spiritual impact that their work and their records have in the world rings true for me. If we are to talk about a holistic approach to archives, we need to recognize that it is attained through symbiosis—accepting the spiritual nature of archival being, understanding the spiritual impact of discovery, and recognizing that records are weighted with spiritual power we cannot begin to fully understand.

Despite the lack of precision in most of his references to spirituality, Taylor is still the bellwether in thinking about spirituality in the archives.[7] The frame outlined in this chapter for a concept of archival spirituality cannot be derived solely from reading Taylor, but can be productively explored outside of our professional literature. In doing this, I first must insist that spirituality need not be seen only as a religious precept. To support this point, I suggest looking to the nursing profession and to studies conducted with college and university students to get a better understanding of what spirituality is and how we can profitably approach it in the archival setting. Turning to these studies, we can build on Taylor's views and gain a better understanding of what spirituality in the archival setting means.

Defining Spirituality

Spirituality has received a great deal of attention in the nursing profession beginning in the mid-1980s up to the present,[8] with an extensive literature from the mid-1990s through the 2000s attempting to develop a standard definition of what spirituality might mean in the context of nursing care. Despite, or maybe because of, the large body of writing, a consensus has not been reached on a universal definition of spirituality. There is concern from some quarters that the term is used so broadly that it might lead to a blanket, broad tent definition that would make the expression meaningless to the point of losing all significance.[9] Nevertheless, several approaches to defining spirituality are useful when thinking about how it might play out in the archival field.

In 1998, Bernice Golberg, applying a nursing study research methodology known as concept analysis in investigating the meaning of spirituality, suggested the descriptors of spirituality were "meaning, presencing, empathy/compassion, giving hope, love, religion/transcendence, touch and healing." These phenomena fall into the relationship categories of physical and/or emotional contact. She argued that spiritual care, physical care, and social and psychological care were inseparable and formed a whole in patient nurturing. She concluded that the physical and emotional categories should be integrated and given the label *connection*.[10] The foregrounding of relationship recalls the feminist ethics of care and the will to connect noted in earlier chapters and situates Golberg's ideas well within my archival paradigm of genuine encounter.

A 2005 study of nursing literature found that professional articles provide many explicit definitions of spirituality, but that there was little agreement in the literature regarding a single definition. The authors of the study synthesized the definitions and argued that spirituality is about meaning and purpose in life, human connection, relationship with a transcendent other, transcendence of self, a force that vitalizes the whole being, a common energy that unifies reality, and is characterized by hope. Even in this synthesis, they recognized that the pluralism of definitions can potentially spiral into relativism and meaninglessness. They suggested a model that brings all definitions into a harmony connecting the personal and the universal, but with the primary focus on love. "The purpose of being is to live the reality of love, that for which we have been fitted. . . . Love is that which is open and receptive to the being of the other, resisting temptations to change otherness." This conception "contemplates the beauty of the otherness."[11] From nursing, then, we draw the idea that spirituality correlates to topics discussed in previous chapters—relationship, empathy, hope, transcendence, the will to connect, and concern for *the other*.

The research on the spiritual experiences and needs of college students is also plagued by widely variant definitions of spirituality. This results from the dynamic nature of the concept, its close association with the theological, and the fact of its fairly recent emergence as a legitimate topic for academic research in the healing arts fields, especially psychology, medicine (including nursing), and social work.[12] Similar to the nursing field, the work related to student spirituality by Patrick Love and Donna Talbot focuses on and defines the concept as the pursuit of meaning and purpose in one's life, the search for personal authenticity and genuineness, ego transcendence, and a desire for profound connection and relationship with others.[13] Likewise, Alexander Astin, a professor of higher education and organizational change, suggests that spirituality: "has to do with the values that we hold most dear, our sense of who we are and where we come from, our beliefs about why we are here—the meaning and purpose that we see in our work and our life—and our sense of connectedness to each other and to the world around us."[14]

The authors cited above, and many more, worry about attaining some consensus of meaning regarding spirituality where none has existed. Their attempts at synthesis raise issues that emerge in archives and mirror many of the issues raised in previous chapters. They all discuss spirituality in terms of relationship and connection, love and the beauty of otherness, duty and obligation. Spirituality is a process of seeking self-awareness and an authentic self-transcendence; it is spirituality that makes us human.[15]

Based on this review of the literature, I have adopted the following definition for my conception of archival spirituality: *It is our inexorable desire and search for meaning and purpose in life, our pursuit of authenticity and genuineness, and an openness to encounter with the other that is characterized by empathy, compassion, and love.*

The elements of the spirituality theory discussed below address compassion, empathy, love, and care. As noted in earlier chapters, these concepts are part and parcel of feminist theory which exerts a powerful impact on twenty-first-century archival thinking. We are always in a state of becoming and spirituality is an essential element in that becoming. Thus, spirituality can be defined not solely as a noun, but more productively as a verb. It is a constitutive part of archival faith, but it is not something we merely have, but rather something we do.

Spirituality as Genuine Encounter

It is the work of Barbara Pesut and Sally Thorne on spirituality in nursing that most closely relates to my definition as well as other central themes presented in this book. They recognize the highly personal nature of spirituality and the inherent challenges of bringing it into the professional-patient relationship. They argue that nurses display three identities in spiritual care, identities that are potentially at odds. "Firstly, they are professionals with a public trust in health promotion and restoration, including those areas that intersect with spiritual health. Secondly, they are citizens of a liberal society where non-judgmental pluralism as it relates to spirituality is enshrined. Thirdly, they are individuals who hold particular beliefs and values about spirituality." The key to an authentic spirituality in the workplace is the balancing of these identities. How the nurse will interact with a patient will depend on whether they view themselves as the expert professional approaching care with the authority that status conveys or with the attitude of a common shared and relational humanity.[16] Their proposition draws on Martin Buber's *Ich und Du*—the same source presented in the discussion of archival covenant.

Without repeating too much from previous discussions, it is important to foreground Pesut and Thorne's central argument. Of Buber's philosophy, the authors note:

> His fundamental premise was that spirit is a relational encounter of living reciprocity. Within that living reciprocity we navigate two worlds simultaneously: the "It" world of human experience and the "I-You" world of relation. The "It" world includes all of those facets of our experiences: perceptions, conceptual knowledge, feelings, needs, intuitions and imaginings. This "It" world represents the cumulative experiences that form the substance of our identities as professionals, citizens and persons. The "I-You" world is a world of relation characterized by immediacy and reciprocity. It is an encounter unmediated except through grace and it is "spoken" with our whole being.[17]

Pesut and Thorne contend that engaging only from the perspective of the "professional" is the I-It encounter, and objectifies *the other* by assigning them the role of dependency. If we engage in the I-You encounter, "we enter a world of sacred relational space characterized by spiritual reciprocity."[18] Similar in many ways to archival covenant, this relational concept translates to archival work which is a series of encounters and an exercise in building genuine relationships. Archivists are experts, especially in a way of archival thinking about the nature and contextual complexities of records, but we must be careful not to adopt a professional posture which excludes relation to *the other*.

Our archival concern should be creating a spiritual narrative that is fluid because a static, unmoving approach will not fit all circumstances and encounters. Archivists can do this by respecting the diversity of needs and cultural makeup of their constituencies, recognizing that reciprocity must be authentic, and that neutrality and impartiality are impossible. Our constituencies, too, have spiritual values and beliefs that are fundamental to their being and we must be cognizant and attentive to those in any genuine encounter of service and obligation. The I-You approach places the need of the constituent foremost. Archivists, then, are challenged to include spirituality as part of their encounter and relationship with others. Yes, it means constructing an identity that appropriately sublimates the "expert" tag, guards against the objectification of others, and foregrounds the sense of shared humanity in our relationships.

Canadian archivist Richard Klumpenhouwer, in a more playful vein than Taylor, also asked whether archives might have a spiritual (or religious) orientation. He suggested that his graduate education "was a kind of quasi-religious initiation into an archival culture and, at the same time, a process of revealing and defining archival culture as a personal identity." He claimed an archival worldview signified by the principle of provenance that gave expression to a professional connectedness with the records archivists keep. He argued that this connectedness is gained through intuition and perception: "It is much like a tenet of systematic theology, which simply attempts to reveal something that, in the end, can only be experienced: the way to God." Echoing several of the studies related to nursing, he defines experience as intangible, "something that is absorbed into the character emotionally and psychologically."[19]

Klumpenhouwer concludes with an observation that is either tongue in cheek or somewhat astonishing:

> I have had the opportunity to climb the mountain of archival exploration, to talk about, feel, and participate in archives as a powerful expression of humanity, and to be and become part of a larger mission, a community, a professional culture that believes in archives. In the end, it is a faith based on identity with something bigger than yourself. And if that is not religion, I do not know what is.[20]

Klumpenhouwer, more directly than Taylor, conflates religion and spirituality, not uncommon among authors who explore spirituality. Archives is not religion, but it does express transcendence, spirituality, and faith. And just as Tom Nesmith posits that archivists are in a state of continuous becoming, these archival conceptions must be expressed not as nouns, but as verbs.

Archival Pluralism

Drawing from the studies above, my argument is that spirituality is a personal search for meaning, transcendence, wholeness, and purpose in one's life. In great measure, a spiritual orientation fosters the ability to consider situations from beyond one's own perspective. Spirituality is the process of seeking patterns, order, and coherence in our lives.[21] This is personal contextualization and its language is not unlike that of the postmodern archival scholars cited in earlier chapters speaking about the quest for an archival discourse that honors lived experience, the search for meaning, and the acceptance of obligation in our relationships. Archival faith and spirituality take form in this context. Archival spirituality, then, evolves from an inner quest for self-understanding and values-clarification to the outer world of self-transcendence and covenant in the search for meaning in the archival endeavour. This archival spirituality defines our individual process, and our profession's collective process, of meaning-making.

Anne Gilliland addresses the distinction of looking beyond one's own perspective in writing about pluralizing archival education: "By pluralism, I mean acknowledging, respecting, and addressing the multiplicity of perspectives, practices, and people involved in the creation, preservation, use, and interrogation of the record in society today."[22] While she notes that scholars have suggested pluralism is motivated by enlightened self-interest and ethical exigency, Gilliland argues that a less frequently discussed but equally important motivation includes "personal moral positions that may be based in religious or other spiritual beliefs or in a cultural or community ethic."[23]

These ideas about values, beliefs, moral development, and self-understanding as pathways to a more culturally sensitive outlook lead Gilliland to ask whether students "see a place for spirituality in the archival classroom, or in archival practice, especially pluralizing practice."[24] My answer is we should not have to ask whether there is a place for spirituality; it is already there. The question is whether we will be poets, as Nhat Hanh suggests, and recognize its existence and embrace its message. One approach to this goal is addressing individual spirituality and then looking at how it plays out in the aggregate.

The Spirituality of Text

Ultimately, Gilliland is talking about spirituality embedded in personal values and beliefs and her sensibilities regarding bringing those values to our work, whether as faculty, students, or archival practitioners. But we must also consider whether there is something inherently spiritual in archival work and in records themselves. Archives is a text-based culture. Texts—in a multiplicity of forms—reveal and re-reveal themselves at every activation, whether through the archivist's encounter with them or through the research and interpretation by users. Each of these activations is a renewal of the text and in this re-contextualizing we are, in a sense, renewing ourselves. The archival actor (archivist, creator, user, etc.) and the archival record interpenetrate in dynamic ways. We are textualized by the records we work with. And, like archival records, we reveal ourselves and our values through our relationships with others and the text. This continual archival renewal of the self is a spiritual activity.[25]

The notion that we are renewed or otherwise impacted by the text emerges from the structure and care that is given to producing the written word. Simcha Cohen, commenting on the work of the religious scribe, notes: "In a writing system, words are formed from a pattern of individual letters grouped in a set sequence. Thus, the manual writing of a Holy Name is a sequential process whereby one letter is formed independently and other letters are added to it, one by one, to crystallize a meaningful word." These creative actions are bound up in rules, codified laws, and careful spiritual preparation.[26] Similarly, Chinese poet and calligrapher Chiang Yee writes, "Affection for the written word is instilled from childhood in the Chinese heart. We are taught never to tear up a sheet of writing, nor misuse any paper with writing upon it."[27]

There are two points to make here. First, it would be understandable that one would shy away from suggesting that the most mundane bureaucratic memoranda be labeled creative or spiritual. Nevertheless, at its core, memo writing contains the elements of intentional word construction described above, thus there is a creativity in play. Second, deliberate and purposeful creativity is an element of spiritual action. David Levy makes this point with his analysis of a cash register receipt. Including brief histories of papermaking, ink production, the development of writing, the invention of numerals and the late-blooming decimal, calligraphy and printing, and the Chinese compassion for the written character, Levy describes this creativity:

> Writing is essentially the marrying of this ability to fix or preserve with the ability to symbolize or represent. It is the creation of stable artifacts and the affixing of meaningful marks to them. . . . It may seem strange to place small, trivial, invisible documents like this one alongside the great ones, and to speak of them in the same breath, but this is exactly what we must do

if we are to see the entire class of documents, all of them, as a
single species; and if we are to see their shared properties and
their joint work in the world.[28]

Levy's treatise on the humble receipt elevates the artefact, confirms its
transcendence, and speaks to the spiritual nature of text.

From here it may not be too great a leap to suggest that archival records
have agency. Jessica Tai et al. do just that in reporting the results of focus
groups with users to determine how they relate to community records as
agents. Between scholars and respondents, the authors found suggestions
of records as actors, records exhibiting longing and desire, and the possibility that records have needs and wants. The authors argue records as
"dynamic, sentient, and generative agents" are capable of "moving people
into new ways of being."[29] Although I am not convinced by arguments that
records are animate and have agency, I certainly concur that they can move
people into new ways of being. To the extent that records have the power to
incite change, it is through the emotional questing of the user who encounters the spirituality of the text. The ability to claim or reclaim the soul of the
text is inherent in the receptivity of those who view it. The literature suggests this is a particularly powerful experience for those communities that
have otherwise historically been removed from archival space.

The spiritual nature of archival work is often hiding in plain sight;
we only need to be open to the possibility of witnessing it. It is sometimes
reflected in the faces of users as noted by David Kingma describing the
reaction of elders during a workshop on Native American sources in the
Gonzaga University archives:

> and here is Felix, repeating softly, "There It Is; ... It's All There,"
> as he discovers with the tribal linguist Father Joset's dictionary
> of "Old" Coeur d'Alene, the original dialect no longer known or
> spoken. Pauline has discovered Father Cataldo's 1866 baptismal
> register, which to her mild shock reveals a line of close relatives
> she knew nothing about 'til now.

Kingma concludes, "Can we not feel, at these moments, there is something
of glory . . . of holiness . . . in our modest profession?"[30] The power of the

user's encounter with records is played out in many different—although generally less dramatic—ways for all of us.

This power of the spiritual event—the event of discovery and joy of exploration—is seen in the posture of users all the time. Or it can surprise you when presented in startling ways you had never conceived, but once stated, seem so real and obvious as to become indelibly part of your conceptual framework. Such is Tamar Zeffren's haunting suggestion of exile and redemption in the archives. Noting that the linguistic flexibility of the biblical Hebrew word *ohel* links it with movable structures, repositories, and communal associations of scholarship and memory, Zeffren suggests that people, institutions, and communities, which also are portable, must fashion themselves as storehouses of knowledge, memory, and narrative construction.[31] Her argument describes a spiritual quest that is part of the endless project of transforming and transcending the finite conditions of our lives, identities, and our knowledge.

Archivists are translators of a records language formed by its context, and the translation of that language and the consequent interpretation of meaning is a spiritual enterprise. According to theologian Michael Fishbane, traditional translation as a spiritual undertaking should "affect or alter the pace of reading so that one's eye and ear can be addressed by the text's words and sounds—and thus reveal an expanded or new sense of life and its dynamics."[32] Archivists should strive for a work rhythm that restores our breathing, so we absorb the text, and elevate our understanding of it to a new level of meaning. It is through this process that we can recognize the sacredness of text and perhaps effect our own self-renewal.

Archival Culture

Whether we are talking about illuminated documents, Abigail Adams' correspondence, nineteenth-century naturalization records, records of slavery, or the most modern digital materials, archives, in great measure, are about death and immortality, hospitality and gift-giving, diversity and commonality, memory and loss; they are about every aspect of life. They chronicle our lives and our stories whether as individuals, institutions, societies, or communities. These are among the essential ideas important to beginning what I view as much-needed discussions of the complex and challenging concept of *archival culture.*

Historian Steven Lubar provided a starting point for that discussion two decades ago when he argued that records are "sites of cultural production." He noted that post-structuralist thinkers point to "archives as a place of language and technology where knowledge and power coalesce and 'instability of textuality' takes place." It is precisely there, in the archives, "where we do the work of culture, that is, the messy work of negotiating power and ideas and memory."[33]

Over a decade later, the Archival Education and Research Institute's (AERI) Pluralizing the Archival Curriculum Group grappled with the idea of archival culture, noting "that the archival field works with a very limited notion of *culture* in that archival practices themselves are not usually recognized as culturally embedded in the way that, for example, museum curatorship and conservation practices have been so recognized." Although this topic was beyond the scope of the curriculum group's task, it still posed the questions: "What is culture? What are the dominant cultural norms in current academic and archival worlds? Do these norms respect all forms of scholarship equally?" Variance in regional and national cultures; the needs and sensibilities of marginalized and underrepresented peoples; and political, social, religious, and economic diversity of the archival community are issues that must be addressed before a mature sense of archival culture can be apprehended. As the participants discussed this topic, they created a list of cultural markers that could be relevant to the broader archival community. Prominent among those components are meaning, religion, tradition, identity, values, relationships, and spirituality.[34] These and the other markers link seamlessly to the attempts at defining spirituality that we see in the nursing field and the academic studies noted earlier.

Sue McKemmish and Michael Piggott, writing about the dichotomy in thinking about theory and practice between institutional archives and personal papers, draw on the work of AERI to suggest that a spiritual orientation regarding these classes of records could enrich archival practice.

They note that Western archival theory has been largely blind to considerations of spirituality and the emotional while focusing on the physical and intellectual dimensions of archival work. Suggesting the potential for a cultural shift in theory and practice, they write: "Consideration of Indigenous views of the emotional, spiritual, physical, and intellectual dimensions present in all forms of recordkeeping and archiving in the archival multiverse could inform richly layered understandings of interconnected corporate and personal recordkeeping behaviours and cultures, and an enriched and more inclusive recordkeeping and archival practice."[35]

Beyond the AERI foray, very little attention has been paid to the possibility of archival culture. This is true not just in the West. Zhiying Lian surveyed Chinese literature and found just five articles that address the definition, function, and construction of archival culture. Yet even from this limited literature, valuable insights include the suggestion that "archival culture was the spiritual fortune created by archivists during the process of archives management." The spiritual profile of archival culture (distinct from the material culture of archives) is characterized by a combination of values, ethics, codes of conduct, ideals, beliefs, and an archives consciousness shaped through the years by archival work.[36]

When considering a vision of archival culture, we need to acknowledge societal and cultural differences across the globe, as well as the structural, legal, and cultural differences between archival institutions. But it may be those very differences, couched as archival pluralism, that allow the possibility of constructing an effective conception of archival culture. One of the principal ideas underpinning the concept of archival pluralism and the archival multiverse is that although Western tradition focuses on the physical protection and intellectual ordering of archives—embodied, for instance, in Jenkinson's "moral defence of archives"—there are multiple other perspectives that should have a place at the archival culture table. As the AERI curriculum group noted, "These perspectives may address aspects of archival theory and practice that are not commonly taught, including reference to the physical, intellectual, emotional, and spiritual dimensions of archival records."[37]

The curriculum group also noted that attendees of "the 2008 Society of American Archivists Native American Roundtable meeting argued that the formation, ongoing care, and use of archives engages four dimensions—intellectual, physical, emotional, and spiritual."[38] Any discussions of the spiritual in archival culture would benefit by drawing on indigenous knowledge systems. The profession as a whole should be guided by Kim Lawson's comment found in the *Protocols for Native American Archival Materials:* "We're not looking at an issue paper by paper or record group by record group. It's a whole system of a way of life. Our knowledge systems don't make sense without spirituality."[39]

American Studies professor Amy Lonetree addresses this subject head-on, and although she is writing about the museum world, her observations are applicable to archival institutions. "For most Native people," she writes, "what is inside tribal museums or any museum that contains Native representations is not a matter of detached, academic interest—something about which we debate as part of our professional careers. We can do this, but the meaning of this work goes much deeper for us. The museum content involves life, ancestors, culture, our continued existence, and future generations."[40] In other words, that content embodies transcendence and spirituality.

Lonetree notes that the Ziibiwing Center of Anishinabe Culture and Lifeways tribal museum in Michigan includes a room for visitors to collect their thoughts and partake in a moment of reflection. The text panel for the room is entitled Mindjimendamowin—Blood Memory—and reads, in part: "Blood memory is an inherent connection we have to our spirituality, ancestors, and all of Creation. Blood memory can be described as the emotions we feel when we hear the drum or our language for the first time. The Creator gives these emotions to us at birth. We use these emotions or blood memories to understand our heritage and our connection to our ancestors. Blood memory makes these connections for us."[41]

Western archival thought and culture would benefit greatly from the integration of multiple ways of knowing and plural spiritualities with our perceived realities and lived experiences. This is not a suggestion that Western archives engage in cultural appropriation,[42] but rather it should embrace the ideal of honest learning from the truths of *otherness*. Culture is not separation, nor is it binary; it is complex and multidimensional. Exploring archival culture by holding fast to the action verb of spirituality could prove productive. After all, it is not out of the question to define archival culture in the same manner that I previously defined archival spirituality: *It is our inexorable desire and search for meaning and purpose in life, our pursuit of authenticity and genuineness, and an openness to encounter with the other that is characterized by empathy, compassion, and love.*

Spirituality and Technology

Discussing spirituality from the perspective of indigenous cultures, biblical texts, ecology, and the ethics of encounter is logical and fitting. But what about the bureaucratic and technocratic essence of twenty-first-century records? Where is the spirituality in the terabytes of information and big data that vex archivists and propel them into all manner of educational programs and workshops with the hope of learning how to manage these resources? The compelling speed of technological change, the rush to keep up with new knowledge, and the demand to manage the incomprehensible volume of digital materials does not seem to provide opportunities for serious reflection on spirituality, transcendence, and the sacred in the archival endeavor. This makes it even more pressing that we find spaces for pondering the fundamental archival questions, and to do it with intention.

The 2015 publication *Leading in the Digital World: Opportunities for Canada's Memory Institutions* asks the following vital questions:

> Is all information worth preserving, or, more specifically, is every story worth remembering? Can the important information be identified in the first place, especially given the fact that digitally born content typically resides in one of numerous communication channels and is collectively stored on innumerable and mostly private digital platforms? Can digitally born information be authenticated and preserved to the traditional

standards? And are libraries, archives, and museums as cultural institutions losing ground to less "authoritative" sources of cultural knowledge?[43]

These questions strike at the heart of archival relevance in the modern world. And they suggest that there is little change in the requirement that we be cognizant of the social and cultural impacts of decisions that archivists make. We need to ask questions about the meaning of what we do and the meaning of who we are. Addressing these questions is crucial both for our individual well-being and our survival as a profession. If we explore the philosophy of technology and develop a specifically archival approach to it, then I believe the issues presented by the digital world can also be framed in spiritual context.

Philosopher and ecologist Alan R. Drengson, writing about various philosophies of technology, first defined philosophy as "a creative activity of conceptual inquiry which frees us of attachment to specific models and doctrines in order to develop more appropriate cultural practices."[44] He further argues that a philosophy of life is developed through the systematic application of attitudes in conceptualizing our experiences and responses to the world in the dimensions of culture, family, and personal life.[45]

Hans Jonas takes this case even further, suggesting the spiritual when asking whether technology has philosophical aspects:

> Of course there are, as there are to all things of importance in human endeavor and destiny. Modern technology touches on almost everything vital to man's existence—material, mental, and spiritual. Indeed, what of man is not involved? The way he lives his life and looks at objects, his intercourse with the world and with his peers, his powers and modes of action, kinds of goals, states and changes of society, objectives and forms of politics (including warfare no less than welfare), the sense and quality of live, even man's fate and that of his environment: all these are involved in the technological enterprise as it extends in magnitude and depth. The mere enumeration suggests a staggering host of potentially philosophic themes.[46]

He notes the distinction between form and matter—the former being the abstract movement or laws of motion that advance technology, the processes by which technology moves forward. Matter, on the other hand, is basically the content "of the things it puts into human use, the powers it confers, and the altered manner of human action by which these objectives are realized." According to Jonas, there is a third element that he calls "the moral side of technology." He portrays this element "as a burden on human responsibility, especially its long-term effects on the global condition of man and environment."[47] Yet, while Jonas raises the question of the moral burden and responsibility around issues of the common good, his scrutiny of technology embraces spirituality in a way that can inform how we approach the digital world.

In 1992, the theme of the annual meeting of the Society of American Archivists in Montreal was Vision 2020. The meeting included a five-session track with experts who were asked to predict where the profession might be in the year 2020 in the areas of technological development, organizational structure, social and cultural change, and research trends. Hugh Taylor was selected to provide the closing summation and commentary. Ruminating on the presentations and the prospects of archives in 2020, Taylor mused:

> And so to our vision. If we are to live effectively and creatively in the new paradigm, which all the authors . . . endorse in their own way, we have to become more balanced in the use of our brains. Centuries of literacy and print have all but resulted in a Faustian pact that can be resolved only by greater use of our holistic, artistic, symbolic, intuitive, emotional, and yes, playful right brain over our sequential, analytic, reductionist, and intellectual left brain. I personally believe that we need once more an overarching cosmology with a spiritual dimension if we are to have something approaching 20/20 vision.[48]

The imperatives of technology and the digital world have, indeed, changed archival workflows and the tools of our trade. Working with digital records has in many ways changed how we look at the historical record moving forward. The demands on archival education have necessarily expanded to ensure that our students can be successful in the (no longer so) new information environment. But we need also to ensure that they and we do not become obsessed with the *how* of the digital world at the expense of all of our *why* questions. Taylor cautioned that we not become slaves to technological processes. He was hopeful that archivists (individually and collectively) could find a way "to deal with the 'technological imperative' more effectively through the insights of a spiritual approach, whatever the tradition, as we seek a reality beyond the material *real*."[49] Taylor gave us some guidance nearly three decades ago for how to cope with the pace of change in the information ecology. The attention to "inner work," recognition of the need for a spiritual grounding, and embracing the holistic, emotional side of ourselves can certainly be applied in the workplace of today and tomorrow.

"Laws of quite another order"

Many of his readers (myself included) were, no doubt, initially puzzled by what Taylor meant in his call for "an overarching cosmology with a spiritual dimension" to guide archivists as they help society preserve the records it needs to nurture our cultural, social, and personal futures. Well before it gained widespread acceptance, Taylor used the term *information ecology* to describe the complex interplay of records, communication, technology, and information.[50] But he also stepped beyond the notion of records systems, and, as he often did, incorporated both biological and metaphysical elements into his meaning. In a flight of eloquence that must have made some of his colleagues uncomfortable, Taylor proclaimed, "We should remember that we are subject to laws of quite another order. We are part of all life on earth, subject to mysteries, rhythms, and cycles whose meaning may be revealed by the great myths distilled from human experience. This is the law beyond our control, but not necessarily beyond our understanding, which the archivist as shaman should seek to reflect and recognize in that which we preserve for the postliterate future."[51]

Taylor was an environmentalist as well as an archivist and saw no contradiction in combining his thinking in both realms, being, in a sense, an early activist archivist. Terry Cook noted that Taylor was a Platonist who conceived of a "holistic universe that united spirit and nature, mind and matter." Taylor was trying to restore a balance between Platonic holism and spirit, and Cartesian empiricism and rationalism. Of the latter, Cook observed: "With justification, many view it as the foundation for this century's ecological nightmare, its particularly violent patriarchal hegemony, and its widespread spiritual ennui in the face of technocratic and cultural homogenization and moral and intellectual relativism."[52]

If we are moved to seek meaning, authenticity, purpose, wholeness, and self-transcendence in all that we do, and to build genuine, obligatory, and reciprocal relationship with those we serve, then we must seriously concern ourselves with spirituality and the culture of archives.

Linda Long and Geoff Wexler have argued that archivists have a sacred mission, most clearly recognizable at the intersection of the past and the future with the realities of the human condition. They stress that "when seen from the most mechanistic point of view, our jobs do involve such things as immortality, or afterlife, or even salvation in its most literal sense." Archivists are the conduits of information—of dreams, fears, hatreds, loves, plans, failures, and successes—across generations. Long and Wexler suggest this is the definition of salvation. "If one chooses to define the soul as the very essence of the person—her or his thoughts, ideas, misconceptions, prejudices, delusions, aspirations—archivists are certainly in the business of saving souls."[53] And, I would argue, not least their own.

In all aspects of our lives, both work and nonwork, we should recognize that how we perform each action is a statement of its relative worth, and in some measure, a statement about what is in our hearts. The self-examination we engage and that our actions require is a longing for connection and for meaning. These are quintessentially spiritual pursuits. Returning to the idea of creativity as an element of spiritual action, we can turn to theologian Paul Tillich's argument that "spiritual self-affirmation occurs in every moment in which man lives creatively in the various spheres of meaning."[54] The archival profession (and all of its functions) is such a sphere. Tillich goes on to say, "Everyone who lives creatively in meanings affirms himself as a participant in these meanings. He affirms himself as receiving and transforming reality creatively. He loves himself as participating in the spiritual life and as loving its contents."[55] When archivists seriously consider personal context and its effect on the archival record and archival service, they are engaging in the creativity that signals archival spirituality.

Over two decades ago, Ann Pederson wrote a commentary on the influential work of David Bearman, focusing on the essays "Archival Methods" and "Archival Strategies."[56] The essays presented perhaps the most comprehensive critiques and suggestions for change aimed at the archives field up to the mid-1990s. They were among the early deconstructions of archival thinking, were debated at annual meetings, and became staple readings assigned by archival educators. In her critical, but positive review essay, Pederson pointed to what Bearman's work had missed. His strategies failed to include allowance for "a parallel record-keeping regime for the world of personal endeavor, the locus of human inspiration, contemplation, and spirituality. . . . A temporary oversight, perhaps, but a very serious one indeed for a proposal which depends so heavily on individual and societal morality."[57]

Pederson was, perhaps, ahead of her time in focusing on the personal, especially those elements that speak to meaning and purpose. It is time to redeem and reinterpret some language from the likes of Hilary Jenkinson in the realization that the words themselves are not positivist anachronisms, and to recognize that our discourse should not be couched in "either-or" rhetoric. Concepts such as spirituality, faith, truth, and morality must have their place in the archival lexicon.

> *If Job speaks truth, as God admits, the truth may be this one: There is no moral order in the world as it is, and there ought to be some. If God speaks truth, as Job admits, it may be to say that creating moral order in the world is just what we're meant to give back to it.*
>
> — SUSAN NEIMAN

CHAPTER EIGHT

Moral Order

Radio Golf, chronologically the final chapter in August Wilson's ten-play sequence of African American history and culture set in the Hill District of Pittsburgh, involves two developers who plan to tear down a historic home and replace it with a new shopping mall as an economic boost for the neighborhood and a financial windfall for the two men. A handyman, Sterling Johnson, who knows the history of the house, the people who have lived in it, and its cultural and spiritual significance to the neighborhood, confronts the developers demanding that they leave the house alone. One of them responds "Rightly or wrongly we're going to tear down the house." Sterling cannot believe it would not matter whether the action was wrong. He replies:

> It's got to matter. If it don't matter than nothing don't work. If nothing don't work than life ain't worth living. See, you living in a world where it don't matter. But that's not the world I live in. The world I live in, right is right and right don't wrong nobody.[1]

Like many of the characters in Wilson's Pittsburgh Cycle who are trying to decipher their world, Sterling Johnson insists on the weight of moral order.

Moral Order

It is not too bold to say everything in this book, to this point, rests on Sterling Johnson's rebuke of the developers. Faith, integrity, truth, duty, wisdom, trust, and all of the other virtues expressed heretofore lay claim that all of life, including archives, is relationship and obligation; and for our field the aim of acquiring a mature sense of archival being is to act with agency—individually and collectively—in the pursuit of moral order. At the end of the day, my argument concludes that moral order is the culmination of those virtues put into action, not just theoretically or ideally, but practically.

Johnson's concern that moral order is both personal and communal recognizes that society's moral development should be measured by assessing its basic decency and determining what each member of that society is able to do and become. In this argument, justice, human dignity, and moral order cannot be separated. Indeed, moral order depends on putting human dignity at the center of any discussion of justice.[2]

If we are to speak of justice, classify it in the archival lexicon, and make it an essential part of our archival being, we must unequivocally and without embarrassment recapture the moral language justice demands. A moral philosophy-based justice must explain the demands that morality makes on humans and the obligations to ourselves and others; and to speak, more or less intelligently, about how one might go about satisfying those demands and obligations. Moral language should be integral to an archival discourse that is thoughtful and passionate, yet free of unnecessary rancor. This does not negate controversy nor suggest that there will not be contested ideas.

Moral Order in Archival Thought

The explicit use of moral language in archival literature over the past two decades is lean in quantity, but strong in conviction. Kay Mathiesen, in focusing on Native American moral rights in traditional cultural expressions, "seeks a reasoned defense of a moral viewpoint" using "considered judgments and moral frameworks to distinguish justified moral claims from unjustified ones."[3] As noted earlier, David Wallace, a consistent voice on behalf of justice theory in archives, argues that our professional codes of ethics should "be based more affirmatively on human morality as our core professional value." He suggests that archivists should "embrace a broader vision of morality over the narrow orientation of codes of ethics."[4] An encouraging development for bringing the explicit language of morality into archival discourse is a growing body of literature based on feminist theory and the ethics of care.

With the exceptions scattered throughout this book, archival scholars do not write about moral philosophy nor do they use the language of morality in relation to the archivist's existential disposition. Some have written about moral reasoning as a necessary activity in the development of ethics codes[5] or expounded on questions of moral rights,[6] but moral disposition and moral action, when presented, are generally abstracted to the profession itself and seldom laid at the doorstep of the archivist as a moral agent. As stated earlier, Hilary Jenkinson is a notable exception with his language around "The Moral Defence of Archives."[7] Jenkinson's formulations have been challenged by postmodern sensibilities, perhaps the most insightful being Terry Cook's suggestion that Jenkinson was less a positivist than "a relic of an orientation of morals belonging to a less cynical era."[8] That is not to say that all postmodern scholars, including Cook, are prepared to cast off concerns of archival morality. Even Verne Harris, one of the most vocal and eloquent deconstructionist thinkers in the profession, allows that although "the boundary between right and wrong is blurred. . . . There is no knowing of right without giving account to personal morality."[9]

We attempt to bring a magnitude of moral order to our work when we perform duties with professionalism and the urgency of obligation and care. The drive for order requires examination of both the archives and archivists. If archivists weigh the emotion and experience of archival work, we cannot help but be compelled "to look at who we are."[10] This engagement in radical self-understanding, coupled with attention to the other virtues that are inherent in archival being, is fundamentally a search for moral order.

Perhaps we need to reframe Jenkinson's "moral defence of archives." Yes, we do have a moral obligation to defend the historical records in our care, but our moral duty does not end there. We must defend archives as a moral endeavor—opening the archives to all users, ensuring archivists mirror the pluralistic nature of society, including records that reflect all social and cultural groups, and welcoming all communities. Cultivating professionals who display the virtues inherent in a moral disposition is imperative for building a just and representative profession.

Truth and Faith

If we are intent on exploring questions of moral order, it must be done with a commitment to speaking truth. Truth takes at least two forms that should concern archivists—facts and cultural narrative. The former is about understanding what facts are and getting them right—the argument being, facts are facts. Indeed, relativism is not an excuse for asserting false facts;[11] nor is it a pretext for asserting that truth is an intuition.[12] The second form of truth, the one this book is most concerned with, points to truth as a deep historical, cultural, social, and mythic phenomenon.

Historian Jill Lepore, discussing the nature of the American creation story, frames a plural understanding of truth and our responsibility to it: "The truths on which the nation was founded are not mysteries, articles of faith, never to be questioned, as if the founding were an act of God, but neither are they lies, all facts fictions, as if nothing can be known, in a world without truth."[13] The truths Lepore suggests are products of constructed cultural narrative and the animating stories of specific groups. Recognition and acceptance of facts is still vitally important, but it is the interpretation of what those facts (or lies) mean that concerns me; it is upon interpretation of the facts of our existence, and through collective memory, that groups fashion their binding narratives. Historical facts can be in conflict with the cultural and political stories communities create in the process of memory making, and one group's narrative may differ from that of another. This suggests that truth is plural; and if there can be many truths, it is logical that they may come into conflict.

Truths are fair game for questioning. Indeed, we are obligated to question the truths we hold dear, even those truths that are *self-evident.* This moral questioning necessitates reliance on evidence, evaluation, and intellectual honesty. Where truths diverge or clash, we must run toward the conflict using fairness and the common good as our beacons. Archivists, who are adept at discovering and explaining the context and the content of records, should be especially interested in truths as a moral pursuit. Just as developing a moral disposition is a necessary and ongoing professional journey for archivists, so too is developing an understanding of truths. Recognizing the limitations of positivist truth and the all-too-often homely state of postmodern relativism, we must labor to mediate truths and truth claims in the archives.

Heather MacNeil suggests connecting truths "to the notion of good faith, the idea that truth is an agreed upon stopping point in a certain kind of inquiry." For those who associate truth with "the integrity of archival practice" and an ordered world, her suggestion provides little solace for it tolerates multiple perspectives, debate, and imperfect solutions.[14] But that is precisely the point. When we talk about truths, we should not be comfortable; we should be wrestling with the enormity of the questions and, with some good luck, holding our own in the struggle.

Kierkegaard offers a difficult, but exquisite, definition of truth that might help archivists form the basis of a mature understanding of truth: "*An objective uncertainty, held fast through appropriation with the most passionate inwardness, is the truth,* the highest truth there is for an *existing* person."[15] He then continues: "But the definition of truth stated above is a paraphrasing of faith. Without risk, no faith. Faith is the contradiction between the infinite passion of inwardness and the objective uncertainty."[16] Kierkegaard opens two lines of thought: truth as faith (one can then say: *without risk, no truth*) and the idea, not explicitly stated, of dialectical truth, or, at the very least, the complexity of plural truth.

There exists in the world at the same time, the truths of good and evil, joy and grief, pleasure and pain. Holding fast to dialectical truths and embracing their complexity is the goal. Admittedly, Kierkegaard is discussing the existence of the divine; nevertheless, he returns us to chapter one and the discussion of archival faith. As archivists—indeed, as members of the human community—we cannot know the future. In the era of climate change and pandemic, the future is an objective uncertainty. Yet, we engage our work with a subjective passion that expresses faith in the continued use of archives. This faith is the most profound cultural truth of the archives profession. If we embrace the idea of intertwined truth and faith, then we commit to the belief that the world should have some moral order. Wrestling with truth, faith, and moral order is fundamental to creating a vibrant archival future.

Moral Complexity

Archival ideals transcend mere experience; and archival experience needs to live up to the ideals we conceive. We are left to ask: What ought the human experience to be? I am convinced this question sums up the sweep of archival thinking starting with Gerald Ham and Hugh Taylor and continuing full force today through the work of Marika Cifor, Eira Tansey, Ben Goldman, Dominique Luster, and others.

Early in my career, I used the story of Sisyphus as a metaphor for dealing with the intractable and endless problem of preserving local government records. I have since reconsidered this metaphor because the Sisyphean task had no real meaning, other than as a punishment exacted by Zeus. I now couch archival work in the language of meaning and as the quest to achieve an ideal. The reality of our work resides in the necessary process of striving in pursuit of moral order, a process of relentless struggle for moral order in the human experience.

One of the consequences of defining human agency in terms of moral virtue is to direct our actions toward the common good.[17] Determining what constitutes the common good in a pluralistic society (and profession) is a heady challenge. Immanuel Kant believes that people choose moral action because the action is categorically right. Yet human experience is full of moral complexity in which individuals and groups differ in their notions of what constitutes moral right and moral wrong, not to mention moral action.[18] Nearly four decades ago Robert Bellah identified the challenge in a society that lacks "a way of making moral sense of significant cultural, social, and economic differences between groups," noting that "we also lack means for evaluating the different claims such groups make." But Bellah saw this challenge as an opportunity, optimistically asserting that "a conception of society as a whole composed of widely different, but interdependent, groups might generate a language of the common good that could adjudicate between conflicting wants and interests." On the other hand, he also noted that Americans do not cope well with complexity, especially around morally charged ideas.[19]

Moral Consensus and Archival Kindness

The archives field must exhibit enough essential *alikeness* coupled with enough respect for *dissimilarity* that it is possible to build a moral consensus around the important values that motivate our work, institution building, and community engagement. The archival profession is strongest when its members commit to it, to each other, and to those whose lives we touch. The virtues proposed in the preceding chapters are moral excellences we can (mostly) agree on; they are learned dispositions that prompt us to act in certain ways. But they must be more than just inclinations, just as our actions must be more than mere habits. Archival virtue confronts the daily "competing demands of morality, politics, professional standards, and funding imperatives" that can vex archivists. But virtue can also broker a needed equilibrium between the practical demands of our work and the ideals we hold. In attempting to accomplish this, Jimerson maintains, "archivists need to heed the call to honesty, fairness, accountability, justice, and transparency in their professional practice."[20]

When I speak of moral order in the archival context, it encompasses attention and commitment to a variety of ideals and human needs including rights and obligations, human dignity, and care and relationship. The use of this language moves us away from John Rawls' "veil of ignorance," the neutral framework in which he locates justice and individual rights. The archival endeavor is not morally neutral, therefore, we cannot (nor should we want to) avoid a professional discourse that encompasses justice, emotion, truth, and the common good.

Philosopher Joseph DeMarco argues that moral theory needs a balanced perspective on the entirety of human experience. In reviewing feminist ethics, he notes that in the past the concept of care was ignored or undervalued by philosophers, and suggests that it should be brought into conversation with all other theories to eliminate bias in moral systems. He quotes Annette C. Baier who claims that "women theorists will need to connect their ethics of love with what has been the men theorists' preoccupation, namely obligation."[21] Here, I would argue that we need to reverse the gaze—should it not also be incumbent upon male theorists to locate obligation in the sacred and put it in conversation with love and joy and care? Perhaps more than anywhere else this plays out in the concepts of *relationship* and *obligation*, which taken together are ultimately about directing one's gaze into the face of *the other*.

Moral excellence becomes so through the practice of genuine encounter, hospitality, and kindness. Living the virtues in concert with commitments to moral order and moral action are powerful political and cultural ideas that we need to approach with humility and strength. If we permit ourselves to be small enough to experience the awe and wonder in archival work and large enough to embrace relationship with *the other*, then we unlock the possibility of transcendent and spiritual archival experience. Relationship (characterized by genuine encounter) and sacred obligation, when taken seriously, are the stuff of moral order.

Employing virtues in a values-laden manner (the only way they can be used!) with the cover fully removed from our moral compass, positions us to imaginatively and authentically create—or approach creating—the just archive. If we do not associate archival work with broader efforts at making our part of the world manifestly kinder and more just, then the project of archives is a failure.

The foregoing chapters have been musings on archival virtues, derived from philosophical leanings more than a practical point of view, although I have tried to relate the philosophical to the very practical side of the archival endeavor. Nevertheless, there is much work still to be done in the area of archival philosophy. This book is, I hope, a constructive beginning for archivists to form a general representation of our place in the world and a different perspective for expanding our understanding of the archival endeavor.

I am not suggesting that we attempt to be more than we can be. Yes, we work in the real world where kindness is not always valued, and yes, we are all flawed in our actions at times. But if we strive toward these ideals, we can reach for and perhaps touch the protective garments of the angels.

About the Author

Scott Cline is a Distinguished Fellow of the Society of American Archivists (SAA), two-time winner of the SAA Fellows' Ernst Posner Award for an outstanding essay in *American Archivist*, and a recipient of SAA's C. F. W. Coker Award for innovative finding aids. His scholarly interests are in the areas of virtue theory, ethics and morality, and relationship in the archival setting. He was the founding archivist and served as director of the Seattle Municipal Archives from 1985 to 2016. He was a lecturer at the University of Washington's Information School for two decades. Cline is a former member of the SAA Council and past president of the Academy of Certified Archivists and Northwest Archivists. He serves on the SAA Foundation Board and completed three terms as board president.

Notes

PREFACE

1   Ernest Hemingway, *A Moveable Feast* (New York: Scribner and Sons, 1964), 131.
2   Terry Cook and Gordon Dodds, eds., *Imagining Archives: Essays and Reflections by Hugh A. Taylor* (Chicago: Society of American Archivists, 2003). The editors pulled together fifteen of Taylor's most influential writings. When referencing these articles, I will use citations from *Imagining Archives*.

INTRODUCTION

1   The Greek word *arete* means excellence; the Romans translated it as *virtus*.
2   Andre Comte-Sponville, *A Small Treatise on the Great Virtues: The Uses of Philosophy in Everyday Life*, trans. Catherine Temerson (New York: Henry Holt, 2001), 3–4.
3   Kwame Gyekye, "African Ethics," *Stanford Encyclopedia of Philosophy* (Fall 2011), ed. Edward N. Zalta, https://plato.stanford.edu/archives/fall2011/entries/african-ethics/, captured at https://perma.cc/HE82-ER3R.
4   Michèle Lamont, "Who Counts as 'Them'? Racism and Virtue in the United States and France," *Contexts* 2 (Fall 2003): 36–41.
5   Lamont, "Who Counts as 'Them'?" 37.
6   Dismas Masolo, *Self and Community in a Changing World* (Bloomington: Indiana University Press, 2010), 251.

7   Sidney J. Levy and Albert G. Robles, *The Image of Archivists: Resource Allocators' Perceptions* (Chicago: Social Research, December 1984), https://www2.archivists.org/sites/all/files/Image-of-Archivists-Levy1984.pdf, captured at https://perma.cc/7522-DJLJ. Scott Cline, "Things of the Spirit: Professionalism as an Archival Virtue," in *Archival Values: Essays in Honor of Mark A. Greene*, ed. Christine Weideman and Mary A. Caldera (Chicago: Society of American Archivists, 2019), 257–67.

8   Fobazi Ettarh, "Vocational Awe and Librarianship: The Lies We Tell Ourselves," *In the Library with the Lead Pipe* (January 10, 2018), http://www.inthelibrarywiththeleadpipe.org/2018/vocational-awe/, captured at https://perma.cc/4E2T-R8RU.

9   Philippa Foot, *Virtues and Vices and Other Essays in Moral Philosophy* (Oxford: Oxford University Press, 2002). Originally published in 1978.

10 Lawrence Blum, "Racial Virtues," in *Working Virtue: Virtue Ethics and Contemporary Moral Problems*, ed. Philip J. Ivanhoe and Rebecca L. Walker (Oxford: Oxford University Press, 2007). Blum cites Philippa Foot, "Virtues and Vices," in *Virtue Ethics*, ed. Roger Crisp and Michael Slote (Oxford: Oxford University Press, 1997), 163–77.

11 Blum, "Racial Virtues," 228.

12 Gyekye, "African Ethics."

13 Odumayak Okpo, "Leadership Ethics: An African Virtue Ethics Approach to Leadership Ethics," *Journal of Philosophy and Ethics* 1, no. 3 (2019): 29–41. In *The Republic*, Plato identified those qualities that came to be known as the cardinal virtues: courage, temperance, wisdom, and justice. Benjamin Franklin, in *The Autobiography of Benjamin Franklin*, lists thirteen moral virtues that he attempted to master. Franklin's list is strikingly similar to that of Rabbi Menachem Mendel Levin in a later work, *Cheshbon haNefesh (A Reckoning of the Soul)*, a book about the ethics philosophy known as Mussar. Comte-Sponville included eighteen virtues in *A Small Treatise on the Great Virtues*; and Susan Neiman in *Moral Clarity: A Guide for Grown-Up Idealists* (Orlando: Harcourt Books, 2008) focuses on happiness, reason, reverence, and hope. Lists of virtues are found in almost every culture.

14 Kedar Nath Tiwari, *Classical Indian Ethical Thought: A Philosophical Study of Hindu, Jaina, and Buddhist Morals* (Delhi: Motilal Banarsidass, 1998), 52–55. The list includes courage, temperance, wisdom, truthfulness, among other recognizable virtues. *The Bhagavad Gita* is perhaps the most famous Hindu discussion of virtues. See Bina Gupta, "Bhagavad Gita as Duty and Virtue Ethics," *Journal of Religious Ethics* 34 (2006): 373–95.

15 David Wong, "Chinese Ethics," *Stanford Encyclopedia of Philosophy* (Summer 2020), ed. Edward N. Zalta, https://plato.stanford.edu/archives/sum2020/entries/ethics-chinese/, captured at https://perma.cc/UH7D-9VZC.

16 Paul Woodruff, *Reverence: Renewing a Forgotten Virtue* (New York: Oxford University Press, 2001), 6.

17 Luc Ferry, *A Brief History of Thought: A Philosophical Guide to Living* (New York: Harper Collins, 2011), xii–xiv. See also Luc Ferry, *On Love: A Philosophy for the Twenty-First Century* (Cambridge: Polity Press, 2013).

18 Ferry, *A Brief History of Thought*, 2–15. Ferry identifies finitude with loss and endings. His examples include the end of childhood, end of school, and the end of a job. Thus, philosophy is also about overcoming our fear of the irreversible.

[19]   In general, what is called Western philosophy became Eurocentric in the eighteenth century and developed a condescending view toward other philosophical thinking. On the erasure of non-Western philosophy, see Susan E. Babbitt and Sue Campbell, eds., *Racism and Philosophy* (Ithaca: Cornell University Press, 1999); Peter K. J. Park, *Africa, Asia, and the History of Philosophy: Racism in the Formation of the Philosophical Canon* (Albany: SUNY Press, 2014); Bryan Van Norden, *Taking Back Philosophy: A Multicultural Manifesto* (New York: Columbia University Press, 2017).

[20]   Lester wrote the first book about the Black Power movement by someone within the movement. See, *Look Out, Whitey! Black Power's Gon' Get Your Mama!* (New York: Dial Press, 1968).

[21]   I discuss the complexity of identity in chapter three. Lester's evolution is captured with frankness in Julius Lester, *Lovesong: Becoming a Jew* (New York: Arcade, 1988).

[22]   Quoted in Charles Johnson, "How the Humanities Help Us through Crisis," *Spark: The Magazine of Humanities Washington* 1 (2020): 16. Lester's comments are from the essay "The Cultural Cannon," in *Falling Pieces of the Broken Sky* (New York: Arcade, 1990).

[23]   Thaddeus Metz, "Ethics in Africa and in Aristotle: Some Points of Contrast," *Phronimon* 13, no. 2 (2012): 99–117. Metz, a South African philosopher, points to African theorists John Mbiti, Ifeanyi Menkiti, N. K. Dzobo, Desmond Tutu, and Mogobe Ramose as seminal proponents of *ubuntu*. See also Jacoba Mugumbate and Andrew Nyanguru, "Exploring African Philosophy: The Value of Ubuntu In Social Work," *African Journal of Social Work* 3 (August 2013): 82–100.

[24]   Kwasi Wiredu, "The Moral Foundation of an African Culture," in *The African Philosophy Reader*, ed. P. H. Coetzee and A. P. J. Roux (London: Routledge, 1998), 210.

[25]   Comte-Sponville, *A Small Treatise on the Great Virtues*, 60.

[26]   David A. Wallace, "Historical and Contemporary Justice and the Role of Archivists," *Arkiv, Demokrati Og Rettferd* (Oslo: ABM-Utvikling, 2006): 14.

[27]   Wendy M. Duff, Andrew Flinn, Karen Emily Suurtamm, and David A. Wallace, "Social Justice Impact of Archives: A Preliminary Investigation," *Archival Science* 13 (2013): 324–25.

[28]   David A. Wallace, "Locating Agency: Interdisciplinary Perspectives on Professional Ethics and Archival Morality," *Journal of Information Ethics* 19, no. 1 (2011): 184. For a more recent and detailed exploration of justice, see David A. Wallace, Wendy M. Duff, Renee Saucier, and Andrew Flinn, eds., *Archives, Recordkeeping, and Social Justice* (New York: Routledge, 2020).

[29]   Michelle Caswell, Giso Broman, Jennifer Kirmer, Laura Martin, and Nathan Sowry, "Implementing a Social Justice Framework in an Introduction to Archives Course: Lessons from Both Sides of the Classroom," *InterActions: UCLA Journal of Education and Information Studies* 8, no. 2 (2012).

[30]   Ricardo Punzalan and Michelle Caswell, "Critical Directions for Archival Approaches to Social Justice," *Library Quarterly* 86, no. 1 (2016): 27.

[31]   Lae'l Hughes-Watkins, "Moving Toward a Reparative Archive: A Roadmap for a Holistic Approach to Disrupting Homogenous Histories in Academic Repositories and Creating Inclusive Spaces for Marginalized Voices," *Journal of Contemporary Archival Studies* 5, no. 1 (2018): 2, https://elischolar.library.yale.edu/jcas/vol5/iss1/6/, captured at https://perma.cc/ZGC7-8R3E.

32 Hannah Alpert-Abrams, David A. Bliss, and Itza Carbajal, "Post-Custodialism for the Collective Good: Examining Neoliberalism in US-Latin American Archival Partnerships," *Journal of Critical Library and Information Studies* 2, no.1 (2019): 18–21, https://journals.litwinbooks.com/index.php/jclis/article/view/87/54, captured at https://perma.cc/AY2X-L926.

33 Robert B. Reich, *The Common Good* (New York: Alfred A. Knopf, 2018), 18, 49.

34 Gyekye, "African Ethics."

35 Alpert-Abrams, Bliss, and Carbajal, "Post-Custodialism for the Collective Good," 20.

36 This information is derived from the SAA Foundation's Archival Workers Emergency Fund website at https://www2.archivists.org/groups/saa-foundation-board-of-directors /archival-workers-emergency-fund, captured at https://perma.cc/U93M-GNKN; Lisa Peet, "Emergency Fund Launches to Help Archival Workers Facing Financial Difficulties During COVID-19," *Library Journal* (April 29, 2020), https://www .libraryjournal.com/?detailStory=Emergency-Fund-Launches-to-Help-Archival -Workers-Facing-Financial-Difficulties-During-COVID-19, captured at https://perma .cc/QE6W-DGNJ; and Foundation Board conversations and correspondence. In the interest of full disclosure, I was the Foundation Board president at the time the Fund was established.

37 We cannot downplay the impact of other factors triggering economic hardship, including universities graduating more people with archival degrees than there are full-time jobs that pay a living wage; and the precarity caused by overreliance on undergraduate and graduate student labor (sometimes unpaid), and soft money for temporary grant-funded positions. I believe AWEF's mutual aid effort quickly gained traction because the pandemic exacerbated these factors and created a material crisis of need.

38 Jacques Derrida, *Archive Fever: A Freudian Impression* (Chicago: University of Chicago Press, 1996).

39 For a few examples, see: Eric Ketelaar, "Archival Temples, Archival Prisons: Modes of Power and Protection," *Archival Science* 2 (2002): 221–38; Joan M. Schwartz and Terry Cook, "Archives, Records, and Power: The Making of Modern Memory," *Archival Science* 2 (2002): 1–19; Terry Cook and Joan M. Schwartz, "Archives, Records, and Power: From (Postmodern) Theory to (Archival) Performance," *Archival Science* 2 (2002): 171–85; Elisabeth Kaplan, "Many Paths to Partial Truths: Archives, Anthropology, and the Power of Representation," *Archival Science* 2 (2002): 209–20; several essays in Francis X. Blouin Jr. and William G. Rosenberg, eds., *Archives, Documentation and Institutions of Social Memory* (Ann Arbor: University of Michigan Press, 2006); Verne Harris, *Archives and Justice: A South African Perspective* (Chicago: Society of American Archivists, 2007); and Randall C. Jimerson, *Archives Power: Memory, Accountability, and Social Justice* (Chicago: Society of American Archivists, 2009).

40 A very small sample of recent works includes: Alexandrina Buchanan and Michelle Bastian, "Activating the Archive: Rethinking the Role of Traditional Archives for Local Activist Projects," *Archival Science* 15 (2015): 429–51; Michelle Caswell and Ricardo L. Punzalan, "Archives and Human Rights: Questioning Notions of Information and Access," *Advances in Librarianship* 41 (2016): 287–301; Marika Cifor and Stacey Wood, "Critical Feminism in the Archives," *Journal of Critical Library and Information Studies* 1, no. 2 (2017), https://journals.litwinbooks.com/index.php/jclis/article/view/27/26,

captured at https://perma.cc/XEA2-5UNZ; Joanne Evans, Sue McKemmish, Elizabeth Daniels, and Gavan McCarthy, "Self-determination and Archival Economy: Advocating Activism," *Archival Science* 15 (2015): 337–68.

41   John J. Grabowski, "Keepers, Users, and Funders: Building an Awareness of Archival Value," *American Archivist* 55, no. 3 (1992): 472, https://doi.org/10.17723/aarc.55.3 .r9gmpj0rj8530811.

42   F. Gerald Ham, "The Archival Edge," *American Archivist* 38, no. 1 (1975): 13, https:// doi.org/10.17723/aarc.38.1.7400r86481128424.

43   "'There Is No Such Thing as Past or Future': Physicist Carlo Rovelli on Changing How We Think about Time," *Guardian*, April 14, 2018.

44   Laurie Goldstein, "Liberals Fighting for Their Faith," *New York Times,* June 11, 2017.

45   Many recent works illustrate how moral philosophy can be applied in a practical fashion in everyday life, including: Holly M. Smith, *Making Morality Work* (Oxford: Oxford University Press, 2018); Todd May, *A Decent Life: Morality for the Rest of Us* (Chicago: University of Chicago Press, 2019); Todd Osiel, *The Right to Do Wrong: Morality and the Limits of Law* (Cambridge: Harvard University Press, 2019). The two works that most influence my thinking are Neiman, *Moral Clarity: A Guide for Grown-Up Idealists,* and Michael J. Sandel, *Justice: What's the Right Thing to Do?* (New York: Farrar, Strauss and Giroux, 2009).

46   Terry Cook, "Electronic Records, Paper Minds: The Revolution in Information Management and Archives in the Post-custodial and Post-modernist Era," *Archives & Social Studies: A Journal of Interdisciplinary Research* 1 (March 2007): 409.

CHAPTER ONE: BEING AND FAITH

1   Lawrence Kushner, *God Was in This Place and I, i Did Not Know: Finding Self, Spirituality and Ultimate Meaning* (Woodstock, VT: Jewish Lights Publishing, 1991), 86. I have used Kushner's version because it is more poetic. Martin Buber's version is in *Tales of the Hasidim: The Early Masters,* trans. Olga Marx (New York: Schocken, 1947), 191–92.

2   Hilary Jenkinson, "Reflections of an Archivist," in *A Modern Archives Reader: Basic Readings on Archival Theory and Practice*, ed. Maygene F. Daniels and Timothy Walch (Washington, DC: National Archives and Records Service, 1984), 21.

3   Sarah Bakewell, *At the Existentialist Café: Freedom, Being, and Apricot Cocktails* (New York: Other Press, 2016), 195–96.

4   Richard J. Bernstein, *Radical Evil: A Philosophical Interrogation* (Cambridge: Polity Press, 2002), 179.

5   Gyekye, "African Ethics."

6   Bernstein, *Radical Evil*, 179. Bernstein's analysis is derived from an interview given by Levinas that appears in "The Paradox of Morality: An Interview with Emmanuel Levinas," in *The Provocation of Levinas: Rethinking the Other*, ed. Robert Bernasconi and David Wood (London: Routledge, 1988), 168–80.

7   Jean-Paul Sartre, *Being and Nothingness: A Phenomenological Essay on Ontology*, trans. Hazel E. Barnes (New York: Washington Square Press, 1992).

8   Bakewell, *Existentialist Café,* 6–10. For a good discussion of the philosophical concept of *being* and its definition through time, see John Dillon, "The Question of Being" in *Papers in Hellenistic Philosophy,* ed. Jacques Brunschwig and Geoffrey E. R. Lloyd (Cambridge: Harvard University Press, 2000), 51–71.

9   Philip E. Devenish and George L. Goodwin, eds., *Witness and Existence: Essays in Honor of Schubert M. Ogden* (Chicago and London: University of Chicago Press, 1989), 12–20.

10 Terry Baxter, "The Doorway from Heart to Heart: Diversity's Stubbornly Persistent Illusion," *Journal of Western Archives* 10, no. 1 (2019): 5.

11 Baxter, "The Doorway from Heart to Heart," 6.

12 I use the term *maintain* in the sense of maintenance theory. See The Information Maintainers (multiple authors), *Information Maintenance as a Practice of Care: An Invitation to Reflect and Share,* June 17, 2019, http://themaintainers.org/info-mc-work, captured at https://perma.cc/5ASR-SVBX. See also Hillel Arnold, "Practicing Care: Constructing Social Responsibility through Feminist Care Ethics," in Weideman and Caldera eds., *Archival Values,* 30–41; and Samantha R. Winn, "Dying Well in the Anthropocene: On the End of Archivists," *Journal of Critical Library and Information Studies* 3, no. 1 (2020): 1–20, https://journals.litwinbooks.com/index.php/jclis/article /view/107/61, captured at https://perma.cc/HTN5-2YAU.

13 Ben Goldman, "It's Not Easy Being Green(e): Digital Preservation in the Age of Climate Change," in Weideman and Caldera, eds., *Archival Values,* 174–87; Winn, "Dying Well," 1–20; Eira M. Tansey, "Review of *Archival Futures,*" *Journal of Contemporary Archival Studies* 6 (2019); Itza Carbajal and Ted Lee, "If Not Now, When? Archivists Respond to Climate Change," *Archival Outlook* (November/December 2019): 6, 17; Rachel Vagts, "The Five-Ton Elephant: How Student Loans Are Crushing Our Profession," *Off the Record,* March 9, 2020, https://offtherecord.archivists.org/2020/03/09/the-five-ton -elephant-how-student-loans-are-crushing-our-profession/, captured at https://perma .cc/5UWS-DYDA.

14 Søren Kierkegaard, *Fear and Trembling,* trans. Alastair Hannay (New York: Penguin Books, 2006), 52–53. Originally published in 1843.

15 James M. O'Toole and Richard J. Cox, *Understanding Archives and Manuscripts* (Chicago: Society of American Archivists, 2006), xiii.

16 Kenneth E. Foote, "To Remember and Forget: Archives, Memory, and Culture," *American Archivist* 53, no. 3 (1990): 380, https://doi.org/10.17723/aarc.53.3 .d87u013444j3g6r2. See also Reine Rydén, "Archivists and Time: Conceptions of Time and Long-Term Information Preservation among Archivists," *Journal of Contemporary Archival Studies* 6 (2019), https://elischolar.library.yale.edu/jcas/vol6 /iss1/6/, captured at https://perma.cc/2X2L-EN66.

17 Duff, Flinn, Suurtamm, and Wallace, "Social Justice Impact of Archives," 324.

18 Abraham Joshua Heschel, *God in Search of Man: A Philosophy of Judaism* (Northvale, NJ: Jason Aronson, 1987), 5–6.

19 Heschel, *God in Search of Man,* 5–9.

20 Heschel, *God in Search of Man,* 6–7.

21 Heschel, *God in Search of Man,* 6.

22 Heschel, *God in Search of Man,* 5–9.

23 Edmund Husserl, *The Crisis of European Sciences and Transcendental Phenomenology*, trans. David Carr (Evanston: Northwestern University Press, 1970), 17.

24 David Carr, *Interpreting Husserl: Critical and Comparative Studies* (New York: Springer, 1987), 73.

25 Mark A. Greene, "The Power of Archives: Archivists' Values and Values in the Post-Modern Age," *American Archivist* 72, no. 1 (2009): 13–41, https://doi.org/10.17723 /aarc.72.1.k0322x0p38v44l53. This article is an expanded version of Greene's presidential address at the annual meeting of the Society of American Archivists, August 29, 2008.

26 "Core Values of Archivists," Society of American Archivists, adopted May 2011, https:// www2.archivists.org/statements/saa-core-values-statement-and-code-of-ethics, captured at https://perma.cc/BE4A-ZVX9.

27 See the essays in Weideman and Caldera, eds., *Archival Values*.

28 David Levy, "No Time to Think," Google Tech Talks, March 5, 2008, available at http:// www.youtube.com/watch?v=KHGcvj3JiGA; David M. Levy, "No Time to Think: Reflections on Information Technology and Contemplative Scholarship," *Ethics and Information Technology* 9 (December 2007): 237–49.

29 Richard J. Cox, *Archives and Archivists in the Information Age* (New York: Neal-Schuman, 2004), 121. This trope is an underlying concern in a more recent work in the library field: Karen P. Nicholson and Maura Seale, eds., *The Politics of Theory and the Practice of Critical Librarianship* (Sacramento: Library Juice Press, 2018).

30 David M. Levy, *Mindful Tech: How to Bring Balance to Our Digital Lives* (New Haven: Yale University Press, 2016), 182–83.

31 Heschel, *God in Search of Man*, 314–16. In another work he notes that "all deeds . . . have to be performed not mechanically but while meditating upon their mystical significance." See Heschel, "The Mystical Element in Judaism," in Louis Finkelstein, ed., *The Jews: Their History, Culture, and Religion* (Philadelphia: Jewish Publication Society of America, 1949): 617.

32 Michelle Caswell, "The Archive is Not an Archives: Acknowledging the Intellectual Contributions of Archival Studies," *Reconstruction* 16, no. 1 (2016), https://escholarship .org/uc/item/7bn4v1fk, captured at https://perma.cc/5L2A-7DW3.

33 Sartre, *Being and Nothingness*, 76–77.

34 Taylor, "A Life in Archives: Retrospect and Prospect," in Cook and Dodds, *Imagining Archives*, 220.

35 Cheshire Calhoun, "Standing for Something," *Journal of Philosophy* XCII (1995): 235–60.

36 See, for example, Mark Halfon, *Integrity: A Philosophical Inquiry* (Philadelphia: Temple University Press, 1989); and Lynne McFall, "Integrity," *Ethics* 98 (1987): 5–20.

37 A few examples of where the terms *moral* or *morality* are applied in their value or virtue sense include Hughes-Watkins, "Moving Toward a Reparative Archive"; Gauld, "The End of Archival Ideas?" in *Archival Futures*, ed. Caroline Brown (London: Facet, 2018), 137–54; The Information Maintainers, *Information Maintenance as a Practice of Care*; Cline, "Things of the Spirit," 257–67.

38 On trust, see Heather MacNeil, "Trust and Professional Identity: Narratives, Counter-Narratives and Lingering Ambiguities," *Archival Science* 11 (2011): 175–92; and Glenn

Dingwall, "Trusting Archivists: The Role of Archival Ethics Codes in Establishing Public Faith," *American Archivist* 67, no. 1 (2004): 11–30, https://doi.org/10.17723 /aarc.67.1.mw0914r2p52xx2t4.

[39] Immanuel Kant, *The Critique of Pure Reason* (London: Macmillan, 1929), B832–833. Originally published in 1781.

[40] Abraham Joshua Heschel writes, "Justice is as much a necessity as breathing is, and a constant occupation." See Heschel, *The Prophets*, Volume 1 (New York: Harper and Row Paperbacks, 1969), 198. Originally published in 1962.

[41] Stephan Fuchs, *Against Essentialism: A Theory of Culture and Society* (Cambridge: Harvard University Press, 2001), 15.

[42] Dolf Zillmann and Hans-Bernd Brosius, *Exemplification in Communication: The Influence of Case Reports on the Perception of Issues* (Lawrence Erlbaum Associates, 2000), 2. The authors write: "The stipulation that all exemplars be identical . . . need not be applied to all features of an entity. We can speak of New Yorkers as identical entities in that their domicile is New York. They may differ in any other regard. It is important, then, to distinguish a set of features for which inter-exemplar similarity is required from a set of features that are free to vary."

[43] Richard J. Cox, *Ethics, Accountability, and Recordkeeping in a Dangerous World* (London: Facet, 2006), 16–17.

[44] Andrea Hinding, "Of Archivists and Other Termites," *American Archivist* 56, no. 1 (1993): 60, https://doi.org/10.17723/aarc.56.1.a752462722210517.

[45] See, for example: Michelle Caswell, Joyce Gabiola, Jimmy Zavala, Gracen Brilmyer, and Marika Cifor, "Imagining Transformative Spaces: The Personal-Political Sites of Community Archives," *Archival Science* 18 (2018): 73–93; Marika Cifor, Michelle Caswell, Alda Allina Migoni, and Noah Geraci, "What We Do Crosses Over to Activism: The Politics and Practice of Community Archives," *Public Historian* 40, no. 2 (May 2018): 69–95; Gracen Brilmyer, Joyce Gabiola, Jimmy Zavala, and Michelle Caswell, "Reciprocal Archival Imaginaries: The Shifting Boundaries of 'Community' in Community Archives," *Archivaria* 88 (Fall 2019): 6–48.

[46] Heschel, *God in Search of Man*, 315.

[47] O'Toole and Cox, *Understanding Archives and Manuscripts*, xiv–xv. See also James M. O'Toole, "The Archivist's Perspective: The History of an Idea," in *Controlling the Past: Documenting Society and Institutions—Essays in Honor of Helen Willa Samuels*, ed. Terry Cook (Chicago: Society of American Archivists, 2011), 329–44.

[48] John A. Fleckner, "Dear Mary Jane: Some Reflections on Being an Archivist," *American Archivist* 54, no. 1 (1991): 12, https://doi.org/10.17723/aarc.54.1.3607610316t66j42.

CHAPTER TWO: ARCHIVAL COVENANT

[1] Ruth 1:16. This translation is from *Tanakh: A New Translation of the Holy Scriptures According to the Traditional Hebrew Text* (Philadelphia: Jewish Publication Society, 1985), 1420.

[2] I am grateful to Brien Brothman, Joan Schwartz, Susan Davis, and the late Terry Cook who generously discussed *covenant* with me and helped deepen my conviction about it as an archival ideal.

[3] Louis Jacobs, "Covenant," *The Jewish Religion: A Companion* (Oxford: Oxford University Press, 1995), 103–4.

[4] Rabbi Lord Jonathan Sacks, "Exposition of the Hebrew Scriptures: The Relationship between the People and God—the Covenant" (address, Lambeth Conference, 28 July 2008), http://rabbisacks.org/address-by-the-chief-rabbi-to-the-lambeth-conference/, captured at https://perma.cc/NQ5J-7UN5.

[5] Shai Held, "On Walking in God's Ways and the Path of Lovingkindness" (lecture at Mechon Hadar, New York City, 12 May 2010), https://www.hadar.org/torah-resource /god-faith-and-path-lovingkindness, captured at https://perma.cc/NWM9-EQH7.

[6] Covenant has had negative applications both in legal and political settings. Prior to the passage of fair housing laws in the United States in the late 1960s, it was common for urban neighborhoods to impose *restrictive covenants* that excluded ethnic, racial, and religious minorities from owning property. See examples at Seattle Civil Rights and Labor History Project, "Racial Restrictive Covenants," http://depts. washington.edu/civilr/covenants.htm, captured at https://perma.cc/9KLL-QQUL. In addition, according to some scholars, the Afrikaner Covenant, declared before the battle of Blood River in 1838, was the basis of Afrikaner nationalism and thus the root of apartheid. See Bruce Cauthen, "The Myth of Divine Election and Afrikaner Ethnogenesis," in *Myths and Nationhood*, ed. Geoffrey Hosking and George Schopflin (London: Taylor and Francis, 1997), 107–31.

[7] Daniel J. Elazar, *Covenant and Polity in Biblical Israel: Biblical Foundations and Jewish Expressions, Vol. 1 of The Covenant Tradition in Politics* (New Brunswick, NJ: Transaction Publishers, 1995), 1–19; David L. Lieber, "The Covenant and the Election of Israel," *Etz Hayim: Torah and Commentary* (Philadelphia: Jewish Publication Society, 1999), 1416–19; Trevor Bryce, "The 'Eternal Treaty' from the Hittite Perspective," *BMSAES* 6 (2006): 1–11, https://perma.cc/89WE-PTED.

[8] James L. Kugel, *How to Read the Bible: A Guide to Scripture, Then and Now* (New York: Free Press, 2007), 101–3.

[9] Elazar, *Covenant and Polity,* 22–23.

[10] Elazar, *Covenant and Polity,* 1–29. For Elazar's extensive exploration of covenant in political theory, see his three-volume study *The Covenant Tradition in Politics* (New Brunswick, NJ: Transaction Publishers, 1995–2000); and Elazar and John Kincaid, eds., *The Covenant Connection: From Federal Theology to Modern Federalism* (Lanham, MD: Lexington Books, 2000).

[11] Elazar, *Covenant and Polity,* 1–19; Lieber, "Covenant and Election," 1416–17; Bryce, "The 'Eternal Treaty,'" 1–11; and David Hartman, *A Living Covenant: The Innovative Spirit in Traditional Judaism* (New York: Free Press, 1985), 4. See also Norman K. Gottwald, *The Hebrew Bible: A Socio-Literary Introduction* (Philadelphia: Fortress Press, 1985); and William L. Holladay, *Long Ago God Spoke: How Christians May Hear the Old Testament Today* (Minneapolis: Augsburg Fortress, 1995).

[12] James M. O'Toole, "Archives and Historical Accountability: Toward a Moral Theology of Archives," *Archivaria* 58 (Fall 2004): 1–19. The questions I have included here appear in various places throughout O'Toole's essay and have been collapsed into one quotation for ease of presentation.

[13] Michelle Caswell and Marika Cifor, "From Human Rights to Feminist Ethics: Radical Empathy in the Archives," *Archivaria* 81 (Spring 2016): 28–29. See also Arnold,

"Practicing Care"; and the 2016 special issue of *Archival Science* edited by Marika Cifor and Anne J. Gilliland titled "Affect and the Archive, Archives and their Affects." As I am writing this, the *Journal of Critical Library and Information Science* is producing a special issue, "Radical Empathy in Archival Practice." Three articles and a perspective are available in preprint, including Michelle Caswell, "Dusting for Fingerprints: Introducing Feminist Standpoint Appraisal," in which she moves feminist ethics from theory to archival practice.

[14] The term *genuine encounter* is adapted from Eugene Borowitz, *Renewing the Covenant* (Philadelphia: Jewish Publication Society, 1991).

[15] Martin Buber, "The Way of Man According to the Teachings of Hasidism," in *Religion from Tolstoy to Camus*, ed. Walter Kaufman (New Brunswick, NJ: Transaction Publishers, 2007), 425–41. The quotation is on page 439.

[16] Martin Buber, *I and Thou*, trans. Walter Kaufmann (New York: Simon and Schuster, Touchstone Edition, 1996). Originally published in 1923. The quotation is on page 124. English translations of *Ich und Du* always result in a title of *I and Thou*, and in most of those works, the genuine encounter is also translated as I-Thou. However, Kaufmann argues that *Du* cannot be translated as anything other than *You*. That is why I use the less familiar I-You formulation.

[17] The event of relation passage is found in Buber, *I and Thou*, 84. The "never only as a means" formulation is from Immanuel Kant, but I am quoting from Kaufmann, "I and You: A Prologue," in *I and Thou*, 16.

[18] Linda Long, "Experience with a Dying Donor: The Case of Tee Corinne." This essay is the second half of a larger piece: Geoff Wexler and Linda Long, "Lifetimes and Legacies: Mortality, Immortality, and the Needs of Aging and Dying Donors," *American Archivist* 72, no. 2 (2009): 478–95, https://doi.org/10.17723/aarc.72.2 .u84p72872w461264. The quotations are on pages 488 and 489.

[19] Borowitz, *Renewing the Covenant*, 221–23, 254, 286.

[20] See Verne Harris, "Ethics and the Archive: An Incessant Movement of Recontextualisation," in Cook, ed., *Controlling the Past*, 345–62. Harris uses the phrase about the archivist, "She is a purveyor of context," on page 346. For more of Harris's discussion of hospitality, see *Archives and Justice*, especially 4–6, 76–77. The concept appears in several essays in the book.

[21] Brien Brothman, "Perfect Present, Perfect Gift: Finding a Place for Archival Consciousness in Social Theory," *Archival Science* 10 (June 2010): 141–89.

[22] David B. Gracy, "Archivists, You Are What People Think You Keep," *American Archivist* 52, no. 1 (1989): 74, https://doi.org/10.17723/aarc.52.1.73j6730385023k87.

[23] Richard J. Cox and Helen W. Samuels, "The Archivist's First Responsibility: A Research Agenda to Improve the Identification and Retention of Records of Enduring Value," *American Archivist* 51, nos. 1–2 (1988): 28–42, https://doi.org/10.17723/aarc.51.1-2. gkw6742413344ug8.

[24] Christine K. Cassel, MD, "The Patient-Physician Covenant: An Affirmation of Asklepios," *Annals of Internal Medicine* 124 (15 March 1996): 604–6. The quotation is on page 604.

[25] Cassel, "The Patient-Physician Covenant," 604.

[26] Cassel, "The Patient-Physician Covenant," 606.

[27] Mary Jo Pugh, *Providing Reference Services for Archives and Manuscripts* (Chicago: Society of American Archivists, 2005), 27–28, 111–30. The quotation is on page 28.

[28] Wendy Duff, "Archival Mediation," in *Currents of Archival Thinking*, ed. Terry Eastwood and Heather MacNeil (Santa Barbara, CA: ABC-CLIO, 2010), 115–36. The quotation is on page 120.

[29] Stacie Mari Williams, "Color of Knowledge: Diversity and Librarianship," Hack Library School (Blog), July 21, 2011, https://hacklibraryschool.com/2011/07/21/the-color-of-knowledge-diversity-and-librarianship/, captured at https://perma.cc/SYW5-HKE3.

[30] William F. May, "Code, Covenant, Contract, or Philanthropy," in *Cross-Cultural Perspectives in Medical Ethics*, ed. Robert M. Veatch (Jones and Bartlett Publishers, 2000), 116–34. The quotation is on page 124.

[31] For a sampling of the works on archival power, see footnotes 4 and 5 in the Introduction.

[32] Baruch Spinoza, *A Theological-Political Treatise,* trans. Michael Silverthorne, ed. Jonathan Israel (Cambridge: Cambridge University Press, 2007; originally published in 1670); Gottfried Leibniz, "Meditation on the Common Concept of Justice," in *Leibniz: Political Writing*, ed. and trans. Patrick Riley (Cambridge: Cambridge University Press, 1988; originally published in 1702).

[33] Comte-Sponville, *A Small Treatise on the Great Virtues*, 60–85.

[34] The growing literature on justice in archival theory and practice is too great to list here. A subjective sampling includes: Wallace, "Historical and Contemporary Justice"; Harris, *Archives and Justice*; Jimerson, *Archives Power*; Anne J. Gilliland, "Neutrality, Social Justice and the Obligations of Archival Education and Educators in the Twenty-first Century," *Archival Science* 11 (2011): 193–209; Duff, Flinn, Suurtamm, and Wallace, "Social Justice Impact of Archives"; Michelle Caswell, *Archiving the Unspeakable: Silence, Memory, and the Photographic Record in Cambodia* (Madison: University of Wisconsin Press, 2014); Michelle Caswell, "Seeing Yourself in History: Community Archives and the Fight Against Symbolic Annihilation," *Public Historian* 36, no. 4 (November 2014): 26–37; Punzalan and Caswell, "Critical Directions"; Caswell and Punzalan, "Archives and Human Rights"; Marika Cifor and Jamie A. Lee, "Towards an Archival Critique: Opening Possibilities for Addressing Neoliberalism in the Archival Field," *Journal of Critical Library and Information Studies* 1 (2017): 1–22; Hughes-Watkins, "Moving Toward a Reparative Archive"; Cifor, Caswell, Migoni, and Geraci, "What We Do Crosses over to Activism"; Jarrett M. Drake, "Diversity's Discontents: In Search of an Archives of the Oppressed," *Archives and Manuscripts* 47, no. 2 (2019): 270–79; Alpert-Abrams, Bliss, and Carbajal, "Post-Custodialism for the Collective Good." In addition, virtually all of the written work on community archives is a form of justice literature.

[35] See Sandel, *Justice.*

[36] Gyekye, "African Ethics."

[37] Neiman, *Moral Clarity*, 187–88.

[38] Gordon S. Wood, *The Idea of America: Reflections on the Birth of the United States* (New York: Penguin Press, 2011), 16.

[39] Buber, "The Way of Man," 438.

[40] Colleen McFarland Rademaker, "Archival Bonds: Love and Friendship in the Archives—Part 1: Finding Love in the Archives," *Archival Outlook* (November/December, 2016): 12–13, 29.

[41] David McCartney, "Archival Bonds: Love and Friendship in the Archives—Part 2: Uncovering Friendship in the Archives," *Archival Outlook* (January/February, 2017): 8–9, 23.

[42] Rademaker, "Finding Love in the Archives," 29.

[43] Sacks, "Exposition of the Hebrew Scriptures."

[44] See especially chapter 1 in Massimo Rosati, *Ritual and the Sacred: A Neo-Durkheimian Analysis of Politics, Religion and the Self* (Farnham, U.K.: Ashgate Publishing, 2009); Elizabeth Burns Coleman and Kevin White, "Stretching the Sacred," in *Negotiating the Sacred: Blasphemy and Sacrilege in a Multicultural Society*, ed. Elizabeth Burns Coleman (Canberra: ANU E Press, 2006), 65–77.

CHAPTER THREE: THE ARCHIVAL CITIZEN

[1] Laura Visser-Maessen, *Robert Parris Moses: A Life in Civil Rights and Leadership at the Grassroots* (Raleigh: University of North Carolina Press, 2016). See also the many passages about Moses in Taylor Branch, *Parting the Waters: America in the King Years, 1954–1963* (New York: Simon and Schuster, 1988) and *Pillar of Fire: America in the King Years, 1963–1965* (New York: Simon and Schuster, 1998). In *Moral Clarity: A Guide for Grown-Up Idealists*, philosopher Susan Neiman profiles Moses in a chapter titled "Enlightenment Heroes." See the Algebra Project's website and links to other projects at https://algebra.org/wp/, captured at https://perma.cc/T5PW-4Y3D.

[2] Michael J. Sandel, *Democracy's Discontent: America in Search of a Public Philosophy* (Cambridge: Belknap Press, 1996), 4.

[3] Sandel, *Democracy's Discontent*, 5.

[4] Terry Eastwood, "Reflections on the Goal of Archival Appraisal in Democratic Societies," *Archivaria* 54 (January 2002): 63. See also, Eastwood, "Archives, Democratic Accountability, and Truth," in *Better off Forgetting? Essays on Archives, Public Policy, and Collective Memory*, ed. Cheryl Avery and Mona Holmlund (Toronto: University of Toronto Press, 2010). Robert A. Dahl was one of the foremost political theorists of the last century. See especially *A Preface to Democratic Theory* (Chicago: University of Chicago Press, 1956); *Democracy and Its Critics* (New Haven: Yale University Press, 1989); and *On Democracy* (New Haven: Yale University Press, 1998).

[5] Gordon S. Wood, *The Radicalism of the American Revolution* (New York: Alfred A. Knopf, 1992), 232.

[6] For a sampling of the growing body of archival literature dealing with justice, see footnote 34 in chapter two.

[7] Dominique Leydet, "Citizenship," *Stanford Encyclopedia of Philosophy* (Fall 2017), ed. Edward N. Zalta, https://plato.stanford.edu/entries/citizenship/, captured at https://perma.cc/876C-MPU9.

[8] Michael Schudson, *The Good Citizen: A History of American Civic Life* (New York: Free Press, 1998), 182–85.

9   Sandel, *Democracy's Discontent*, 5–6.

10   Schudson, *The Good Citizen*, 289–92. Schudson quotes at length from Mary Ann Glendon, a conservative law professor at Harvard. See Glendon, *Rights Talk* (New York: Free Press, 1991).

11   Robert N. Bellah, Richard Madsen, William M. Sullivan, Ann Swidler, and Steven M. Tipton, *Habits of the Heart: Individualism and Commitment in American Life* (Berkeley: University of California Press, 1985), 196–218. The quotation is on page 200.

12   Gyekye, "African Ethics."

13   Bee Piang Tan, Noor Banu Mahadir Naidu, and Zuraini Jamil Osman, "Moral Values and Good Citizens in a Multi-Ethnic Society: A Content Analysis of Moral Education Textbooks in Malaysia," *Journal of Social Studies Research* 42 (April 2018), 119–34. The concern of these researchers is with the questions of national unity in a multi-ethnic nation.

14   Marika Cifor and Jamie A. Lee, "Towards an Archival Critique: Opening Possibilities for Addressing Neoliberalism in the Archival Field," *Journal of Critical Library and Information Studies*, 1, no. 1 (2017): 5.

15   Yascha Mounk, *The Age of Responsibility: Luck, Choice, and the Welfare State* (Cambridge: Harvard University Press, 2017). Both quotations are on page 22.

16   Jimerson, "Embracing the Power of Archives," 19–32. Quotations are on pages 24 and 29.

17   Fleckner, "Dear Mary Jane," 12.

18   Jimerson discusses the issues of neutrality and objectivity in the archival realm throughout *Archives Power*, but especially on pages 290–95. A useful analysis of the concepts drawn from journalism are in Wesley Lowery, "A Reckoning over Objectivity, Led by Black Journalists," *New York Times*, June 23, 2020, at https://www.nytimes.com /2020/06/23/opinion/objectivity-black-journalists-coronavirous.html.

19   Andrew Flinn and Ben Alexander, "Humanizing an Inevitably Political Craft," *Archival Science* 15 (2015): 332.

20   Alexis de Tocqueville, *Democracy in America*, ed. Richard D. Heffner (New York: New American Library, 1956, 12th printing), 194.

21   Emmanuel Levinas, *Totality and Infinity: An Essay on Exteriority*, trans. Alphonso Lingis (Pittsburgh: Duquesne University Press, 1969). Levinas described responsibility as the experience of transcendence.

22   For the use of the term *citizen archivist* in this meaning, see Stacie M. Williams and Jarrett M. Drake, "Power to the People: Documenting Police Violence in Cleveland," *Journal of Critical Library and Information Studies* 1, no. 2 (2017), https://journals .litwinbooks.com/index.php/jclis/article/view/33/25, captured at https://perma.cc /44SM-J4KE. The term *citizen archivist* gained some usage over a decade ago with the idea of personal archives and the proliferation of lay-managed collections. See, for example, Richard J. Cox, *Personal Archives and a New Archival Calling: Readings, Reflections and Rumination* (Duluth, MN: Litwin Books, 2009).

23   For a sampling, see Laura Millar, "An Obligation of Trust: Speculations on Accountability and Description," *American Archivist* 69, no. 1 (2006): 60–78, https:// doi.org/10.17723/aarc.69.1.v88wl1m57382087m; Creighton Barrett, "Building Trust in Information: Perspectives on the Frontiers of Provenance," *American Archivist*

80, no. 2 (2017): 466–70, https://doi.org/10.17723/0360-9081-80.2.466; William Rosenberg, "Politics in the (Russian) Archives: The 'Objectivity Question,' Trust, and the Limitations of Law," *American Archivist* 64, no. 1 (2001): 78–95, https://doi.org /10.17723/aarc.64.1.9454828761277787; Glenn Dingwall, "Trusting Archivists: The Role of Archival Ethics Codes in Establishing Public Faith," *American Archivist* 67, no. 1 (2004): 11–30, https://doi.org/10.17723/aarc.67.1.mw0914r2p52xx2t4; Heather MacNeil, "Providing Grounds for Trust: Developing Conceptual Requirements for the Long-Term Preservation of Authentic Electronic Records," *Archivaria* 50 (Fall 2000): 52–78; Heather MacNeil, "Trust and Professional Identity: Narratives, Counter-Narratives and Lingering Ambiguities," *Archival Science* 11 (2001): 175–92; Geoffrey Yeo, "Trust and Context in Cyberspace," *Archives and Records* 34 (2013): 214–34.

24 MacNeil, "Trust and Professional Identity," 190.

25 Eastwood, "Reflections on the Goals of Archival Appraisal in Democratic Societies," 71.

26 Yeo, "Trust and Context in Cyberspace," 216.

27 Yeo, "Trust and Context in Cyberspace," 226–27.

28 See Glenn Dingwall, "Trusting Archivists," 11–30.

29 Many of the questions raised here about archival trust and trustworthiness are adapted from Shai Held's discussion of emunah. See Held, "On Walking in God's Ways and the Path of Lovingkindness."

30 Jarrett Drake, "I'm Leaving the Archival Profession: It's Better This Way," Medium: On Archivy, June 26, 2017, https://medium.com/on-archivy/im-leaving-the-archival -profession-it-s-better-this-way-ed631c6d72fe, captured at https://perma.cc/95FY -Q9KA. Duff et al. make a similar argument that a "narrowly construed professionalism obliquely reinforces racial, class, and gender privileges and biases." See Duff, Flinn, Suurtamm, and Wallace, "Social Justice Impact of Archives," 325.

31 Dominique Luster, "Professionalism: As Pursuit of Archivist Identity," in Weideman and Caldera, eds., *Archival Values*, 249.

32 Luster, "Professionalism: As Pursuit of Archivist Identity," 254–55.

33 Professionalism was included among the Core Values adopted in 2011, but was removed from the revised list in 2020. I argued for that change in "Things of the Spirit" in Weideman and Caldera, eds., *Archival Values*.

34 For a more fulsome discussion of my views on professionalism, see Cline, "Things of the Spirit," 257–67. The quotation is on page 265.

35 Ruby Sales, "How We Can Start to Heal the Pain of Racial Division," September 2018, at https://www.ted.com/talks/ruby_sales_how_we_can_start_to_heal_the_pain_of _racial_division/transcript, captured at https://perma.cc/N57G-MGC2.

36 Mellody Hobson, "Color Blind or Color Brave?" March 2014, at https://www.ted.com /talks/mellody_hobson_color_blind_or_color_brave/transcript, captured at https:// perma.cc/59PX-DSJ8.

37 The best discussion of critical race theory and archives is Anthony W. Dunbar, "Introducing Critical Race Theory to Archival Discourse: Getting the Conversation Started," *Archival Science* 6 (March 2006): 109–29. His justice framework has been central to others including Duff, Flinn, Suurtamm, and Wallace, "Social Justice Impact of Archives"; and Punzalan and Caswell, "Critical Directions."

38   Kimberlé Crenshaw, "Demarginalizing the Intersection of Race and Sex: A Black Feminist Critique of Antidiscrimination Doctrine, Feminist Theory and Antiracist Politics," *University of Chicago Legal Forum, Special Issue on Feminism in the Law: Theory, Practice and Criticism* (University of Chicago Law School, 1989): 139–68. For a brief introduction to intersectionality, see Crenshaw's keynote address at the 2016 Women of the World Festival at https://www.youtube.com/watch?v=-DW4HLgYPlA.

39   The City of Seattle Race and Social Justice Initiative is an ongoing program that requires each city agency to apply a racial equity analysis to proposed annual budgets and to create internal SJI work plans. The Office of Civil Rights has developed an RSJI Tool Kit for departmental use, reviews the city's comprehensive plan, and conducts community outreach to underserved communities to gather input and feedback on city programs. For more information on RSJI, see https://www.seattle.gov/civilrights/what-we-do/race-and-social-justice-initiative, captured at https://perma.cc/QLP9-HHFU.

40   This matrix is adapted from Maurianne Adams, Lee Anne Bell, and Pat Griffin, eds., *Teaching for Diversity and Social Justice* (New York: Routledge, 2007), and training materials from the Seattle Office of Civil Rights' Race and Social Justice Initiative. The Adams, Bell and Griffin matrix includes a fifth column titled *Border Group*. This recognizes groups who may not suffer the same degree of oppression as the targeted groups. For example, in the Citizenship category, "Naturalized" citizens are listed as a border group because they are foreign-born.

41   Michelle Caswell, "On Archival Pluralism: What Religious Pluralism (and Its Critics) Can Teach Us about Archives," *Archival Science* 13 (2013): 286.

42   There are many great works, both fiction and nonfiction, on race and racism by Frederick Douglass, W. E. B. Du Bois, Zora Neale Hurston, Richard Wright, Harlan Ellison, James Baldwin, Lorraine Hansberry, August Wilson, Toni Morrison, and a host of others. A few recent examples include: Jason Reynolds and Ibram X. Kendi, *Stamped: Racism, Antiracism, and You* (New York: Little, Brown and Company, 2020); Ijeoma Oluo, *So You Want to Talk about Race* (New York: Seal Press, 2018); Safiya Umoja Noble, *Algorithms of Oppression: How Search Engines Reinforce Racism* (New York: New York University Press, 2018); Henry Louis Gates, Jr., *Stony the Road: Reconstruction, White Supremacy, and the Rise of Jim Crow* (New York: Penguin Press, 2019); and Jennifer L. Eberhardt, *Biased: Uncovering the Hidden Prejudice that Shapes What We See, Think, and Do* (New York: Viking, 2019). Isabel Wilkerson, *Caste: The Origins of Our Discontents* (New York: Random House, 2020) provides a complex analysis that speaks to the intersection of race and class.

43   Caswell, Broman, Kirmer, Martin, and Sowry, "Implementing a Social Justice Framework."

44   Alpert-Abrams, Bliss, and Carbajal, "Post-Custodialism for the Collective Good."

45   The Information Maintainers, *Information Maintenance as a Practice of Care.*

46   Archives for Black Lives in Philadelphia Anti-Racist Description Working Group, "Archives for Black Lives in Philadelphia: Anti-Racist Description Resources," October 2019, https://archivesforblacklives.files.wordpress.com/2019/10/ardr_final.pdf, captured at https://perma.cc/CW4Z-YW8N.

47   David James Hudson, "Diversity as Anti-Racism in Library and Information Studies: A Critique," *Journal of Critical Library and Information Studies* 1, no.1 (2017): 5, https://journals.litwinbooks.com/index.php/jclis/article/view/6/2, captured at https://perma.cc/26Q6-RL59.

[48] Drake, "Diversity's Discontents," 270.

[49] Nel Noddings, *Caring: A Feminine Approach to Ethics and Moral Education* (Berkeley: University of California Press, 1982); and *Starting at Home: Caring and Social Policy* (Berkeley: University of California Press, 2002). In *Caring*, Noddings developed the notion of "caring for," but suggested it applied in its full measure to those who were proximate and less so to others. Criticism of this construct led her two decades later to write that "caring about" humanity was an obligation.

[50] Andrea Hinding, "Of Archivists and Other Termites," 54–61. All quotations are on page 60.

[51] Caswell and Cifor, "From Human Rights to Feminist Ethics," 30. The authors note that empathy asks us to imagine our body in the place of another. The power of radical empathy is experiential and emotional; we are asked to feel, not cognize.

[52] Caswell and Cifor, "From Human Rights to Feminist Ethics," 42.

[53] Hillel Arnold, "Practicing Care: Constructing Social Responsibility through Feminist Care Ethics," in Weideman and Caldera, eds., *Archival Values*, 30–41.

[54] Schudson, *The Good Citizen*, 301–6. Any such measurement would necessarily require qualitative analysis, although some of the measures do lend themselves to the collection of statistical data.

[55] Although the discussion of internal and external measures of the health of archival citizenship might appear to focus primarily on formal structures such as professional associations, I contend that they apply in equal measure to other groups such as community archives, collectives that engage in archival work, and archivists who work in arenas previously not considered as being within the "profession."

[56] See Steven Sloman and Philip Fernbach, *The Knowledge Illusion: Why We Never Think Alone* (New York: Riverhead Books, 2017).

[57] Sandel, *Democracy's Discontent*, 350–51.

CHAPTER FOUR: MEMORY AS JUSTICE

[1] Yehuda Amichai, *Amen* (Minneapolis: Milkweed Editions, 1977), 33.

[2] Verne Harris, "A Shaft of Darkness: Derrida in the Archives," in *Archives and Justice*, 47.

[3] Amichai, *Amen*, 22. The allusion is to a pivotal battle against the invading Egyptian army during Israel's 1948 War of Independence.

[4] A sample of the archival literature on memory that has been particularly useful for me includes: Jimerson, *Archives Power*; Blouin Jr. and Rosenberg, *Archives, Documentation and Institutions of Social Memory*; Harris, *Archives and Justice*; Barbara L. Craig, "Selected Themes in the Literature on Memory and Their Pertinence to Archives," *American Archivist* 65, no. 2 (2002): 276–89, https://doi.org/10.17723/aarc.65.2 .362773030n128265; Jeannette A. Bastian, "Flowers for Homestead: A Case Study in Archives and Collective Memory," *American Archivist* 72, no. 1 (2009): 113–32, https:// doi.org/10.17723/aarc.72.1.k751734304667050; Foote, "To Remember and Forget," 378–92; Trond Jacobsen, Ricardo L. Punzalan, and Margaret L. Hedstrom, "Invoking Collective Memory: Mapping the Emergence of a Concept in Archival Science," *Archival Science* 13 (April 2013): 217–51; Jeannette A. Bastian, "Memory Research/ Archival Research," in *Research in the Archival Multiverse*, ed. Anne J. Gilliland, Sue

McKemmish, and Andrew J. Lan (Monash University Publishing, 2017), 269–87, http://library.oapen.org/handle/20.500.12657/31429, captured at https://perma.cc /H5T5-FT7N; and Noam Tirosh and Amit M. Schejter, "The Regulation of Archives and Society's Memory: The Case of Israel," *Archival Science* 21 (2020).

5   Margaret Hedstrom, "Archives and Collective Memory: More than a Metaphor, Less than an Analogy," in Eastwood and MacNeil, *Currents of Archival Thinking*, 163–79.

6   Craig, "Selected Themes in the Literature on Memory," 279.

7   Hedstrom, "Archives and Collective Memory," 164–66.

8   Joan van Albada, "Archives: Particles of Memory or More?" in Blouin Jr. and Rosenberg, *Archives, Documentation and Institutions of Social Memory*, 217.

9   Indeed, these are definitions derived from the 1970 Funk & Wagnalls dictionary.

10 van Albada, "Archives: Particles of Memory or More?" 217.

11 Yosef Hayim Yerushalmi, *Zakhor: Jewish History and Jewish Memory* (Seattle and London: University of Washington Press, 1996 edition), 5.

12 See Jeffrey Burds, "Ethnicity, Memory, and Violence: Reflections on Special Problems in Soviet & East European Archives," in Blouin Jr. and Rosenberg, *Archives, Documentation and Institutions of Social Memory*, 466–79.

13 Most archival writing on collective memory is influenced by French sociologist Maurice Halbwachs' 1950 study. A good English translation is Maurice Halbwachs, *On Collective Memory*, trans. Lewis A. Coser (Chicago: University of Chicago Press, 1992).

14 Richard White, *Remembering Ahanagran: A History of Stories* (New York: Hill and Wang, 1996), 30–31.

15 White, *Remembering Ahanagran*, 6. Also quoted in Jimerson, *Archives Power*, 193.

16 Yerushalmi, *Zakhor*, xxxiv.

17 Tywanna Whorley, "The Tuskegee Syphilis Study: Access and Control Over Controversial Records," in *Political Pressure and the Archival Record*, ed. Margaret Procter, Michael Cook, and Caroline M. Williams (Chicago: Society of American Archivists, 2005), 173.

18 Yerushalmi, *Zakhor*, 5, 11, 108.

19 Quoted in Yerushalmi, *Zakhor*, 107.

20 Geoffrey C. Bowker, "Lest We Remember: Organizational Forgetting and the Production of Knowledge," *Accounting, Management and Information Technology* 7 (1997): 113–38.

21 Janet Carsten, "The Politics of Forgetting: Migration, Kinship and Memory on the Periphery of the Southeast Asian State," *Journal of the Royal Anthropological Institute* 1 (1995): 317–18.

22 Eva Moseley, "Visiting Archives in China," *American Archivist* 50, no. 1 (1987): 137, https://doi.org/10.17723/aarc.50.1.n6t5271u105mq231; Beatrice S. Bartlett, "Qing Statesmen, Archivists, and Historians and the Question of Memory," in Blouin Jr. and Rosenberg, *Archives, Documentation and Institutions of Social Memory*, 424. In 1999, I visited several Chinese archives as part of an international seminar on local records and was surprised when confronted first-hand with the paucity of documentary evidence of China's ancient civilizations. Only a relative handful of documents of the Ming Dynasty (1368–1643) remained.

23 David A. Wallace, "Introduction: Memory Ethics—or the Presence of the Past in the Present," *Archival Science* 11 (2011): 6.

24 Caswell, "Seeing Yourself in History," 26.

25 A useful work on the types of silences and possible solutions to this form of forgetting in the archives is David Thomas, Simon Fowler, and Valerie Johnson, *The Silence of the Archive* (London: Facet Publishing, 2017).

26 J. M. Coetzee, *Foe* (London: Martin Secker & Warburg, 1986; Penguin edition, New York, 1987), 121–22.

27 Verne Harris, "Contesting Remembering and Forgetting: The Archive of South Africa's Truth and Reconciliation Commission," in *Archives and Justice*, 289.

28 Bastian, "Flowers for Homestead," 113–32. See also Bastian's *Owning Memory: How a Caribbean Community Lost Its Archives and Found Its History* (Westport, CT: Libraries Unlimited, 2003).

29 Catherine Hall, Introduction to "Remembering 1807: Histories of the Slave Trade, Slavery and Abolition," *History Worskshop Journal* 64 (Autumn 2007): 1.

30 Jessica Tai, Jimmy Zavala, Joyce Gabiola, Gracen Brilmyer, and Michelle Caswell, "Summoning the Ghosts: Records as Agents in Community Archives," *Journal of Contemporary Archival Studies* 6 (2019), https://elischolar.library.yale.edu/jcas/vol6/iss1/18/, captured at https://perma.cc/M8L7-E7P5.

31 Coetzee, *Foe*, 17.

32 Terry Cook, "Remembering the Future: Appraisal of Records and the Role of Archives in Constructing Social Memory," in Blouin Jr. and Rosenberg, *Archives, Documentation and Institutions of Social Memory*, 169; and Cook, "From the Record to Its Context: The Theory and Practice of Archival Appraisal Since Jenkinson," *South African Archives Journal* 37 (1995): 33, quoted in Brian Williams and William K. Wallach, "Documenting South Africa's Liberation Movements: Engaging the Archives at the University of Fort Hare," in *Archives, Documentation and the Institutions of Social Memory*, 323. Elsewhere, Harris points out how absorption of apartheid ideology by the South Africa State Archives Service supported silence and affected the construction of social memory through its appraisal practices. See "Redefining Archives in South Africa: Public Archives and Society in Transition, 1990–1996" in *Archives and Justice*, 176–78.

33 Harris, influenced by Derrida, coined the term *recordmaking* and uses it in several essays in *Archives and Justice*.

34 Several articles documenting ethnic collecting programs appear in Ethnic Forum: Bulletin of Ethnic Studies and Ethnic Bibliography, including manuscripts by Joseph R. Anderson, John Grabowski, Rudolph J. Vecoli, and Joel Wurl. Representative studies in *American Archivist* include: Rudolph J. Vecoli, "The Immigration Studies Collection of the University of Minnesota," *American Archivist* 32, no. 2 (1969): 138–45, https://doi.org/10.17723/aarc.32.2.c434218317665xw5; Robert M. Warner and Francis X. Blouin, "Documenting the Great Migration and a Century of Ethnicity in America," *American Archivist* 39 (July 1976): 319–28; Richard N. Juliani, "The Use of Archives in the Study of Immigration and Ethnicity," *American Archivist* 39, no. 3 (1976): 469–77, https://doi.org/10.17723/aarc.39.3.1318m268q80275w2; Nicholas V. Montalto, "The Challenge of Preservation in a Pluralistic Society: A Report on the Immigration History Research Center, University of Minnesota," American Archivist 41, no. 4 (1978): 399–404,

https://doi.org/10.17723/aarc.41.4.f827024663561mwp. A 1985 special issue of *American Archivist* on ethnic records collecting contains five essays by Joseph R. Anderson, Jacqueline Goggin, John Grabowski, Susan Grigg, and Thomas H. Kreneck. A good overview of the history of archival concern for immigrant and ethnic records is Dominique Daniel, "Documenting the Immigrant and Ethnic Experience in American Archives," *American Archivist* 73, no. 1 (2010): 82–104, https://doi.org/10.17723/aarc .73.1.k2837h27wv1201hv. For an excellent analysis of the impact social history had on archival collecting practices, see Fredric Miller, "Social History and Archival Practice," *American Archivist* 44, no. 2 (1981): 113–24, https://doi.org/10.17723/aarc.44.2 .r5x54qq0r71275w4.

35 Hedstrom, "Archives and Collective Memory," 171.

36 Hedstrom, "Archives and Collective Memory," 171–73. For a brief review of appraisal theories that were developed in the 1970s to 1990s, see Frank Boles, *Selecting and Appraising: Archives and Manuscripts* (Archival Fundamentals Series II) (Chicago: Society of American Archivists, 2005).

37 Two good examples of ethnic and social history collection development that depended on engagement with communities and that stressed policy reassessment are John J. Grabowski, "Fragments or Components: Theme Collections in a Local Setting," *American Archivist* 48, no. 3 (1985): 303–14, https://doi.org/10.17723/aarc.48.3 .j552384783776157; and R. Joseph Anderson, "Managing Change and Chance: Collecting Policies in Social History Archives," *American Archivist* 48, no. 3 (1985): 296–303, https://doi.org/10.17723/aarc.48.3.r841l17518244654.

38 Hedstrom, "Archives and Collective Memory," 172–73.

39 A small sample of the community archives literature from this time period includes: Andrew Flinn, Mary Stevens, and Elizabeth Shepherd, "Whose Memories, Whose Archives? Independent Community Archives, Autonomy and the Mainstream," *Archival Science* 9 (2009): 71–86; Lyndon Ormond-Parker and Robyn Sloggett, "Local Archives and Community Collecting in the Digital Age," *Archival Science* 12, no. 2 (2012): 191–212; Anne Gilliland and Andrew Flinn, "Community Archives: What Are We Really Talking About?" CIRN Prato Community Informatics Conference (2013), https://www.monash.edu/__data/assets/pdf_file/0007/920626/gilliland_flinn_keynote .pdf, captured at https://perma.cc/4FTL-4DAJ; Ricardo L. Punzalan, "Understanding Virtual Reunification," *Library Quarterly* 84, no. 3 (2014): 294–323; Caswell, "Seeing Yourself in History," 26–37; Michelle Caswell, Marika Cifor, and Mario H. Ramirez, "To Suddenly Discover Yourself Existing: Uncovering the Impact of Community Archives," *American Archivist* 79, no. 1 (2016): 56–81, https://doi.org/10.17723/0360 -9081.79.1.56; Caswell, Gabiola, Zavala, Brilmyer, and Cifor, "Imagining Transformative Spaces," 73–93; Cifor, Caswell, Migoni, and Geraci, "What We Do Crosses over to Activism," 69–95; Brilmyer, Gabiola, Zavala, and Caswell, "Reciprocal Archival Imaginaries," 6–48; Tai, Zavala, Gabiola, Brilmyer, and Caswell, "Summoning the Ghosts"; Williams and Drake, "Power to the People."

40 Deuteronomy 16:20. This translation from the Hebrew is in *Tanakh: The Holy Scriptures.* The Hebrew is in the command form. Various Christian bibles translate the verse differently, but usually in the same command form.

41 See commentary on this verse in *Etz Hayim: Torah and Commentary*, 1088–1089.

42 Yerushalmi, *Zakhor*, 117.

[43] For a sample of important archival literature on justice, see footnote 34 in chapter two.

[44] Harris, "Something Is Happening Here and You Don't Know What It Is: Jacques Derrida Unplugged," in *Archives and Justice*, 76–77; Harris, "A World Whose Horizon Can Only Be Justice: Toward a Politics of Recordmaking," in *Archives and Justice*, 256–66. Among more recent authors who write about justice as process, see, for example: Alpert-Abrams, Bliss, and Carbajal, "Post-Custodialism for the Collective Good"; Caswell, Broman, Kirmer, Martin, and Sowry, "Implementing a Social Justice Framework"; and Punzalan and Caswell, "Critical Directions."

[45] I am in no way suggesting that Harris takes a passive position in the pursuit of justice. His career bears witness to his activist commitment to seeking and sustaining justice.

[46] Harris, "Introduction," in *Archives and Justice*, 4–6. Harris makes this philosophical statement based on his reading of Derrida and Levinas.

[47] For a small sample of the work on these topics, see: Dunbar, "Introducing Critical Race Theory to Archival Discourse," 109–29; Caswell, "Seeing Yourself in History," 26–37; Caswell, *Archiving the Unspeakable*; Jennifer R. O'Neal, "The Right to Know: Decolonizing Native American Archives," *Journal of Western Archives* 6, no. 1 (2015); Caswell and Cifor, "From Human Rights to Feminist Ethics," 23–83; Marika Cifor, "Affecting Relations: Introducing Affect Theory to Archival Discourse," *Archival Science* 16 (2016): 7–31; Marika Cifor and Anne J. Gilliland, "Affect and the Archive, Archives and their Affects: An Introduction to the Special Issue," *Archival Science* 16 (2016): 1–6; Punzalan and Caswell, "Critical Directions," 25–42; Stacie M. Williams and Jarrett M. Drake, "Power to the People"; Hughes-Watkins, "Moving Toward a Reparative Archive"; Jarrett M. Drake, "Diversity's Discontents," 270–79.

[48] Gudmund Valderhaug, "Memory, Justice and the Public Record," *Archival Science* 11 (2001): 20.

[49] Valderhaug, "Memory, Justice and the Public Record," 21.

[50] See Williams and Drake, "Power to the People." This relationship is replicated throughout the many community archives.

[51] Wendy M. Duff and Verne Harris, "Stories and Names: Archival Description as Narrating Records and Constructing Meanings," *Archival Science* 2 (2002): 145.

[52] Wallace, "Historical and Contemporary Justice," 14, 23. Wallace makes a distinction between historical justice and contemporary justice. The former "can be enabled through the reevaluations and retellings of the stories of the past"; the latter is "normally located in the realm of law and legal procedure."

[53] Sandel, *Justice*, 241–42. The classical conception of the good life focuses on the individual. According to Aristotle, the good life occurs when one is able to function well in ways essential to humans, when one is flourishing. See Aristotle, *Nicomachean Ethics*, trans. W. D. Ross (Oxford: Clarendon Press, 1908), http://classics.mit.edu /Aristotle/nicomachaen.html, captured at https://perma.cc/JAM4-P7BY.

[54] Gyekye, "African Ethics."

[55] Sandel, *Justice*, 261–69.

[56] Wallace, "Historical and Contemporary Justice," 24.

[57] O'Toole, "Archives and Historical Accountability," 8–10.

[58] Duff, Flinn, Suurtamm, and Wallace, "Social Justice Impact of Archives," 323–24.

[59] Artspace Editors, "Art 101: How the Art World Caught Archive Fever," January 22, 2014, https://www.artspace.com/magazine/art_101/art_market/the_art_worlds_love _affair_with_archives-51976, captured at https://perma.cc/Q8MK-QRY9.

[60] Hal Foster, "An Archival Impulse," *October* 110 (Fall 2004), 7. I want to thank my students at the University of Washington for pointing me toward this article.

[61] Foster, "An Archival Impulse," 21–22.

[62] Heather Fraser and Dee Michell, "Feminist Memory Work in Action: Method and Practicalities," *Qualitative Social Work* 14 (2015): 321–37. The quotation is on page 322.

[63] Fraser and Michell, "Feminist Memory Work," 324.

[64] Hedstrom, "Archives and Collective Memory," 176.

[65] Wallace, "Introduction: Memory Ethics," 7. The quotation includes within it a quotation from Jeffrey Blustein, *The Moral Demands of Memory* (New York: Cambridge University Press, 2008), 229.

[66] Amichai, *Amen*, 107.

CHAPTER FIVE: ARCHIVAL VALIDITY

[1] Hemingway, *A Moveable Feast*, 13.

[2] Hemingway, *A Moveable Feast*, 12.

[3] Maurice Merleau-Ponty, *Sense and Non-Sense*, trans. Hubert L. Dreyfus and Patricia Allen Dreyfus (Evanston: Northwestern University Press, 1964), 9–25. Merleau-Ponty noted that Cézanne's depiction of nature was "capable of such a vision which penetrates right to the root of things beneath the imposed order of humanity." The quotation is on page 16.

[4] An excellent example of the application of metrics to archival value is the Archival Metrics Project, a joint project of the University of Michigan, University of North Carolina, and University of Toronto.

[5] See the various essays in the special issue, "Evidences, Implications, and Critical Interrogations of Neoliberalism in Information Studies," *Journal of Critical Library and Information Studies* 2, no. 1 (2019), https://journals.litwinbooks.com/index.php/jclis /issue/view/6, captured at https://perma.cc/Z8PL-LLPM.

[6] American Evaluation Association, "About AEA," https://www.eval.org/p/cm/ld/fid=4, captured at https://perma.cc/4LMV-S3KQ.

[7] Society of American Archivists, "Core Values of Archivists." I prefer this introductory passage over the newer version adopted in 2020 as it gives greater currency to the notion of obligation to community.

[8] Michael Scriven, *Evaluation Thesaurus*, 4th ed. (London: Sage Publications, 1991), 372.

[9] Ernest R. House, *Evaluating with Validity* (Beverly Hills: Sage, 1980), 249–55. See also James C. Griffith and Bianca Montrosse-Moorehead, "Editors' Notes," *Revisiting Truth, Beauty, and Justice: Evaluating with Validity in the 21ˢᵗ Century: New Directions for Evaluation* 142 (Summer 2014): 1–8. Hereafter, all citations to articles in *New Directions for Evaluation* volume 142 are listed as *NDE*.

[10] House, *Evaluating with Validity*, 94; Griffith and Montrosse-Moorehead, "Editors' Notes," *NDE*, 4.

11 House, *Evaluating with Validity*; the quotation is on page 255. The staying power of House's work is illustrated by the republication of the book in 2010, the dedication of an issue of *New Directions for Evaluation* (2014) to it, and inclusion of the three chapters of the book that deal with truth, beauty, and justice on the website of the American Evaluation Association at http://comm.eval.org/coffee_break_webinars /viewdocument/evaluating-with-vali, captured at https://perma.cc/AH93-BB32.

12 House, "The Origins of the Ideas in Evaluating with Validity," *NDE*, 10.

13 Griffith and Montrosse-Moorehead, "Editors' Notes," *NDE*, 5.

14 E. Jane Davidson, "Visible Values: Striving for Truth, Beauty, and Justice in Evaluation," paper presented to Anzea Auckland Branch, December 2, 2010; and "How Beauty Can Bring Truth and Justice to Life," *NDE*, 36–37.

15 Terry Cook, "Macroappraisal in Theory and Practice: Origins, Characteristics, and Implementation in Canada, 1950–2000," *Archival Science* 5 (2005): 101–61; Ham, "The Archival Edge," 5–13.

16 Davidson, "How Beauty Can Bring Truth and Justice to Life," 32.

17 Griffith and Montrosse-Moorehead, "Editors' Notes," 6.

18 Griffith and Montrosse-Moorehead, "Editors' Notes," 6.

19 House, "The Origins of the Ideas in Evaluating with Validity," 14.

20 Davidson, "How Beauty Can Bring Truth and Justice to Life," 32.

21 Davidson, "How Beauty Can Bring Truth and Justice to Life," 32, 42.

22 John Rawls, *A Theory of Justice*, rev. ed. (Cambridge, MA: Harvard University Press, 1999).

23 Rodney K. Hopson, "Justice Signposts in Evaluation Theory, Practice, and Policy," *NDE*, 86.

24 House, "The Origins of the Ideas in Evaluating with Validity," 13.

25 Bianca Montrosse-Moorehead, James C. Griffith, Pamela Pokorny, "House With a View: Validity and Evaluative Argument," *NDE*, 103.

26 For a sample of important works on justice, see footnote 34 in chapter two. On the concept of the multiverse, see Gilliland, McKemmish, and Lau, *Research in the Archival Multiverse*.

27 House, "The Origins of the Ideas in Evaluating with Validity," 11.

28 James C. Griffith and Bianca Montrosse-Moorehead, "The Value of Validity," *NDE*, 28.

29 House, "The Origins of the Ideas in Evaluating with Validity," 10. For discussions of how the impossibility of reaching the ideal plays out in professional lives, see Deborah Kerdeman, "Why the Best Isn't So Bad: Moderation and Ideals in Educational Reform," *Educational Theory* 50 (2009): 511–31; and Scott Cline, "Archival Ideals and the Pursuit of a Moderate Disposition," *American Archivist* 77, no. 2 (2014): 444–58, https://doi.org /10.17723/aarc.77.2.c1221u1183p6vh27.

30 Woodruff, *Reverence*, 182–85. Woodruff identifies "good judgment" as an important virtue required in expressing genuine reverence.

31 Barry Schwartz and Kenneth Sharpe, *Practical Wisdom: The Right Way to Do the Right Thing* (New York: Riverhead Books, 2010), 35.

32 Schwartz and Sharpe, *Practical Wisdom*, 6–8.

33 Schwartz and Sharpe, *Practical Wisdom*, 25–26.

34   Schwartz and Sharpe, *Practical Wisdom,* 5–19.

35   Schwartz and Sharpe, *Practical Wisdom,* 20–21.

36   Schwartz and Sharpe, *Practical Wisdom,* 22–26.

37   Aristotle, *Nicomachean Ethics.*

38   Schwartz and Sharpe, *Practical Wisdom,* 24–25.

39   Andrea Hinding, "Of Archivists and Other Termites," 59–60.

40   John Kekes, *Moral Wisdom and Good Lives* (Ithaca: Cornell University Press, 1995),
     1–21, 208. Kekes describes the goods required to live the good life as self, intimacy, and
     social order.

41   Kekes, *Moral Wisdom,* 4–11. "Right, sound, or just" seems to parallel Ernie House's
     truth, beauty, and justice.

42   Comte-Sponville, *A Small Treatise on the Great Virtues,* 368.

43   Schwartz and Sharpe, *Practical Wisdom,* 20–21, 135–136.

44   Caswell and Cifor, "From Human Rights to Feminist Ethics," 24.

45   Henry Greenspan, *On Listening to Holocaust Survivors: Beyond Testimony,* 2nd ed.
     (St. Paul, MN: Paragon House, 2010), 244.

46   Greenspan, *On Listening to Holocaust Survivors,* 42.

47   Greenspan, *On Listening to Holocaust Survivors,* 42.

48   Greenspan, *On Listening to Holocaust Survivors,* 211.

49   David Levy, *Scrolling Forward: Making Sense of Documents in the Digital Age* (New
     York: Arcade Publishing, 2001), 21–38.

50   Fleckner, "Dear Mary Jane," 9–10.

51   O'Toole and Cox, *Understanding Archives and Manuscripts,* 132.

52   Jennifer Douglas, "Toward More Honest Description," *American Archivist* 79, no. 1
     (2016): 26–55, https://doi.org/10.17723/0360-9081.79.1.26.

53   This is also Verne Harris's argument. See several of his essays in *Archives and Justice.*

54   Taylor, "Towards the New Archivist: The Integrated Professional," in Cook and Dodds,
     Imagining Archives, 154.

55   Greenspan defines knowledge as "knowing with," an ongoing project developed in
     conversation and relationship, and engaging survivors as "partners in conversation."

CHAPTER SIX: ARCHIVAL TRANSCENDENCE

1   Thich Nhat Hanh, *The Heart of Understanding: Commentaries on the Prajnaparamita
    Heart Sutra,* ed. Peter Levitt (Berkeley: Parallax Press, 1988), 3-5.

2   Taylor, "The Archivist, the Letter, and the Spirit," in Cook and Dodds, *Imagining
    Archives,* 230, 233. Several of Taylor's essays include his ideas on spirituality, reverence,
    and the sacred in relation to archives. Prominent among those are "My Very Act and
    Deed: Some Reflections on the Role of Textual Records in the Conduct of Affairs";
    "Recycling the Past: The Archivist in the Age of Ecology"; and "The Totemic Universe:
    Appraising the Documentary Future." These are also included in *Imagining Archives.*

3   "Letter from Birmingham City Jail," in *A Testament of Hope: The Essential Writings and Speeches of Martin Luther King, Jr.*, ed. James M. Washington (New York: HarperCollins, 1986), 290.

4   King and Nhat Hanh knew and admired one another. In 1967, King nominated Nhat Hanh for the Nobel Peace Prize.

5   Woodruff, *Reverence*, 233. A dictionary example is *Webster's Ninth New Collegiate Dictionary* (Springfield, MA: Merriam-Webster, 1988), which defines *transcendent* as "being beyond comprehension" and "transcending the universe or material existence."

6   Heschel, *God In Search of Man*, 51, 75, 105, 117. See also, Shai Held, *Abraham Joshua Heschel: The Call of Transcendence* (Bloomington: Indiana University Press, 2013). Held explores Heschel's conception of self-transcendence of humans and God.

7   Thomas R. Flynn, "Sartre," in *A Companion to Continental Philosophy*, ed. Simon Critchley and William R. Schroeder (Malden, MA: Blackwell Publishing, 1998), 256–68. See especially pages 259–61.

8   Neiman, *Moral Clarity*, 97–98.

9   Peter L. Berger, *A Rumor of Angels: Modern Society and the Rediscovery of the Supernatural* (Garden City: Doubleday and Company, 1969), 53.

10   I hope it is apparent in all cases where I take religious concepts and apply them in a secular fashion that I do so humbly and with all due respect.

11   Berger, *A Rumor of Angels*, 53–54. The quotation is on page 54.

12   Berger, *A Rumor of Angels*, 54–57. The quotation is on page 56.

13   Brien Brothman, "Orders of Value: Probing the Theoretical Terms of Archival Practice," *Archivaria* 32 (Summer 1991): 81.

14   Schwartz and Cook, "Archives, Records and Power," 13–14.

15   Baxter, "The Doorway from Heart to Heart," 9.

16   Hughes-Watkins, "Moving Toward a Reparative Archive," 3.

17   Tom Nesmith, "Seeing Archives: Postmodernism and the Changing Intellectual Place of Archives," *American Archivist* 65, no. 1 (2002): 32–33, https://doi.org/10.17723/aarc .65.1.rr48450509r0712u.

18   Hans-Georg Gadamer, *Truth and Method*, 2nd ed. (London and New York: Continuum, 1975), 534.

19   Terry Cook, "Archival Science and Postmodernism: New Formulations for Old Concepts," *Archival Science* 1 (2001): 10.

20   Eric Ketelaar, "Tacit Narratives: The Meanings of Archives," *Archival Science* 1 (2001): 138.

21   Berger, *A Rumor of Angels*, 57–60.

22   Gadamer, *Truth and Method*, 101–134. Berger and Gadamer both cite Johan Huizinga, *Homo Ludens: A Study of the Play Element in Culture* (Boston: Beacon Press, 1955).

23   Berger, *A Rumor of Angels*, 58.

24   Maygene Daniels, "On Being an Archivist," *American Archivist* 59, no. 1 (1996): 10–11, https://doi.org/10.17723/aarc.59.1.94q023738n718216.

25   Fleckner, "Dear Mary Jane," 13.

26 "A Year of Living Dangerously for Archives: Call to Action #4: Why I Am an Archivist," Society of American Archivists, https://www2.archivists.org/living-dangerously/why-i-am-an-archivist, captured at https://perma.cc/VD83-J72X.

27 Eric Ketalaar, "Cultivating Archives: Meanings and Identities," *Archival Science* 12 (2012): 24.

28 Berger, *A Rumor of Angels,* 61.

29 Berger, *A Rumor of Angels,* 62.

30 Berger, *A Rumor of Angels,* 60–65.

31 Cook and Dodds, *Imagining Archives,* 18.

32 Kierkegaard, *Fear and Trembling,* 53.

33 Terry Cook, "What's Past is Prologue: A History of Archival Ideas Since 1898, and the Future Paradigm Shift," *Archivaria* 43 (Spring 1997): 19, 49.

34 Berger, *A Rumor of Angels,* 65-69.

35 Susan Neiman, *Evil in Modern Thought: An Alternative History of Philosophy* (Princeton, NJ: Princeton University Press, 2002), 7–8.

36 For Harris's use of the phrase "the call of justice," see several essays in *Archives and Justice.* Harris uses the phrase "the call to justice" in "Jacques Derrida Meets Nelson Mandela: Archival Ethics at the Endgame," *Archival Science* 11 (2011): 113–24. The quotation is on page 121.

37 Harris, "The Archive is Politics," in *Archives and Justice,* 249.

38 Berger, *A Rumor of Angels,* 70.

39 Berger, *A Rumor of Angels,* 70-71.

40 See, for example, Inge Bundsgaard and Michael H. Gelting, "What To Be or Not to Be? Evolving Identities for State and Grassroots Archives in Denmark," *American Archivist* 55, no. 1 (1992): 46–57, https://doi.org/10.17723/aarc.55.1.5r77m1126454mh0q; John Roberts, "Archival Theory: Much Ado About Shelving," *American Archivist* 50, no. 1 (1987): 66–74, https://doi.org/10.17723/aarc.50.1.l357257455776g52.

41 Hinding, "Of Archivists and Other Termites," 54–61, and "In a Slightly Different Voice, or Perspectives," *American Archivist* 48, no. 1 (1985): 24, https://doi.org/10.17723/aarc.48.1.l104m5t2732h17r5.

42 Comte-Sponville, *A Small Treatise on the Great Virtues,* 221.

43 Hinding, "Of Archivists and Other Termites," 60–61.

44 Hinding, "In a Slightly Different Voice, or Perspectives," 22–25.

45 Cifor, "Affecting Relations," 12.

46 Cifor and Gilliland, "Affect and the Archive, Archives and Their Affects," 1.

47 Caswell, Gabiola, Zavala, Brilmyer, and Cifor, "Imagining Transformative Spaces"; Tai, Zavala, Gabiola, Brilmyer, and Caswell, "Summoning the Ghosts."

48 Kovner's life is documented in Rich Cohen, *The Avengers: A Jewish War Story* (New York: Alfred A. Knopf, 2000).

49 Gadamer, *Truth and Method,* 297.

50 Gadamer, *Truth and Method,* 217.

51 Nesmith, "Seeing Archives," 35.

52 Neiman, *Moral Clarity,* 97.

53 Taylor, "The Archivist, the Letter, and the Spirit," 235.

54 Berger, *A Rumor of Angels*, 94–95.

CHAPTER SEVEN: SPIRITUALITY AND ARCHIVAL CULTURE

1   Taylor, "The Archivist, the Letter, and the Spirit," in Cook and Dodds, *Imagining Archives*, 226–43.

2   Taylor, "The Archivist, the Letter, and the Spirit," 230–35.

3   Taylor, "The Archivist, the Letter, and the Spirit," 229.

4   "The Archivist, the Letter, and the Spirit" is the clearest example of Taylor's inclusion of spirituality in his writing, but several other essays in *Imagining Archives* address or allude to spirituality, faith, and religion.

5   Taylor, "The Archivist, the Letter, and the Spirit," 232–34.

6   Taylor, "The Archivist, the Letter, and the Spirit," 237.

7   Other than Taylor, most explorations of spirituality in the archives relate to religious archives. Jared Warkentin's master's thesis describes spirituality in church archives with a focus on digital preservation, but in chapter one he includes a section on the secular concept of spirituality. Jared Warkentin, "I Have Become All Things to All People: Spirituality in Church Archives & Digital Preservation" (master of arts thesis, University of Manitoba, 2020).

8   The following brief review of the attempts at definitions of spirituality in the nursing literature is not meant to be comprehensive. I reviewed several representative articles whose viewpoint creates a framework that can, at least in part, be applied to archives.

9   Wilfred McSherry and Keith Cash, "The Language of Spirituality: An Emerging Taxonomy," *International Journal of Nursing Studies* 41 (February 2004): 151–61.

10 Bernice Golberg, "Connection: An Exploration of Spirituality in Nursing Care," *Journal of Advanced Nursing* 27 (April 1998): 836–42. Concept analysis is a linguistic methodology for clarifying ambiguous ideas in a theoretical framework by deconstructing and rebuilding the concept into a more precise definition. See, for example, Lorraine Olszewski Walker and Kay Coalson Avant, *Strategies for Theory Construction in Nursing*, 6th ed. (New York: Pearson, 2019).

11 Pam McCarroll, Thomas St. James O'Connor, and Elizabeth Meakes, "Assessing Plurality in Spirituality Definitions," in *Spirituality Health: Multidisciplinary Explorations*, ed. Augustine Meier, Thomas St. James O'Connor, and Peter L. Van Katwyk (Waterloo: Wilfrid Laurier University Press, 2005), 43–60. The quotations are on pages 44–47 and 56.

12 Patrick G. Love, Marianne Bock, Annie Jannarone, and Paul Richardson, "Identity Interaction: Exploring the Spiritual Experiences of Lesbian and Gay College Students," *Journal of College Student Development* 46 (2005): 193–209. The quotation is on page 196.

13 Love et al., "Identity Interaction," 196–97. See also, Patrick Love, "Differentiating Spirituality from Religion," *Character Clearinghouse*, Florida State University, https://characterclearinghouse.fsu.edu/article/differentiating-spirituality-religion, captured at https://perma.cc/53SP-UCND. In this article, Love summarizes elements of his work with Talbot in Patrick Love and Donna Talbot, "Defining Spiritual Development: A

Missing Consideration for Student Affairs," *NASPA Journal* 46 (2009): 614–28. Their definition of spirituality also includes a more overtly religious aspect that I do not include here, not because I think personal religious conviction is an unimportant potential source of spirituality, but rather because I do not want to make the argument that archives is a religious endeavour.

14   Anne Gilliland, "Pluralizing Archival Education: A Non-Zero-Sum Proposition," in Mary A. Caldera and Kathryn M. Neal, eds., *[Through the] Archival Looking Glass: A Reader on Diversity and Inclusion* (Chicago: Society of American Archivists, 2014), 267. Gilliland quotes the Astin study. Part of Astin's definition falls outside my conceptual framing of archival spirituality. He notes: "Spirituality can also have to do with aspects of our experience that are not easy to define or talk about, such things as intuition, inspiration, the mysterious, and the mystical."

15   Love et al., "Identity Interaction," 196. They draw on the scholarship of Daniel A. Helminiak. See *Spiritual Development: An Interdisciplinary Study* (Chicago: Loyola University Press, 1987) and *The Human Core of Spirituality: Mind as Psyche and Spirit* (Albany: SUNY Press, 1996).

16   Barbara Pesut and Sally Thorne, "From Private to Public: Negotiating Professional and Personal Identities in Spiritual Care," *Journal of Advanced Nursing* 58 (2007): 396–403.

17   Pesut and Thorne, "From Private to Public," 401.

18   Pesut and Thorne, "From Private to Public," 401.

19   Richard Klumpenhouwer, "The MAS and After: Transubstantiating Theory and Practice into an Archival Culture," *Archivaria* 95 (Spring 1995): 89–93.

20   Klumpenhouwer, "The MAS and After," 95.

21   Love, "Differentiating Spirituality from Religion." See also Sharon Daloz Parks, *Big Questions, Worthy Dreams: Mentoring Young Adults in their Search for Meaning, Purpose, and Faith,* (San Francisco: Jossey-Bass, 2000).

22   Gilliland, "Pluralizing Archival Education," 236.

23   Gilliland, "Pluralizing Archival Education," 235–38. For this conclusion, Gilliland draws on Robert Wright, *The Evolution of God* (New York: Little, Brown and Company, 2009).

24   Gilliland, "Pluralizing Archival Education," 268.

25   The construction of this idea is influenced by Michael Fishbane, "A Note on the Spirituality of Texts," *Etz Hayim: Torah and Commentary,* 1503–1504.

26   Simcha J. Cohen, *The 613th Commandment: An Analysis of the Mitzvah to Write a Sefer Torah* (New York: Ktav Publishing House, 1983), 61.

27   Chiang Yee is quoted in David M. Levy, *Scrolling Forward: Making Sense of Documents in the Digital Age* (New York: Arcade Publishing, 2001), 15.

28   Levy, *Scrolling Forward*, 7–20. The quotation is on page 20.

29   Tai, Zavala, Gabiola, Brilmyer, and Caswell, "Summoning the Ghosts," 1.

30   David Kingma, "It's All There! Reflections on a Workshop with Native American Elders" (paper presented at the annual meeting of the Society of American Archivists in San Diego, August 9, 2012). I am grateful to David Kingma for sharing the text of his presentation.

31   Tamar Zeffren, "Learning to Carry One's Home on One's Back: The Workings of Exile in Jewish History and Archival Theory" (paper presented at the annual meeting of the

Society of American Archivists in San Diego, August 9, 2012). I am grateful to Tamar Zeffren for sharing a copy of her paper.

32 Fishbane, "A Note on the Spirituality of Texts," 1504.

33 Steven Lubar, "Information Culture and the Archival Record," *American Archivist* 62, no. 1 (1999): 12–18, https://doi.org/10.17723/aarc.62.1.30x5657gu1w44630.

34 "Educating for the Archival Multiverse: The Archival Education and Research Institute (AERI), Pluralizing the Archival Curriculum Group (PACG)," *American Archivist* 74, no. 1 (2011): 69–101, https://doi.org/10.17723/aarc.74.1.hv3396471l2745684. All quotations in this paragraph are on page 81.

35 Sue McKemmish and Michael Piggott, "Toward the Archival Multiverse: Challenging the Binary Opposition of the Personal and Corporate Archive in Modern Archival Theory and Practice," *Archivaria* 76 (2015): 111–44. The quotation is on page 133.

36 Zhiying Lian, "Archives Microblogs and Archival Culture in China," *American Archivist* 78, no. 2 (2015): 361, https://doi.org/10.17723/0360-9081.78.2.357.

37 "Educating for the Archival Multiverse," 90.

38 "Educating for the Archival Multiverse," 81.

39 First Archivist Circle, *Protocols for Native American Archival Materials*, http://www2.nau.edu/libnap-p/protocols.html, captured at https://perma.cc/9B75-26TG.

40 Amy Lonetree, *Decolonizing Museums: Representing Native America in National and Tribal Museums* (Chapel Hill: University of North Carolina Press, 2003), 27.

41 Lonetree, *Decolonizing Museums*, 142–43.

42 Kay Mathiesen argues that one form of cultural appropriation is cultural destruction; it is defined as "the appropriation of that culture through such activities as unethical research practices; collecting and selling stories, art and craft styles, and music; and appropriating elements of native cultures as representations of the "'exotic,' 'authentic,' 'spiritual,' or 'savage.'" See Mathiesen, "A Defense of Native Americans' Rights over Their Traditional Cultural Expressions," *American Archivist* 75, no. 2 (2012): 462, https://doi.org/10.17723/aarc.75.2.0073888331414314.

43 Council of Canadian Academies, *Leading in the Digital World: Opportunities for Canada's Memory Institutions* (Ottawa: Council of Canadian Academies, 2015), 40.

44 Alan R. Drengson, "Four Philosophies of Technology," *Philosophy Today* (Summer 1982): 104.

45 Drengson, "Four Philosophies of Technology," 104.

46 Hans Jonas, "Toward a Philosophy of Technology," in *Technology and Values: Essential Readings*, ed. Craig Hanks (Hoboken: John Wiley and Sons, 2010), 11–25. The quotation is on page 12.

47 Jonas, "Toward a Philosophy of Technology," 12.

48 Hugh A. Taylor, "Some Concluding Thoughts," *American Archivist* 57, no. 1 (1994): 142–43, https://doi.org/10.17723/aarc.57.1.q385p565778211157.

49 Taylor, "The Archivist, the Letter, and the Spirit," 226–30.

50 Taylor, "Information Ecology and the Archives of the 1980s," in Cook and Dodds, *Imagining Archives*, 90–106.

51 Taylor, "Information Ecology and the Archives of the 1980s," 103.

52 The quote appears in the fourth manuscript draft of "Mind Over Matter: Towards a New Theory of Archival Appraisal" dated 3 January 1992. Cook provided this draft to me during a 2012 email exchange regarding archival ideals. The manuscript was published as Terry Cook, "Mind Over Matter: Towards a New Theory of Archival Appraisal," in *The Archival Imagination: Essays in Honour of Hugh Taylor,* ed. Barbara Craig (Ottawa: Association of Canadian Archivists, 1992), 38–70.

53 Wexler and Long, "Lifetimes and Legacies," 478–95. The quotations are on page 479.

54 Paul Tillich, *The Courage to Be* (New Haven: Yale University Press, 1952; 3rd ed. 2014), 43.

55 Tillich, *The Courage to Be,* 44.

56 See David Bearman, "Archival Methods," *Archives and Museum Informatics Technical Report,* vol. 3, no. 1 (Spring 1989); and "Archival Strategies," *American Archivist* 58, no. 4 (1995): 380–413, https://doi.org/10.17723/aarc.58.4.pq71240520j31798.

57 Ann Pederson, "Empowering Archival Effectiveness: Archival Strategies as Innovation," *American Archivist* 58, no. 4 (1995): 449, https://doi.org/10.17723/aarc .58.4.8q1308301728h79x.

CHAPTER EIGHT: MORAL ORDER

1 August Wilson, *Radio Golf* (2007), Act 2, Scene 1. Each play in Wilson's Pittsburgh cycle is set in a different decade of the twentieth century. One of the plays, *Ma Rainey's Black Bottom,* is set in Chicago.

2 This is at the heart of Martha C. Nussbaum's theory of moral philosophy and justice. See *Creating Capabilities: The Human Development Approach* (Cambridge: Belknap Press of Harvard University Press, 2011), 36. For more on the human development approach, see Amartya Sen, *Development as Freedom* (New York: Oxford University Press, 1999).

3 Mathiesen, "A Defense of Native Americans' Rights," 461.

4 Wallace, "Historical and Contemporary Justice and the Role of Archivists," 24. James O'Toole makes a similar argument in "Archives and Historical Accountability," 3–20.

5 See Dingwall, "Trusting Archivists," 11–30 for the best example.

6 See, for example, Mathiesen, "A Defense of Native Americans' Rights," 456–81; and Malcolm Todd, "Power, Identity, Integrity, Authenticity, and the Archives: A Comparative Study of the Application of Archival Methodologies to Contemporary Privacy" *Archivaria* 61 (Spring 2006): 181–214.

7 Hilary Jenkinson, *A Manual of Archive Administration* (London: P. Lund, Humpries and Company, 1937). One section of the manual is headed "Physical Defence of Archives" followed by a section titled "Moral Defence of Archives." Another exception is found in *The Archivist's Code,* promulgated by Wayne Grover at the National Archives in 1955, which began "The archivist has a moral obligation to society." David E. Horn, "The Development of Ethics in Archival Practice," *American Archivist* 52, no. 1 (1989): 65, https://doi.org/10.17723/aarc.52.1.nk661527341j0610. See *"The Archivist's Code,"* *American Archivist* 18, no. 4 (1955): 307–8, https://doi.org/10.17723/aarc.18.4 .g027u80688293012.

8   Quoted in Paige Hohmann, "On Impartiality and Interrelatedness: Reactions to Jenkinsonian Appraisal in the Twentieth Century," *American Archivist* 79, no. 1 (2016): 14–25, https://doi.org/10.17723/0360-9081.79.1.14.

9   The Harris quote is in Randall C. Jimerson, "Archives for All: Professional Responsibility and Social Justice," *American Archivist* 70, no. 2 (2007): 273, https://doi .org/10.17723/aarc.70.2.5n20760751v643m7.

10 Brothman, "Orders of Value," 78–100. The quotations are on page 91.

11 Harry G. Frankfurt, *On Truth* (New York: Alfred A. Knopf, 2006), 15–27.

12 Richard N. Katz and Paul B. Gandel ask the disturbing question: "Is it possible as information becomes so voluminous, the standards of selection so pluralistic, and the content of information so nuanced, that intuitive feeling will replace research analysis as the social barometer of truth?" See Katz and Gandel, "The Tower, The Cloud, and Posterity: Documenting in a Digital World," in *Controlling the Past*, 233–34.

13 Jill Lepore, *These Truths: A History of the United States* (New York: W. W. Norton and Company, 2018), xix.

14 Heather MacNeil, "Trusting Records in a Postmodern World," *Archivaria* 51 (Spring 2001): 46–47.

15 Søren Kierkegaard, *Concluding Unscientific Postscript,* trans. Alastair Hannah (New York: Cambridge University Press, 2009), 171. The emphasis is Kierkegaard's.

16 Kierkegaard, *Concluding Unscientific Postscript*, 171–72.

17 Ferry, *A Brief History of Thought*, 117.

18 Andrew A. Abela, "Digesting the Raisins of Wrath: Business, Ethics, and the Archival Profession," *American Archivist* 71, no. 1 (2008): 204, https://doi.org/10.17723/aarc.71.1 .g674617g204g7142.

19 Bellah, Madsen, Sullivan, Swidler, and Tipton, *Habits of the Heart*, 207.

20 Jimerson, "Archives for All," 273.

21 Joseph P. DeMarco, *Moral Theory: A Contemporary Overview* (Boston: Jones and Bartlett Publishers, 1996), 106–17. The quotation is from Annette C. Baier, "What Do Women Want in a Moral Theory?" *Nous* 19 (1985): 56. Baier argued that men make moral decisions based on a conception of justice and women make them based on trust and the ethics of care.

Index